GO ON, GIRL

Hilary Grossman

D1502113

Published, 2018

Cover Design by Greg Simanson
Edited by Samantha Stroh Bailey

This is a work of fiction. Names, characters, places, brands, media, and incidents are either the product of the author's imagination or are used fictitiously. Any resemblance to similarly named places or to persons living or deceased is unintentional.

PRINT ISBN

ISBN-10: 1725514001

Library of Congress Control Number: ____

To all the moms – Go On, Girls! Keep crushing it!

In loving memory to my own Sidney, my father… Thirty years have passed, but not a day goes by that I don't miss you.

PRAISE FOR HILARY GROSSMAN

"Although a light read, the subject matter was very sad at times and I found myself choking back tears, but in a good way! It was so authentically heart wrenching yet often very funny too. The characters were so well fleshed out and three dimensional - no one was perfect and no one was fatally flawed - like real life. I thought the twist was genius!"
 - *Meredith Schorr Best Selling Author*

"I do not believe there is a mother or daughter who would not enjoy reading Plan Bea. An emotional roller coaster that had me crying, laughing, and feeling pain and sorrow. It is a very real story with very identifiable characters that we all have known."
 - *Readers' Favorite*

"Dangled Carat sparkles with humor and shines with wisdom. It is a gem of a book."
 - *-Christina Baker Kline - New York Times & USA Today Best Selling Author of Orphan Train.*

"Move over mainstream chick-lit authors Jennifer Weiner, Lauren Weisberger, and romance author Nicholas Sparks. Hilary Grossman is just as good as you, and deserves to be out right next to you on the shelf."
 - *The Intellectual Blog*

CHAPTER ONE

WHOEVER HAD THE IDIOTIC IDEA to invent text messages? If I could, I'd strangle them. Back in the day, when people had to rely on the telephone, they were forced to hold back their every insecurity and issue, even if only a bit. But now, with the ease of a few keystrokes, everyone was able to share their thoughts and opinions at breakneck speed, without any consideration for their reputations. Not to mention how it made other people feel.

"They're all freaking crazy!" Disgusted, I tossed my new iPhone with a bit too much force. It landed right on the edge of the kitchen table and dangled precariously, narrowly escaping a sudden death.

My husband, Craig, rescued the device and turned it face down in front of him. It beeped in frantic succession, alerting me to at least three new incoming texts. He picked up his coffee cup and calmly took a sip, completely unaware that during his five-mile run this morning my phone hadn't stopped beeping for one single second.

My pulse raced with every alert. "At this rate, I'm going to have to change my text tone, again." A few months back, after my phone had exploded from a similar incessant group text, I switched the sound because every time I heard the chime, it stressed me out.

Last week, I was in the supermarket, and the woman in front of me at the deli counter had the same melody on her phone I used to. When she'd received a text, I'd instantly had palpitations. It was like some technologically provoked post-traumatic stress disorder. "What's it this time?" my husband asked as he coated his pumpernickel bagel with jalapeño cream cheese.

"A major calamity, apparently." I rolled my eyes. "I never realized organizing a carpool could be so cutthroat. But that's what I'm dealing with."

Craig scratched the dark stubble on his chin before he frowned in sympathy. He'd heard different versions of this same story a hundred times during the last term. But he knew I needed to vent, and he would let me. The mothers of my daughter's classmates were catty and juvenile, constantly at each other's throats over petty situations. I missed out on most of their meltdowns because I wasn't part of the clique, thanks to my full-time job as CFO of a food importer. But sometimes, like now, I couldn't avoid the aftermath of an argument, because the turmoil trickled down to my day-to-day life and impacted my daughter and me.

"I don't understand what's wrong with people." I stood up and refilled my coffee cup. Before I returned to the table, I gazed out the back window. I stared at a cardinal that was perched on top of Amanda's swing set and imagined how wonderful it would feel to be able to fly away. "We're supposed to be adults, but everyone's acting like petulant children." I pointed at our six-year-old daughter, who was sitting cross-legged on the floor in the den. Her dark pig-tailed head was bowed, and she was deep in concentration. She intently colored, despite being surrounded by fifteen Barbie dolls, most of which were naked. "She has more maturity in her little pinky than most of the mothers of her classmates."

"She does take after me, you know." Craig beamed. He was five years my senior, and often acted far older than his forty-one years. He was very rational and levelheaded, perfect for his chosen profession, corporate law, which was how we'd met thirteen years before.

When the company I worked for had undergone their first merger, they had hired Craig's law firm to represent them. They'd assigned him to the case, and he and I had to work closely. I'd managed the finance side of the transaction, and the workload was intense. Craig and I had a bit of a bumpy start. I wasn't in the best state of mind since I was petrified about how the corporate change would affect my day-to-day job. But once the deal was signed, our relationship was sealed as well.

Craig's reasonable side suited me perfectly since I tended to get easily upset over insignificant events. My patience level was low for two reasons. First, I was always stretched so thin. I had more commitments and obligations than I could comfortably juggle, so I hated to waste one second. Also, I was a bit of a control freak who feared change. When situations, regardless of their magnitude, were out of my hands, I felt overwhelmed.

It took everything for me not to throw my spoon at him, and by the smirk on his face, I could tell he knew I was contemplating violence. I wasn't usually this angry and upset on a Sunday morning in the summer, but today my blood was boiling. My next-door neighbor, Suzanne, had warned me about this inevitable drama, but I didn't believe her. I figured she had to be exaggerating. I should have trusted her, though. While her kids were now in college, she did raise three of them in this superficial town where social status, appearances, and wealth meant more than morals, compassion, or real friendship.

"Come on, Sydney," Craig mumbled as he chewed his bagel. "Are you going to tell me what's eating at you?"

Before I could say a word, my phone exploded once again. "Ugh! Can these mothers stop it for five seconds? What would they do if they had a real issue?"

Craig picked up my phone and waved it in front of my face. "Don't you want to check what they said?"

I opened my mouth to reply but shook my head.

"Very well." He did what I should have done an hour ago. He silenced my phone and placed it face down on the table.

I took a deep breath. "School starts in only two weeks. Right before kindergarten ended a bunch of the moms organized a carpool schedule, which was no easy feat, mind you. Apparently, it is almost impossible to juggle long-standing manicure appointments, personal trainers, and yoga classes." I pointed at my chest. "I work, and I was the most flexible woman in the bunch! Eventually, even though it took about three weeks and probably numerous refills of Xanax, we managed to sort everything out. But now the plan's gone up in smoke because two of the moms, Donna and Jackie, got into a huge fight last week at a Pilates class."

"What does one thing have to do with another?" Craig tilted his head.

"It shouldn't. But after they had this knock-down screaming

match, Jackie went home and called the other moms in the carpool and invited them over for lunch." I took a sip of coffee. I was so frustrated. I thought by agreeing to participate in a carpool this year, I would be able to eliminate some stress from my life. I couldn't have been more wrong. The entire experience had been nothing but aggravating.

I'd yank Amanda out of the schedule right now except I knew my little social butterfly was excited to ride back and forth to school with her classmates, and I didn't want her to miss out.

"Did you go?"

"Um, no. Unlike the other moms, I work for a living, remember?" I felt a small smile creep on my face as I thought about our babysitter, Sally. "I'm shocked Jackie didn't call Sally and invite her to the rant session. That way at least someone from the Clayton household could have represented."

"Sally would have enjoyed it." Craig smiled.

We both knew our babysitter was quite the gossip. Craig and I never worried about missing out on anything that happened in the neighborhood when Sally was around. She had the inside scoop on everyone and everything. In her mid-sixties, Sally spent the better part of her life devoted to caring for children living in this town. Although she'd never married or had kids of her own, she had no shortage of family. She was an instrumental part of so many homes in Forest River; the woman probably received more holiday invitations than the mayor.

"I know. So, anyway, Jackie filled them all in on the fight. She told them she wanted nothing more to do with Donna unless she apologized. She rallied the moms with macaroons from La Petite Boulangerie and Ace of Spades champagne. Of course, they all caved like a house of cards."

"What did Donna do anyway?"

I waved my hand in the air. "Believe me, you don't even want to know." I rolled my eyes. "It's all so petty and stupid." I hated that I was so invested in the drama, but I worried about my daughter. She was such an outgoing child, one who loved spending time with her friends. I didn't want to compromise her happiness in any way, especially since I knew firsthand how difficult life was when you didn't fit in as a kid.

"I know I'll regret this but tell me what happened."

I'd won the husband jackpot. Most men wouldn't have the patience for this type of nonsense, but Craig was different. He was a natural problem solver and loved to try to rectify a situation. He also knew it was in his best interest to let me babble right away about what bothered me than hear me harp about it later.

"Donna jumped on the bad-mouthing bandwagon. She and Jackie both have daughters who are entering the fifth grade, and they're part of a tight-knit clique. Right before the school year ended, Jackie's daughter got into a fight with one of the other girls in the group. Instead of letting the battle blow over, this girl's mother decided to make sure the girls weren't in the same class come September."

"How did she plan on managing that?" Craig asked with a mouthful of cookie.

"She apparently called the school psychologist and told him the girls were having issues and requested they be separated."

"That's not so terrible."

"No, it's not. She didn't stop there, though. This woman then called all the other mothers and offered to take their children on an expense-free Caribbean cruise. It's a blatant, conniving attempt to convince them to contact the school's psychologist as well and tell him their girls couldn't get along with Jackie's child either. The other mothers made the calls as quickly as they packed their kids' Louis Vuitton bags. This mother's manipulative tactics guaranteed her daughter was placed in the class with all her friends while Jackie's daughter was left out, alone."

"Nice way to treat a friend. No wonder she's upset."

"Yeah, I get it. I would be hurt too if the roles were reversed. But I'd be able to put things into perspective and move on. There would be no way I'd cause even more drama."

He cocked his head to the side and stared at me with unblinking eyes. "Really?"

I felt my face flush. "Well, I certainly wouldn't refuse to participate in a carpool because Donna's daughter was in it, which is what Jackie did. And of course, her posse is supporting her."

"They're all grown women. I'm sure they had reasons."

"Yeah, right, Craig." I stood up and kissed the top of his wavy jet-black hair. "Bless your heart. For someone who has such book smarts, you're naïve sometimes. I'd be shocked if half the women in Jackie's fan club would even be able to decide what to eat for lunch if their fearless leader wasn't there to direct them. I've seen these women in action. They all idolize her."

"Maybe they have reason to?"

I clenched my teeth.

"I'm simply saying, Syd, I think you're blowing this all out of proportion. It'll take some work, but you ladies will sort out the schedule once again."

Craig seemed ready to end the conversation. He'd rather be outside playing Frisbee with our daughter.

I put my elbows on the table and rested my head in my hands. "What do I do about Julia? Amanda's best friend." I sighed.

"I really couldn't care less if Julia's mom is," I made air quotes, "'out of the carpool,' but I do feel sorry for Julia. She didn't do anything wrong, and now she's going to have to pay the price because of her mother's actions. If the moms aren't accepting Julia into their cars because of this fight, will they invite the girl over for play dates, birthday parties, or sleepovers?" I got up and started to pace around the kitchen. "She and Amanda are in the same first-grade class. I know Amanda is going to want to pal around with her. Do we have to worry these other kids are going to shun her because of their mothers, who are clearly as mature as a toddler? What is wrong with people?"

"You've got me." He raised his arms over his head and stretched. "Unfortunately, I think things are only going to get worse."

"I know." I sat back down and took a bite of my cookie. "This town is so superficial. The people here don't share the same values as us. I worry about how it will effect Amanda growing up here."

"She doesn't have to."

"What do you mean?" My breath hitched in my throat, and I looked around our newly remodeled kitchen. "This is where we live.

This is our home."

Craig pushed his plate away. "It doesn't have to be forever."

I blinked. "What are you talking about?"

He leaned in. "Maybe we should consider making a change, Syd."

I swallowed hard. "What kind of change?"

"A move."

"A move?" I felt my eyes bulge. "Why on earth would we move? We love our house and look at all the work we did. It's finally perfect."

Craig and I were renovation junkies. We'd spent years improving this house and did a lot of the work ourselves.

"I know." I followed his gaze as his green eyes scanned the room. "Our house is wonderful. But let's face it; we don't love this town anymore. Honestly, I'm not sure we ever really did."

Craig and I had decided to settle in Forest River ten years ago, right after we'd gotten married. One of the paralegals in his office grew up here and recommended we visit the community once she'd learned we were in the market to buy a home. We immediately fell in love with all the unique stores and restaurants located in the heart of town. Both Craig and I were lovers of water, so living so close to a lazy river was quite appealing to us.

I instantly regretted eating the cookie, which now sat like a lead weight in the pit of my stomach. "What are you talking about?"

"Come on, Syd. We never were part of this community. We've kept to ourselves, and it was wonderful until Amanda started school. You know as well as I do that the people here are not like us. We don't belong." He folded his arms across his chest. "You carried on all last year about how obnoxious and phony the mothers were. You kept fretting about how you were afraid Amanda would become spoiled by having to keep up with her classmates. This school year hasn't even started yet, and the drama is already in full force. Do we really want to raise our daughter in this type of environment?"

I shifted in my chair. Although he had some valid points, this was my home. "I don't know."

"Consider your commute for a minute. How many hours a

week do you spend in your car?"

"Way too many." I frowned. One of the worst days of my career was when my boss announced he was moving our office. I'd even contemplated resigning as a result.

"If we moved closer to your office, you'd be able to spend more time with Amanda."

"That would be nice." I imagined my life without a two-and-a-half-hour daily ride in bumper-to-bumper traffic.

"You know what else would be nice?" Craig continued. "If we lived closer to your family."

Unlike Craig's siblings who'd dispersed across the country when his parents had retired and moved to Florida, my sister, Bethany, and I remained in New York. In fact, Bethany lived close to where we grew up, near the town where my parents still resided.

"Yes, it would be. I'd love to be able to pop over and visit them rather than always having to plan an excursion, especially now that Dad hasn't been well." My father had had a heart attack a few months before and needed a double bypass. While he was recovering nicely from surgery, it was a wake-up call for my sister and me about our parents' mortality. I stayed with my mom while he underwent the procedure, but it was difficult for me to return home afterward. I did wish I lived closer to them like my sister.

I picked at my cuticle. "But Craig, I love it here."

His eyes narrowed. "Do you really?"

I looked around the room once more. "Of course I do. Where is all this coming from anyway? We've lived here for ten years. Since when have you thought about moving?"

He bit his lip. "I really haven't. Last week I received an email from a local real estate agent. She has someone who's very interested in buying a house in this neighborhood. She asked if we'd consider showing ours. I didn't reply, but it's been gnawing at me ever since." He rubbed his forehead. "This town is very hot right now. People want to live here, and not many houses go up for sale. When they do go on the market, they sell pretty much instantly and usually for more than the asking price."

"I know. It's crazy." A family who'd lived down the street from us had put their house on the market a year ago, and after only a week they found themselves in a bidding war between two prospective buyers.

"Maybe we should consider it, Syd. We can probably get top dollar for this place. Then, we could move into an even bigger house in a more relaxed kind of town."

I picked up my phone. "Crap," I muttered as I scanned the twenty-five text messages I had missed. So much for the ladies sorting anything out. Relaxed they were not. Would I be able to survive a drama-filled term? Would we be better off living someplace else?

CHAPTER TWO

"MOM, I'VE GOT TO GO." I almost dropped my phone as I shoved a basket of stuffed animals and dolls, which had been scattered all over our den floor moments ago, into the hall closet. "Yes, we'll try to come over this weekend. Give Daddy my love."

It was late Wednesday afternoon, and a week after the new school year had started. Craig and I had both come home early from work, although I arrived later than I'd planned. Now I had no time to change out of my work clothes or see Amanda before Sally, our babysitter, took her to the park. Turning to face my husband, I asked, "Tell me again why we're doing this?"

"Why not?" His eyes sparkled as he neatly folded the afghan his grandmother had made us when we'd gotten engaged.

"That's not a good answer, you know." I smoothed my beige pencil skirt and tucked my crisp white blouse back in.

"I mean we have nothing to lose here, Sydney. We're not doing anything. We're only exploring our options." He gently poked me in the ribs. "I think, especially given everything we did around this place, it would be interesting to see what it's worth, don't you?"

"I suppose." I fiddled with my thin, gold necklace that Amanda, meaning Craig, had bought me for Mother's Day last year. "What if she hates the place?"

He shrugged. "Who cares? It won't matter. It's not like we actually want to sell and move, right?"

I closed my eyes. "Right." I felt queasy. I couldn't decide what worried me more: some stranger finding fault with the home we'd built or her falling in love with it. Craig's enthusiasm didn't help calm my nerves, either.

From the moment I'd reluctantly agreed to let him have the real estate agent come to view the house with her client, he'd become completely preoccupied with making sure our home was in tip-top shape. I knew I shouldn't complain too much–he had been a cleaning machine. He'd even fixed the creaky basement step that I had been nagging him about for months. And while he wouldn't admit it, I was petrified he had already made up his mind about where he wanted us to spend our future.

"Come here," Craig said and held out his arms.

I was only in his embrace for a second or two when I heard a car pull into our driveway. I glanced at my watch and exhaled slowly. "They're early."

"Relax." He kissed the top of my head. "Nothing's going on here." As we heard a second car approach our driveway, he added, "I'll go and answer the door."

I nibbled at a cuticle and examined the two women who were now standing on our front porch. It was clear who was whom. The real estate agent was in her early sixties. She was short, barely five feet tall. She had dark blond hair, which was cut in a bob and wore a gray pinstriped power suit. She was holding a clipboard and talking a mile a minute to the other woman, who towered above her. The younger lady, who appeared to be in her late twenties or early thirties, had a long, clearly dyed, brassy blond ponytail. She wore the uniform of the neighborhood: black Lululemon pants, a fitted white tee shirt, and designer sneakers. She nodded her head furiously as she frantically typed on her mobile phone. Thankfully she had the good graces to slip the device into her Prada purse when Craig approached the doorway.

"Hi. Come on in," he said and held open the door for the women.

"Craig?" the broker questioned, her right hand extended. My husband nodded.

"Hi." She turned on the charm and flashed him a killer watt smile. "I'm Rosemary Sanders. We spoke on the phone." Gesturing to the woman beside her, she said, "This is my client, Kara." Her voice was very nasal and high-pitched. "It's nice to finally meet you both."

"This is my wife, Sydney."

I smiled and also shook the women's hands. I was impressed by Kara's strong grip.

"Unfortunately," Rosemary turned to her client, "I don't know much about this house since I've never been in it before. So I suggest we take a look around."

Kara nodded. Her eyes scanned the room as quickly as her fingers had typed on her phone.

Craig placed his hand on Rosemary's shoulder. "I know it's not conventional, but I'd be happy to show you the house, and answer any questions you have since we know this place inside and out." Indicating me, he said, "We've lived here for ten years. And we've put a lot of love into this home. We bought the house right after we were married. I'd be kind if I described it in a state of disrepair." Craig waved his hands as he spoke. "When we first bought the house, there were a lot of little rooms on this floor. We removed as many walls as we could; we wanted an open floor plan."

Kara's eyes lit up. Apparently, she was a fan of open and airy. She hung on Craig's every word. I expected her eyes to have glazed over when he mentioned the house's mechanics, but instead she seemed mesmerized. When we entered the kitchen, she gravitated to our six-burner BlueStar range, which faced the big window. "Wow, I guess you guys like to cook?"

I felt a slight sense of calm come over me and remembered the first meal we'd cooked in the house, chicken Francese with sautéed spinach. "Yes, we actually spend a lot of time in this kitchen, as a family."

Kara turned on two burners. "Oh, you don't mind, do you?"

I folded my arms across my chest and smiled tightly. "No. Go right ahead."

With a gleam in her eyes, she said, "My husband, Jonathan, and I love to cook too. We're so not the norm in this town, huh?"

"You can say that again. Some of our daughter's classmates' mothers store sweaters in their stoves."

Rosemary scratched her forehead as Kara giggled. "Good to know not much has changed around here since I was little."

"You grew up here?" I asked.

"Yep. Three blocks away, actually, on Forest. My older sister is in town too. She lives closer to the high school, though. And while her house is amazing, I like this part of town much better, especially this block." She paused. "Growing up, my best friend lived on the corner." Her eyes clouded over. "I spent most of my childhood in her house. Her mother was like a second mom to me."

My mind skimmed through everyone on my street. "Jane Wilson?"

Kara nodded.

"Oh, she still lives here."

"I know." She gave me a closed mouth smile. "I'm going to stop over and visit with her for a bit when we finish up here." She sniffed. "I remained close with Jane over the years. After her daughter passed away in the car accident, our bond deepened. Caroline was Jane's only child, you know."

I nodded. I couldn't imagine a worse fate, especially since I too only had one kid. The accident took place two years before. Jane's daughter, who lived in Michigan, was home to celebrate Thanksgiving with her family. She went out to pick up bagels for breakfast on Black Friday and was hit by a drunk driver. She died upon impact.

"Obviously, losing Caroline at such a young age was devastating. I've tried very hard to be there for her. I would love nothing more than to live within walking distance of her house."

I raised my hand to my lips as my mouth went dry. "Um, Kara," butterflies filled my stomach, "you're not going to mention to Jane why you were here, are you?

Mrs. Wilson was born and raised in this town. She put Sally's knowledge of the local gossip to shame. Our mail woman even had tea with her every Tuesday.

"No, no. Of course not." She touched my arm for emphasis, and I prayed I could trust her.

The last thing I wanted was the word we were considering moving to spread among the other mommies. I feared they wouldn't want their kids to waste time playing with Amanda if she'd soon be leaving town.

"Rosemary stressed you wanted to keep my visit on the down

low. Don't worry. I won't say a peep. I'll tell her I'm meeting my sister for dinner and I got to town earlier than expected."

Craig led the group upstairs toward the bedrooms. "Who's your sister, anyway?" I asked as I bent down to pick up Amanda's stray sock.

"Mia. Mia Montgomery. Do you know her?"

I squinted and did a mental inventory of all the mothers I had met over the past two years. While the name sounded familiar, I couldn't place it. "Does she have kids who go to Forest River Elementary?"

"Her youngest is in fifth, and her other two are in middle school."

No wonder the name didn't ring any bells. While I did know my fair share of mommies in this town, pretty much all of them had a first grader in their house.

"We have four bedrooms in total." Craig pointed down the hallway. "Right now, we have three set up as bedrooms and the fourth as an office. Like downstairs, all the bathrooms were all recently renovated." A satisfied smile spread across his face. "Oh, and we have two more full bathrooms up here, as well."

Rosemary jotted this tidbit down on her clipboard, where she had been scribbling ever since she'd set foot in the door. She'd barely uttered a word during the entire tour, allowing Craig to do all the talking. I never expected my husband would take such an active role in tonight's festivities. But he appeared to be having the time of his life bragging about our home, so who was I to complain?

"We have this set up as a spare bedroom." Craig slowly opened the first door. Except for when my husband's parents made their annual pilgrimage from Boca Raton, the room usually remained empty. When we'd first moved in, I'd imagined we'd have more than one child and a lot of overnight guests. Sadly, neither came to fruition. I had a few miscarriages after Amanda was born. And when Craig's siblings came to town, occasionally they'd sleep over, although usually they opted to stay at a hotel instead.

Craig then opened the door to my office. "Pardon the mess." He cleared his throat. "Sydney is quite the slob."

"Yeah, I can see." Kara giggled. Her eyes grew wide as she

studied the immaculate room. "Sydney, I need to take organization lessons from you."

I grinned. "Well, clutter drives me bonkers, and this is the only room I have complete control over. I refuse to let Craig work in here because then it would look like a bomb exploded at a convenience store."

"So, Kara, what makes you want to move back to town, now?" I asked.

"Oh, it's the right time." She checked herself out in the bathroom mirror before returning her attention to me. "I had the best childhood in this town. I promised myself when I grew up and started a family, I would come back here to raise my kids." She placed her hand on her flat stomach. "And it's time." She beamed. "We're due in April."

"How wonderful. Congratulations!" I sucked in my stomach. How many hours daily must she spend at the gym to have a killer body like that, especially being over three months pregnant? No more excuses. I would start my diet this week. I knew I should probably lose the extra twenty pounds I had been carrying since Amanda was born. I was comfortable with my weight and appearance for the most part. It was only when I was with the school moms that I felt insecure and self-conscious. Then I felt like I was judged for both working full-time and not being a size two.

"This is our daughter's room," Craig announced.

Kara let out a small yelp when she entered the haven we'd created for Amanda. The room had pale pink walls and a mulberry wool shag carpet. There was a crystal chandelier over our daughter's queen size bed. There was a window bench, also covered in a plush mulberry fabric, in front of the big bay window that faced the backyard. The seat was covered with dolls and stuffed animals. Shelving surrounded the room and contained more toys, dolls, and books.

"It's something special, isn't it?" He put his arm around my waist and squeezed me tightly. "My wife put her heart and soul into designing this room. She painted the mural herself."

Kara walked over and studied the carnival scene that took me over a year to sketch out and paint. Gently she ran her hand over it.

"It's beautiful, Sydney."

"Thanks. Our daughter is the envy of Forest River Elementary School, because of these digs."

"Yes, I know."

My stomach did a somersault. What could she possibly know about Amanda and why? Were there any Forest River family facts not broadcast through the mommy rumor mill?

CHAPTER THREE

CRAIG SLOWLY SHUT OUR DOOR. "Well, that was interesting."

I angled myself, so I was able to see the driveway, while no one outside could see me, or at least I hoped they couldn't. It was impossible to take my eyes off the two women who were huddled together, conspiring. Neither was making a move to leave my front yard. I was probably paranoid, but it looked like they were concocting a plan to take over the world, well, at least my world.

"Want a glass of wine?"

"Um, sure," I muttered. It was five o'clock, and normally I'd still be crunching numbers at work. I knew I should take advantage of a rare afternoon at home, but I was unable to move.

My husband placed two glasses and a bottle of pinot noir on the living room table. "Come on, Syd. Sit down and have a drink."

I couldn't tear myself away. I didn't even budge an inch. "I'll be there in a sec."

"Amanda and Sally will be back any minute from the park. Relax while you can." He patted the sofa.

"Oh my God!" I gasped and did a double take. "I don't believe it!" My voice raised several decibels.

"What?"

My mouth hung open, and I shook my head. "That Kara woman is busy walking around our property taking pictures of our house. And now she's going in the backyard! Who does she think she is anyway?"

He lounged back on the couch and placed his feet on the coffee table. "What's the big deal?"

"What's the big deal?" I ran my fingers through my hair. "Are you dense or something? We're talking about our house! Why does she need pictures of it on her phone?"

"Are you seriously asking me that question?" He smirked at me. "And I'm the dense one. Sydney? Are you blind? Did you not see the expression on her face when she entered the front door? She tried to keep her emotions in check and failed miserably. She fell in love with this place instantly, not that anyone could blame her."

I grunted in reply and kept watch for about ten more minutes. I sighed loudly. "Finally, they're gone." I picked up the glass Craig had poured me and took a giant gulp of wine before sitting down next to him on the couch. Then I addressed his comment. "I know. Kara looked like a kid in a candy store the entire time she was here. Did you see her face when you pointed out the Jacuzzi tub in the master bathroom? I thought she was going to rummage in the vanity for some eucalyptus Epsom salts and strip down to her skivvies so she could enjoy a soak."

Sally opened our front door, and Amanda raced in and squealed, "Mommy and Daddy are home!" She threw her arms around my neck. "I had the best time at the park today with Cassidy!"

I beamed. School had only been in session for a couple of weeks, and she'd already made new friends. I was the opposite of my daughter growing up. I was very quiet and shy. It took me forever to make my first friend, Kelly, who was also socially awkward. We were joined at the hip and hung out exclusively with each other. I'd be lying if I said I hadn't wished I was one of the popular girls, but at least initially, I was happy with the way things were.

I kissed the top of Amanda's head; she was growing up so fast. She was such a confident little girl. I prayed she'd remain that way forever.

Amanda bounced her legs. "You won't believe what happened at the park." Her excitement was contagious, providing a reprieve from all the real estate talk until the house phone rang.

I stood up. "I'll get it. It's probably a telemarketer."

"Hello," I practically whispered, expecting a digital recording to inform me how I could lower my heating costs by switching to solar power.

Instead, a high-pitched enthusiastic shriek bombarded me.

"Sydney? Hi! I didn't expect to reach you. I thought you'd still be at work and I'd have to leave a message with Sally. It's Jackie. Jackie Martin, Cassidy's mom! How are you?"

I walked toward the kitchen. "Good, and you?" My heart skipped a beat. I crossed my fingers Jackie hadn't gotten into an argument with another mother. The last thing I wanted to do right now was revamp the carpool schedule yet again since it finally seemed to be settled.

"Me too! So, listen. Cassidy was at the park playing with Amanda. The girls had such an amazing time together," Jackie gushed.

"I know. Amanda was just filling us in."

"I'm delighted that Cassidy seems to have taken a liking to your daughter. I hope they can get even closer this year. Wouldn't that be wonderful for all of us?"

"Sure." All I cared about was my daughter's happiness. I didn't care who her friends were as long as they were good kids, and she enjoyed spending time with them.

She cooed, "My Cassidy's birthday party is going to be in two weeks, on Saturday at noon. I haven't picked up the invitations yet, but it will be the birthday bash of the year! Definitely one not to miss."

"Amanda was blown away by Cassidy's party last year."

Although my daughter wasn't in the same kindergarten class as Cassidy, and barely knew her, she'd received an invitation. The Martins must have invited the entire grade. When I'd picked Amanda up, I'd been shocked at how over the top the event was. Between the fun house, cotton candy stand, and professional face painters it felt more like a school carnival than a birthday party for a five-year-old.

"Oh, well, last year was nothing compared to what I have up my sleeve this year." Her voice raised several octaves. "Of course, I've scheduled the fun house again. How could I not? It's always such a hit with the children. I've arranged to have two magicians and a clown come. There will also be a petting zoo set up in the backyard. The pièce de résistance is I managed to get Yesterday's Yogurt to come by in a truck. After the cake is served the kids can have their pick of any one of eighteen flavors either in a cup or cone, with as many toppings as their little hearts desire."

"Wow," I replied, repulsed. If a first grader had a party like this now, what did they have to look forward to when they got older? I couldn't help but imagine what type of wedding Cassidy would one day have.

"Oh, yes. It will be wonderful. Truly a memory she'll never forget. I digress, though." In a second her tone turned icy. "The reason I called is I wanted to let you know that Cassidy was *planning* on inviting Amanda."

The way she said "planning" sent a chill down my spine. "Thank you. I'm sure Amanda will have a blast."

"Oh, no doubt she will. I like to expose my daughters to all children, but once they enter first-grade, we narrow the selection." She giggled. "I know the moms of this town pray their kids are lucky enough to make the cut."

I rested my head in my hands. I was all for having confidence. But the way she carried on rubbed me the wrong way.

"Did you know I'm the PTA president of Forest River Elementary, Sydney, and have been for years?"

A lump formed in my throat as her agenda became crystal clear to me. "Yes, I'm aware."

"Oh, good. So, after the whole Donna debacle went down, she decided it was best not to participate this year. She was our treasurer."

I absentmindedly thumbed through a fashion magazine I had flung on the kitchen table this morning. The designer clothing couldn't defuse the panic I felt radiating through my veins. "Oh, that's too bad."

"Yes, and no." Her voice softened. "Of course, it's always a loss when someone leaves the team, but it's also an amazing opportunity for the group as a whole. After all, when you get new members, you get fresh eyes and innovative ideas."

I swallowed hard. "Mmm hmm."

"Well, the ladies and I had an impromptu meeting and decided you'd be the perfect replacement for Donna!"

I closed the magazine with such force it fell off the table. The last thing in the world I wanted to do was get involved in the PTA. The thought of spending my free time with that bunch of self-centered phonies, who disguised their need for power as concern for the kids, made me break out into hives. "I don't think so, Jackie."

"Oh, don't be silly! I know you're a bookkeeper or something."

I rubbed my forehead. "I'm a CPA and the CFO of a large international food distributor, which is why I can't commit to helping. My position is a bit more than merely a nine-to-five job. I put in a lot of hours at the office and home."

"Oh, yes, how unfortunate you have to work so hard." She made a clucking sound. "Don't worry, though. The position won't require a lot of your time. We don't meet too often, and when we do, we usually have so much fun! And as for time management, you can accomplish most of your actual duties remotely, so your career won't get in the way. You'll be magnificent!"

"I truly appreciate you all thinking of me, and of course your vote of confidence makes me feel wonderful, but I don't know if I can do this." No, I knew I couldn't. I needed to figure out a way to get more free time, not less.

"Come on, Syd. I know you'll enjoy every second of it. And besides, you should be thinking about Amanda, not yourself."

Even though I had figured out her end-game a while ago, I decided to play dumb. Trying to sound as sweet and innocent as Jackie had pretended to be during most of this call, I said, "I'm sorry. I don't understand how my joining the PTA would affect my daughter."

"Oh, Sydney. I thought you were a smart woman. Must I spell it out for you? The PTA moms and their children are, let's just say, a very a close-knit group. We look after our own, and we stick together, if you know what I mean. Of course, I don't want to pressure you. You can take some time and think about joining. I can wait another few days for an answer, which, wow," she paused, and her tone turned frigid again, "coincides perfectly with the exact time I will have to pass out invitations to Cassidy's birthday party. It would be a crying shame if Amanda weren't able to join, wouldn't it?"

My blood began to boil at the audacity of this woman, who took the word "bitch" to a whole new level. I closed my eyes and took a deep breath to calm myself and steady my voice. All I wanted to do was tell her to go to hell, but I knew that would have disastrous ramifications for my daughter. Putting Amanda first, I said, "You know, Jackie, I think you're right. I'm sure I can figure out a way to juggle things around to make time for the PTA."

"Excellent!" She began to clap. I scratched at the hives that now dotted my arms, as she gushed, "Oh, the other ladies will be delighted when I tell them the spectacular news. And of course, my Cassidy will be thrilled when I tell her Amanda will be able to attend her party after all!" Without even stopping for a breath of air, "Now, getting down to business, the first meeting is coming up. Check your email. I just sent you the details. You made the right decision, Sydney."

"Thanks," I muttered and rested my head in my hands.

"Well, I got to go! Ta-ta for now!"

I splashed some cold water on my face before rejoining my family in the den. I hugged Amanda tightly. Then Craig whispered something into her ear and she took off like a bullet, leaving us alone.

"What's wrong with you?" Craig wrinkled his brow and studied me. "Your face is beet red."

I picked up my almost full glass of wine and downed it, wishing it were vodka. "I'm in a little shock. I was just manipulated into managing the treasury function for the PTA."

"Manipulated?" Craig sat up straight in his seat. His mouth hung open, and he leaned forward. "I don't understand. How is that even possible?"

I wrung my hands. "Believe it or not, that's what happened. It was Jackie, Cassidy's mom, on the phone. She coerced me; I didn't have a choice."

He raised an eyebrow. "You always have a choice."

I wish he didn't always see everything in black and white.

"Not really."

He shrugged. "Big deal. She doesn't need to go to the birthday party."

"Yes, but she wants to. The party is only the tip of the issue.

Jackie insinuated Amanda's acceptance with her classmates would be contingent on my participating. I really didn't have a choice."

"This is ridiculous. Call Jackie back and tell her you changed your mind."

"I can't, and I won't. Don't you get it? I. Didn't. Have. A. Choice! Amanda likes Cassidy and her friends."

"True, but one thing doesn't have to do with another."

"Seriously?" I placed my hands on his chest. Bless his heart. He was so naïve. "How are you not able to see what goes on here?"

He stared at me blankly.

"The kids are in first grade. They can't pick themselves up and go hang out with their friends anytime they like. They need their parents to take them. The parents are in control! The women of this town are concerned with who their children associate with for all the wrong reasons. They don't give a darn about who their children like the most. They are only interested in whether the other parents seem cool or worthwhile. If they want to foster friendships, they will.

"And if they desire to sabotage it, they will do that too. We're talking about social engineering at its finest! Come on, look at poor Julia. I'm sure she's going to pay the price for Donna's fight with Jackie. I'm not about to put Amanda in that position. If it means I have to volunteer my time for the PTA, so be it. I'll do what I have to for our daughter. And you my friend," I gently kissed his cheek, "will be her soccer coach."

His eyes grew wide. "I'm going to be her what?"

"You heard me. Everyone is planning on playing soccer this year, so Amanda wants to as well." I snuggled up next to him and massaged his neck. "I want a member of our home team with her."

"This is going to be one very long year."

CHAPTER FOUR

"WHERE'S THE FIRE?" Craig asked as I raced into the house. He didn't even bother to look up from his laptop. He had to be taking his frustrations out on his keyboard because I'd never seen anyone pound so hard while they typed. It shocked me he didn't break his computer. As usual, he had manila folders spread out all over the sofa, across the coffee table, and on the floor. I came home to this exact scene every evening. But despite the mess, I had no complaints. I was thankful that Craig was able to leave his office early enough to relieve Sally since my work schedule wasn't as predictable.

Slightly out of breath from sprinting from my Lexus SUV to my front door, I called out, "I'm late!"

He arched his eyebrow and I carelessly kicked off my high heels, happy I didn't twist my ankle, again, when I made my mad dash. "I left my office later than I'd planned. I couldn't get this confused client off the phone, then traffic was torturous. There was a little fender bender on the parkway, so everyone and their uncle had to slow down and gawk." I looked down at my watch and exhaled. "Crap. It's even later than I thought it was."

"What's the big deal? So you're home a half hour later than normal. Sally defrosted the baked ziti, and I put it in the oven. Want a glass of wine?" he asked although he didn't get off the couch.

I shook my head. "Not tonight."

He tilted his head to the side. "Are you sick?"

"Oh, that's a loaded question." I pursed my lips. "Physically I'm fine, but I do have a case of the jitters. Did you forget? Tonight's my first PTA meeting. I have to be at Jackie's house at eight-thirty," and then imitating her, I added *"sharp!"* I sighed. "Which was why I wanted to get home early. I'm barely going to have a chance to hang out with Amanda tonight. Speaking of which, where is she?"

Usually, when I came home from work, I'd find Amanda sitting cross-legged on the floor next to her dad doing some sort of arts and crafts project.

"Her room," Craig replied without taking his eyes off his laptop.

"Is she okay?" I asked, but I didn't stick around long enough for him to answer. I took the stairs two at a time and immediately went to my daughter's room. She must have sensed my presence because she discarded her stuffed bunny and ran right into my arms. "Mommy, you're home. I missed you so, so much!"

I squeezed her tightly and kissed the top of her head. When she didn't break the embrace after a few seconds, my heart filled with dread. While my daughter was affectionate, she was far from clingy. She preferred to kiss and run rather than have a loving linger.

I scooped her up, carried her to her bed, and placed her down in the center. I sat next to her and realized she had changed clothes from this morning.

"What's wrong, baby?" I absently played with her pigtails.

She looked up at the ceiling. Her lip quivered. "Nothing."

"Come on. I know something is troubling you." I tickled her slightly. "So, spill it."

She placed the palm of her hand against her forehead. "I've had a very rough day, Mommy."

I bit my lip to suppress my smile. She totally got her drama queen streak from me. "What happened, baby?"

She looked me square in the eyes. "It was all my tee-shirt's fault."

"I'm sorry, sweetheart. I'm not following you. What could your shirt possibly have done?"

"*Everyone* wore the same one to school today, just like we planned at Cassidy's party."

I picked up the wrinkled hot pink shirt she had carelessly tossed on the floor. On the front of the shirt, in big bold letters, it said: "We had the best time at Cassidy Martin's sixth birthday party." Saturday's date was noted, as well. Then in a font designed to resemble children's handwriting, about fifty kids' names were listed.

On the back of the shirt, there was a picture of a petting zoo, clown, musician, and a yogurt truck.

"It was so cool to see everyone in the same shirt!" My daughter's face lit up. "It was so much fun. I loved it! But then..." Amanda ran her fingers over her lips before continuing. "At recess, we all were hanging out with Cassidy. We were laughing and talking about the party. It was so great." Amanda's green eyes filled with tears. "Until it stopped being fun. All of a sudden Julia came from nowhere. She tugged at my shirt and dragged me away from my friends. She was very angry, Mommy."

"What did she say?" My heart hurt. I hated when my little girl was upset. But what made me feel worse was that I wasn't here to comfort her when she came home from school. Craig didn't even notice she was troubled; he just kept working, business as usual.

"Julia said I have a lot of new friends, so I don't need to be her friend anymore. She said she's going to find a new best friend. And she told me she's never going to let me come over to her house to play again. EVER!"

Life was ironic. Only a few weeks ago I'd tossed and turned all night long, worried sick my daughter would be shunned because of her friendship with Julia, and now Julia was rejecting her? I wondered how much of today's drama was Julia's anger. Did her aggression stem from the fact that her mother, Donna, had brainwashed her as a form of retaliation for being excluded from Cassidy's birthday party?

Amanda's silent tears transformed into full-blown sobs. I hugged her tightly. "Let it out, sweetie." And as my daughter cried, I did too. I couldn't even imagine how horrible she'd felt when Julia had confronted her. She must have been so scared too. It couldn't have been easy to see such resentment from someone she thought was her friend.

Finally, her tears slowed, but she continued to hiccup as she gasped for air.

"Amanda, look at me and listen carefully."

"Okay." Her bottom lip quivered.

I twirled her pigtail. "Julia was feeling very sad today. Do you know why she wasn't at Cassidy's party?"

Amanda shrugged her tiny shoulders.

"She wasn't at the party because she wasn't invited. How would you feel if all your friends went to a super fun party and no one asked you to go too?"

She furrowed her brow. "I'd feel sad?"

"Yeah, you'd be sad, upset, and angry. It wasn't very nice of Julia to take her frustration out on you, but you're her friend. Sometimes you treat those you love the most the worst because you can. Because you know they care about you too and always will. Most of the time you don't mean what you say. Remember the time when you got so mad at Daddy for not letting you watch the scary movie with your cousins when we were staying at Grandma's? You said some mean things to Daddy, but he knew you were only upset, remember?"

She nodded.

"Don't worry, sweetie. I'm sure in a few days Julia will calm down, and everything will be okay with you guys. And if it makes you feel any better, I can call her mommy."

CHAPTER FIVE

"SYDNEY, HELLO," Jackie sang out when she opened the thick wood door of her large Colonial home.

I looked up at Jackie since she was a good three inches over my five-foot-five frame. Even with limited makeup, and her ash blond hair pulled back into a loose ponytail, she was stunning, with the most mesmerizing blue eyes. Jackie was ten years my senior but didn't look her age in the slightest.

I took in my surroundings. Jackie's house was the complete opposite of what I had expected. She was one of the most cutting-edge, fashion-wise, ladies I knew. Yet her home was extremely formal, with dark wood moldings, marble floors, and crystal chandeliers. Long and heavy draperies covered all the windows, and there were antiques everywhere.

"I'm so glad to see you." She took my worn black sweater and hung it in the hall closet. She glanced at the grandfather clock in the corner of the room. "We were getting worried about you since you were late."

I looked at my watch. Probably for the first time this year, I managed to get someplace precisely on time. "What do you mean, late? You said to come over at eight-thirty."

"Yes, I know." Jackie walked down the corridor. Her shoes clicked loudly with every step she took. "Being on time would have brought you here five minutes early." With a dismissive nod, she trilled, "Anyhoo, don't worry about it. It's your first meeting, after all. You'll get into the groove in no time, I'm sure."

She opened the door to the den where four ladies already sat. They were deep in conversation. On the coffee table, there were three different bottles of red wine, and two bottles of white were chilling in silver ice buckets. Also, there was a large cheese platter, three different types of hummus, cut-up vegetables, as well as assorted crackers and nuts.

"Everyone," Jackie announced and clapped her hands, "Sydney is here."

In stereo, four women answered, "Hi, Sydney!"

Pointing around the room, Jackie nodded. "You know everyone, right?"

I nodded, too, and greeted the women. I felt like I had just entered Barbie's dream house. With the exception of one woman, everyone resembled a living doll. They were all perfectly toned, meticulously made up, and had chemically created long, light locks.

"Excellent." Jackie beamed. "Now go on, girl. Help yourself to a glass of wine. Take your pick. I've got a cabernet, a pinot noir, a merlot, a sauvignon blanc, and a pinot grigio, and they're all open."

"Thanks." I'd never been so relieved to see booze in my life. I poured myself a glass of cabernet and sat down on the sofa next to one of the other mothers, Trisha Dickens.

"This is for you." Jackie danced in place before she handed me a cloth swag bag, embroidered with the words: "Proud Forest River Elementary PTA Mom!" "Go on, open it!" Jackie squealed, and her smile grew even wider. The other women stared at me.

Inside the bag was a leather notebook, five pens, a plastic bracelet, a water bottle, three tee shirts, a fleece hoodie, and a pair of yoga pants. Each item was hot pink and labeled with "Proud Forest River Elementary PTA Mom."

"Wow. Thanks." I wondered if I was expected to go out in public in this getup.

Jackie waved her hand in the air. "No thanks needed. You're one of us now!" She grinned, the other women cheered, and my stomach cramped.

"So, first things first," Jackie addressed the group. "We have a tremendous year ahead of us. The school board has already confirmed the date for the penny auction. It will take place on March nineteenth."

The women clapped enthusiastically. I was clueless. I felt I had no choice but to join in, half-heartedly. I couldn't help but wonder if my husband had his way, would we still be living in Forest River come springtime?

My lame attempt at applauding didn't go unnoticed, unfortunately. "Oh, Sydney. I forgot." Jackie patted my thigh. "Amanda is your only child, and you probably haven't been properly exposed to a penny auction yet." She tapped her pen against her hot pink clipboard. "Of all the fundraising events the PTA hosts, the auction is the most important. It benefits the first graders and sets the tone for the rest of their tenure at Forest River Elementary School. Usually, the PTA is made up of mommies with kids scattered all about the school, but this year out of the entire team, everyone here except for Stacey has a first grader! Which is superb, because that means unless there's a hiccup, and someone doesn't live up to her potential, we'll be working together for the next five years." She let out a little whoop. "I digress. Since almost all of us have a personal connection to the first-grade class, it is our opportunity to make this year's penny auction simply unforgettable!"

The ladies all hooted, cheered, and clapped again. I nodded and joined in more enthusiastically, even though I was still confused.

Stacey Williams turned to face me. When she pulled her dark blond hair into a ponytail, I couldn't take my eyes off her perfect biceps. "Amanda was in kindergarten last year. Surely you attended last year's event, didn't you?"

Before I could reply, Jackie chimed in, "No!" She pointed a manicured finger at me. "If I recall correctly, last year when the auction took place, you were traveling."

"You're right!" Claire Conroy chimed in. If the moms were to receive titles, Claire should be considered the PTA hottie. She was extremely petite, barely five-feet tall, and didn't have one ounce of fat on her frame, but man, did she have a rack! She pointed a long, magenta fingernail at me. "You weren't there. You were on vacation and totally missed it. Where did you guys go anyway? I hope it was somewhere warm and sunny, and that you had the best time ever. Especially since you missed such an amazing event!"

I licked my lips. "If only…Unfortunately, my husband's uncle passed away. We had to travel to attend his funeral."

"Was it at least somewhere warm and sunny?" Claire asked.

I looked at my lap. "No." I couldn't believe my ears. How could grown women be so callous?

Jackie cleared her throat. "What happened happened. The past is gone, and there's no turning back. We have to focus on the future. And this year the penny auction will be the best one Forest River Elementary has ever seen."

Trisha dipped a carrot into the hummus and rolled her eyes. "I sure hope it's better than last year's debacle. I, for one, don't want to scramble for donations again at the eleventh hour."

"Don't worry, Trisha." Jackie reached over and patted her on the thigh. "I have everything under control. I've already begun collecting donations."

"Good to know," Trisha said with a curt nod.

While I didn't know her well, I liked Trisha. She often dared to be different from the group. Unlike the rest of the ladies, she had dark hair like me, although hers was cut short in a blunt bob, which framed her freckled face. She wore cut-off jeans and flip-flops rather than the standard Lululemon ensemble.

I tilted my head toward her. "What happened last year?"

All the women groaned in unison.

"I've got this," Stacey answered and raised her hand, once again showing off her perfectly toned arms, and winked at our host. "Jackie, in a moment of weakness, relinquished control of the event to her friend, Donna." She paused for a second, her eyes narrowed on Jackie. "Then, Donna, in her infinite wisdom decided to enlist the aid of a non-PTA mother." Stacey dramatically rolled her eyes as if a mortal sin were committed. "Why she did this, we don't know. After all," she placed her hand on her chest, "every one of us would have been more than happy to help. Donna assured us that her friend needed the project. Apparently, this woman just found out her husband was cheating on her, and she was an emotional wreck and needed a distraction. We weren't happy about having an outsider in such a crucial role, but we went along with it."

"Worst decision ever!" Aimee chimed in and topped off her wine glass with some pinot grigio. Aimee, a former model, made

Jackie seem like a little person. She was practically six feet tall and super skinny. Also ten years my senior, Aimee didn't have one line or wrinkle on her face. Instead of being blessed with good genes, she was blessed by being married to a plastic surgeon.

"You can say that again," Jackie said. "At every meeting, we asked Donna to report on the status of the donations. She was never able to give us a straight answer. She just kept assuring us everything was under control. We made a major mistake all right. We trusted her." She closed her eyes briefly and bit her lip. "I should have learned my lesson then." She shook her head. "She had been a PTA mom for years, so I gave her the benefit of the doubt. I figured incorrectly she had a handle on things."

"Not even close." Claire sneered. "About two weeks before the auction was scheduled, we still didn't have any definitive answers as to how many donations we had. We had no idea how to plan for the event. We were completely in the dark! How could we hold an auction and not even know what we had to raffle off? It was insane."

"So desperate times call for desperate actions." Aimee's sapphire eyes twinkled. "Jackie called me, and together we went to this other woman's house." She smirked at our host and shrugged. "Saying that we went over sounds so polite, doesn't it?"

I nodded, as I was expected to. Something about Aimee's tone put me on edge. I couldn't even try to predict what had happened next.

"Yeah." Aimee scrunched her nose. "Well, we were anything but polite. The woman didn't want to let us in, so Chanel-clad commander pushed herself in the door. We pretty much stormed the joint as if we were invading enemy territory."

Jackie giggled.

"As soon as we walked in, I thought I was going to die." Aimee swallowed hard. "Thank God I was dieting for my sister's wedding. Because if I had eaten breakfast or lunch, I would have lost it! The place reeked of cat pee and dog poo."

Jackie shuddered. "I demanded that she turn over the donations, immediately. She looked so frightened and was barely able to form words when she brought us down to her basement. There were only a handful of items there, and they were all covered in pet hair, and..." Jackie grimaced. "Other unmentionables."

Claire grinned. "Miraculously, we were all able to call in some favors, and in less than two weeks, we scored two hundred donations and raised over twenty-five thousand dollars for the first grade."

The women all cheered again. This time I made a point to clap as hard as the rest of them. There was no way I wanted to get called out another time. In my wildest dreams, I could never have imagined a school fundraising event generating such a large sum of money.

Jackie raised her hands to her face. "I still can't believe we pulled it off." She leaned down, picked up her wine glass, and raised it high in the air. "Let's face it, with a dream team like this, anything is possible. Cheers, ladies!"

We all raised our glasses, and I took a long sip.

"Well, last year was enough drama for me." Jackie placed her glass back down on the table. "This year we won't have to worry, and we won't be embarrassed by the small sum of money raised either. We've all learned our lesson the hard way about involving outsiders. We'll never make the same mistake again. We will do everything together!"

All the ladies raised their fists in the air and started to chant, "Together, together, together!"

It was a minor miracle I didn't spit my wine across the room, although I did choke on it.

Stacey was polite enough not to comment on my coughing fit. "So who's doing what?"

Jackie picked up her clipboard but didn't glance down at it. "I say there's no reason to mess with perfection." She made eye contact with everyone, while she smiled widely. "You all did an amazing job with your tasks last year, so you will do the same ones again." She turned and faced me. "Sydney, I know you're new, but I have the utmost faith in you and your talents, so I saved the most important job for you."

I swallowed hard. "You did?" For the thousandth time tonight, I wondered what I'd gotten myself into, and why I was here.

"Oh, yes. You're in charge of getting the donations! Isn't that exciting?" She stared at me so hard I felt as if her gaze would burn a hole in my brain.

I carefully chose my words. "Oh wow, Jackie, thanks. I appreciate your confidence in me, but I don't know if I'm up to the task." I looked down at my sneakers. "It seems very, um, involved."

I might have imagined it, but I could have sworn they all bit their lips in a not-so-subtle attempt to express pity.

"Oh, I'm fully aware of your other obligations, Syd. You won't be alone in this. I'll be right at your side to help. We'll spend so much time together. It'll be great!"

CHAPTER SIX

DURING THE ENTIRE FOUR-BLOCK COMMUTE back to my house, I felt torn. Part of me wanted Craig to still be awake, so I could rehash the ridiculous evening with him. Another part of me, however, wished I'd find him fast asleep, snoring loudly, so that I could try to banish the memory of tonight from my mind. Well, at least until the morning. When I turned my key in our lock, I made up my mind. I prayed he'd be awake, waiting patiently for a play-by-play of the PTA party.

"Hey, sweetie," he called out from the couch then reached for the remote control to shut off the baseball game. He studied me up and down. "I see you survived your first Forest River PTA meeting, and you look like you're in one piece. Good job out of you!" He pointed at my swag bag. "A gift? Should I be jealous?" He smirked. "Here I was stuck home looking after Amanda and catching up on case files, and you were partying it up."

I flopped down next to him, kicked off my sneakers, and surveyed the room. It looked like my husband had enjoyed a party of his own tonight. The room was a complete mess. Potato chip crumbs were all over the couch. He'd spilled iced tea on the table but hadn't bothered to clean it up. And the floor was covered with crumpled up sheets of paper and Amanda's toys. For once, I put the need to tidy up aside. Instead, I sat down beside him and placed my feet on his lap, pinching my nose to ease my tension headache. "Oh, it was a hoot alright." I was still in shock about everything that had happened this evening.

"Come on." He massaged my feet. "You've been at the meeting for hours. There's no way it could have been that terrible."

I reached over and took a gulp of his iced tea, grimacing at the amount of sugar he'd added. "You have no idea. The calm portion of the evening was when I found out what my new role of treasurer would entail."

"I thought when that woman called you she said this wouldn't be time-consuming."

"Yeah, and I should never have believed one word that came out of her mouth." I started to nervously bounce my leg the same way my dad always did when he was upset. "I have no idea how I'm going to do this, but at least I have Jackie to help me." I gave him a small, sad smile. "I know you were joking around tonight about her becoming my new bestie. I think you were onto something, though. I'm pretty sure she's been scouting out a replacement BFF since she and Donna split up. And I have a sinking feeling I'm the chosen one."

He chuckled then opened his mouth to speak. Before he could let out a wisecrack I added, "Jackie seemed nicer than I expected, which isn't saying much." I rolled my eyes. "I don't need to be joined at the hip to her, or anyone else for that matter. Look, she gave me this." I reached into my bag and handed Craig the hot pink sheet of paper she'd slipped into my hand right before I left her house.

He quickly scanned it. His eyes protruded. He rolled up his sleeves and wiped a bit of sweat from his forehead with the palm of his hand. "This is ludicrous, Sydney. She can't honestly expect you to spend the next four Sundays with her traipsing all over town begging merchants for donations."

I chuckled. "Unfortunately, she does. Little does she know, I have a few aces up my sleeve."

Craig arched an eyebrow at me.

"Oh, come on, there's got to be some perks for having family members in retail," I said, thinking about my older sister, who was a buyer for a major department store. "Bethany always receives more samples than she can use. I have no doubt she'd share some with me to spare me a Sunday or two searching for swag."

"Good thinking. With your sister's help, you won't need this nonsense." He ripped up the schedule that Jackie had given me into little pieces. Little did he know the handwritten version wasn't the only copy I had. Jackie had written out the times and dates on the first page of my notebook, as well as forwarded it to me in a text and an email.

"Do you have any more assignments?"

I felt my cheeks flush. "No, but you do."

He narrowed his eyes. "What does that mean?"

I flashed him a tentative smile. "So, the meeting had to be cut short."

Craig glanced at his watch. "Cut short? You've been at Jackie's house for over three hours."

"I guess I should rephrase. The planned portion of the evening came to an abrupt halt when Jackie received a very upsetting text message."

"Do I even want to know what happened?" Craig rubbed his eyes.

"No. But if I had to live through it, you have to hear about it, my friend." I picked up a few kernels of popcorn from the bowl on the coffee table and chewed slowly. "Just as Jackie was about to go over how she pictured us utilizing the private Facebook group she'd created for the PTA, her phone blew up with text messages. They were from the mother of a little girl who was at Cassidy's birthday party this weekend. Apparently, not only did this child have the worst afternoon of her life, but she was also completely traumatized as a result of attending the party. The mother thinks she may even need counseling."

"What?" Craig glared at me. "I don't understand. Wasn't this the..." he paused to make air quotes, "party of the year?"

"Well, for everyone but this kid, apparently it was. According to her mother's account, first off, she was afraid of clowns. Second, when she went to the petting zoo one of the sheep looked at her funny."

"You're making this up." Craig laughed.

"I wish I was. You know I'm not this creative. And besides, like all the other ladies, I read every single text message. Trust me there were enough to write a full book." I patted my husband's thigh. "It gets better. So, after the sheep had scared her senseless, she walked away backward to keep one eye on the killer beast. Unfortunately, in the process, she ended up stepping in some pony poop."

Craig's laughter fueled me. "The little girl was so grossed out about the state of her shoe she was unable to eat lunch. Then, she claimed she wasn't offered any birthday cake, only frozen yogurt, which of course she couldn't eat because she's lactose intolerant."

"You're serious?" Craig wiped a tear away from his eye

My entire body shook with laughter. "After the mother had finished her rant, she demanded Jackie return the gift card she gave Cassidy as a present."

"No way!" Craig placed the bowl of popcorn on his lap and absently ate.

"Yes, way! I wish I could have videoed the reactions of the group for you. It was hysterical. Claire Conroy was the most outraged. She started to pace around Jackie's den, yelling and cursing about this mother's nerve. Spittle was even flying out of her mouth!"

Until that moment when I'd watched them all band together to support Jackie, I'd cursed myself for not being strong enough to have successfully avoided the PTA. Despite how crazy the women acted all night long I now saw the women as people, and not just Barbie dolls brought to life. Honestly, I was glad to be part of a group. I didn't realize until tonight how much I'd missed having friends like I did in college. I was always rushing around, and my friendships suffered. Craig and I socialized with others, don't get me wrong. But we had more acquaintances than true friends.

"Once everyone stopped plotting, Jackie explained that Cassidy didn't even want to invite this kid, but her mother had forced her. Jackie thought it would be nice to have her at the party since Cassidy is friends with her sister and they're all in the same first-grade class."

"Hold up. Now you lost me. Are you trying to tell me a mother of twins is making a fuss because one of her daughters had a bad time at a party? Did she even mention her other kid?"

I struggled to keep a straight face. "I never said the mother had two children, now did I?"

Craig stared at me, blinking his eyes quickly as if he were doing long division in his head. "You just told me her sister was in the same first-grade class."

"Yes, dear. Same father; different mothers. This mommy had an affair with a married man. The gem of a guy got both her and his wife pregnant at pretty much the same time. His wife divorced him as soon as she found out about his extracurricular activities. She's now remarried with a toddler."

"You're not making this up, are you?"

I shook my head.

He ran his fingers through his hair. "This all happened tonight?"

"Yep, scout's honor." I saluted my spouse. "Only Jackie had the inside scoop on this scandal. And once Jackie had finished sharing the entire tale, Trisha suggested we draft a petition to remove this kid from the school since technically she shouldn't be there in the first place. I'm pretty sure Trisha was joking. Jackie fell in love with the idea, just like the other ladies."

Craig buried his head in his hands.

"And since I was the only mommy married to an attorney, you, my love, were elected to draft the petition. Welcome to the team."

CHAPTER SEVEN

"CAN YOU PLEASE COME AND HELP ME?" I called out and tried unsuccessfully to open the screen door to my house.

"Here, give me that." My father reached for the large corrugated box I carried, which was filled to the brim with donations for the penny auction.

"No way, mister." I winked at him. "Just hold the door for me, okay? Craig can get the rest. You're not supposed to lift heavy things, remember?"

My dad sheepishly studied his shoes and held the door. I couldn't even imagine how frustrated he must have felt to have his activities and food choices so limited. As a former New York City police sergeant, who was strong as an ox, he was used to taking care of others, not someone who needed to be cared for.

"Is Mom here?" I asked, panicked I'd forgotten an appointment with my parents.

"Of course. Phyllis is in the kitchen baking cookies with your daughter. We found ourselves with a free afternoon and she needed an Amanda fix."

"Holy cow!" Craig exclaimed when he spotted the size of the box I carried. "Give it to me, babe."

"No, I've got it." I angled my head toward the driveway. "You can go and get the others, though."

"There's more?"

"Yep. Three more boxes. All in a day's work." I narrowed my eyes and whispered, "And make sure my dad doesn't try to help you carry any of them."

"Mommy!" Amanda, who looked like she'd rolled in flour,

screamed at the top of her lungs when she spotted me. "Grandma and Grandpa are here, and we're making cookies!"

"I see." I kissed the top of her head. "They're going to be delicious."

"I know! Grandma let me use extra chocolate." She danced in place as if the excitement was more than she could handle. "I ate some too!"

"I wouldn't expect any less." I playfully swatted her behind. She and my mother were both fully aware there was a no-candy-before-dinner rule in this house.

My mom pulled the tray of cookies out of the oven and put them on the counter. Then she wrapped her arms around me. It was probably my imagination, but I thought she felt a bit frail. "I hope you don't mind we stopped over, Sydney. I did call Craig before we came."

"How could I mind? I love seeing you guys." And I did. I did wish that Craig would have texted me to give me a heads up they were here. I would have cut my time short with Jackie and come home sooner to spend time with them.

It was already after six, and I was bone tired. I didn't want to have a late night. I had an early meeting tomorrow at work and getting Amanda to sleep on Sunday nights was a struggle.

After Craig had placed the last box down on our dining room table, he joined us in the kitchen. "So, I guess you and Jackie had a successful afternoon running around town. I told you that you'd only have to go donation begging for one day. You were so worried about losing all those Sundays for nothing!" He poked me in my arm and caught my father's eye. "One of these days, Carl, your daughter will start to listen to me. And when she does, she'll be so happy she finally saved herself so much unnecessary stress and aggravation."

I scowled at him. "You know, sometimes I totally hate you."

"Sydney, that's not nice," my mom scolded as she scrubbed the kitchen counter.

Amanda burst into laughter. She loved when my mother busted me for using a "bad" word.

"It's okay, Phyllis. It's hard for Syd that I'm right all the time." Craig elbowed my father, who shuffled a deck of cards after being beaten in a round of gin rummy with Amanda.

I snorted and took off my hot pink "Proud Forest River PTA Mom" hoodie that Jackie insisted I wear all day. "It sure is. One day maybe you'll understand how difficult it truly is."

Craig opened his mouth to speak, but I didn't give him a chance. "You think you know everything, don't you? Well, I've got news for you. You're wrong, my friend. While this may look like we hit the motherlode of merchandise, we barely made a dent in our donation requirements. In fact, Jackie was in a panic we may have to step up our game and commit to gallivanting around together for another weekend or two to make up for our shortfall."

He started to rummage through the various boxes. "How much crap do you guys need anyway?"

"Rummy!" Amanda announced with glee and spread out her cards on the table.

My father shuffled the deck and I faced my husband. "I need enough stuff to fill two hundred and fifty baskets with a retail value of between two hundred and one thousand dollars. I hope my sister keeps her word and sends some samples from the store. She told me she had them shipped out on Wednesday, but we've haven't received anything. Have we?"

Craig had a horrible habit of forgetting to tell me when we received certain pieces of mail or packages. I'd once spent forty-five minutes arguing with a customer service representative how they must have shipped my shoes to someone else's house because I never got them. In the middle of my rant, Craig had casually placed the box down in front of me. After I'd apologized profusely to the poor woman, he admitted they'd actually arrived ten days prior.

"No, Syd. I'd tell you if we received anything."

I let his comment pass. I didn't want to argue in front of my parents. "I know. I'm desperate. I'm counting on Bethany to save the day."

My mother sat down next to me and put her hand on my thigh. "Don't worry, honey. Bethany's never disappointed you before."

"Well, there have been a few times, Mom." I laid my head down on the table and exhaled deeply. My mother would never admit it, but her oldest daughter was and always would be her favorite. I'd learned a long time ago that it was pointless to ever make a negative comment about my sister to my mother.

"Are you hungry, sweetie?" my mom asked.

I groaned in response. "I never want to see food again."

Craig raised an eyebrow, and Amanda raised her hands in the air after beating my dad in another round of cards.

"We hit our fair share of bakeries, restaurants, and coffee shops today," I explained.

"All the more for me," my father said with a twinkle in his eye.

My mother glanced at our oven. "Oh, Amanda and I also made fresh tomato sauce and lasagna for dinner. You have to have a little, Syd."

Amanda chimed in, "Grandpa kept trying to eat the cheese when Grandma wasn't looking."

I raised my head and paused long enough to properly appreciate the smell of sautéed garlic and basil that wafted through the house. "No wonder it smells amazing in here."

Craig opened a bottle of wine and brought four glasses to the table. "So, while you were out and about, Rosemary Sanders called," he said while he poured.

"Who?"

"The broker who came here with that woman, Kara."

"Oh, yeah." I'd almost forgotten about the day we'd shown the house. So much had happened in the past few weeks, that afternoon felt like it had taken place a lifetime ago. "What did she want? I figured Kara found a place she liked that was actually on the market."

"Nope." Craig sat down next to me. "Kara fell in love but didn't want to appear too eager. Rosemary asked if they could come back again with Kara's husband."

I wrung my hands. "You didn't agree to it, did you?"

My mother's unblinking eyes spoke volumes. Although she loved the idea of us moving closer to where she and my dad lived, she worried about us uprooting Amanda, especially since she now had so many friends in her grade.

"No, of course not. I wanted to check with you first."

I glanced at my daughter. Even though she was engrossed in her game of rummy with my dad, she had the uncanny ability to pick up on everything Craig and I discussed. I cautiously responded, "Good. Call Rosemary, or better yet, email her tomorrow morning. Tell her we're not selling anything so it's pointless to keep wasting everyone's time." I agreed with my mom's concerns. There was no reason to entertain a move at this moment.

"Aren't you even curious to see what they think it's worth?" Craig asked.

"Sure I am. But what's the point? It's not like we're planning on doing anything. And let's face it. With you coaching Amanda's soccer team, my PTA duties, and both of our jobs, we don't have any time to spare. I do enjoy sleep, you know."

"I know. But…"

"Hold that thought," I said. For once I was thankful for the sound of my ringing cell phone. "Let me get this first." I smiled at my mother. "Maybe it's Bethany with a tracking number." I dug into my handbag and retrieved my mobile phone. My stomach dipped when I saw who was calling me.

"Hey, Jackie." I tried to sound much more upbeat and enthusiastic then I felt. "What's the matter? Are you missing me already?"

"Oh, Sydney. You sure are a funny one, aren't you?" Her voice was pure saccharine.

"I try." I stood up, took my glass of wine, and walked to the counter.

"I'm such an idiot. I spent the entire day with you, and it wasn't until I got home I realized I forgot to ask you something extremely important."

I braced myself. "Um, okay."

"Claire normally would handle this, but she's out of town this week. Did you know it was her birthday on Wednesday?"

"Yes, thank goodness for Facebook." I grimaced. I had a love-hate relationship with social media. Sure, I loved being able to keep up on the comings and goings of all the people who'd touched my life, especially my childhood best friend, Kelly, who lived across the country. But I also hated the way I had become so invested in their situations; especially with individuals I knew I would never have any relationship with in real life if not for the Internet.

"Oh, yes. Her husband surprised her with a trip to Italy. They left for Florence on Thursday afternoon. She won't be back home until next weekend. She hasn't replied to any of my emails or texts, so I'm guessing she has spotty Internet service wherever she's staying. Since I can't rely on her right now, I desperately need your help. I've heard through the grapevine that you're a very gifted writer."

"I don't know about that," I replied, confused.

"Nonsense! Of all the birthday cards my Cassidy received yours was the most articulate and thought-provoking. I wish the other mommies could be as expressive as you. I'm always shocked at how many people simply sign their names to pre-printed cards with no added creativity or sentiment. It's so cold."

Apparently, my mother and Jackie shared the same pet peeve. From the time my sister and I were old enough to hold a crayon, my mother made sure we "signed" our cards. When we'd finally learned how to write, she made us always send out our thank you notes within days of receiving a gift. She instilled in us that the notes had to be at least four sentences long, and personalized. I never thought her courteous intentions could backfire on me.

"Thanks, but I don't understand." I smiled as Amanda beat my dad at another round of rummy.

"Don't worry. I'll explain. Do you have paper and pen handy?"

"No."

"Well, go get some then! You'll need it."

I clutched my forehead and walked over to the junk drawer where we had a small pad of paper and assorted pens, as well as countless paperclips, rubber bands, and rolls of masking tape.

"I'm ready, Jackie." I tucked a loose strand of hair behind my ear.

"Oh, goodie! So here's the deal. There is a serious problem at Forest River Elementary School. A huge problem! I'm still in shock and so aggravated. I barely slept at all last night, in fact. Even Xanax didn't help. I can't get over the audacity! The school is trying to compromise our children's civil rights!"

"What?"

"Yes! You heard me correctly. Things have reached a critical point. Didn't you read the memo Mrs. Hamilton sent home with the kids on Friday afternoon?"

"Yes." I wracked my brain to try to figure out what could have possibly gotten Jackie so up in arms. Everything seemed quite routine to me, but I didn't dare say that.

"So, then you know what's troubling me. How could the school demand our daughter's first-grade class, cafeteria, and playground be turned into a best-friend-free- zone?"

My little tension headache morphed into a full-blown migraine. "I really don't see what the big deal is. It's only a phrase."

There was dead silence on the other end of the phone.

I waited a moment before continuing. "Jackie, seriously, can't you appreciate the need for them to want to prevent kids from feeling isolated or hurt?" As soon as the words were out of my mouth, I realized that Jackie probably would have no sympathy or understanding for any child who felt excluded.

"Of course I do." She cooed. "Poor Julia. I feel sorry for the girl. I'm sure it was hard for her when Amanda and Cassidy admitted to the group at recess the other day they were best friends. I know how close they were last term. But the dramatics that continued were blown completely out of proportion."

From what I knew, a bunch of girls were sitting in a circle playing duck, duck, goose. One of them came up with the idea they should switch up the game and play based on best friend partners. One by one the girls announced who their best friend was. When Amanda named Cassidy, Julia had a meltdown. She carried on so much the teacher had to end recess early.

"Jackie, I really don't understand why you're so upset."

"Sydney, seriously? Did you not read the memo? They want to ban best friends!"

I glanced at my family across the room. Amanda loved the attention her grandparents were giving her. "No, changing the language the kids use will not change the relationships the kids have with each other."

"While you do have a point, Sydney, I see things in a completely different way. Since the beginning of time, children and adults have used the term best friend. It connects them to another person, someone who they care about deeply. Also, people respect the best friend bond."

I opened my mouth to speak, but she was on a roll. "And what about the first amendment? Our children have the right to freedom of speech. If they want to declare they have a best friend, why should they be forced to call that person their close friend instead?"

"Jackie, I think you're too sensitive. I think we should agree to disagree. I don't want to get into an argument with you."

"Great!" she exclaimed. "I knew you'd be reasonable. Oh, Sydney. I thank my lucky stars every day that you're part of our team! Normally if Claire were away, I'd take it upon myself to handle the communications. Given the current state of my relationship with Donna, the email to the parents can't come from me. She'd assume I was being vindictive or something instead of concerned for the rest of the children's happiness. Which is why I need you to handle writing the email."

"Why can't you get Aimee, Stacey, or Trisha to do it?" I whined. I couldn't look at Craig and my father, who were making faces at me. Both men struggled to suppress their laughter.

"Like I explained, Sydney, you are the best writer of the bunch. And this notification is critical, just as significant as the petition was. Look how great that worked out. I heard the zoning officials are about to remove that crazy woman's child from the school!" Jackie let out a whoop.

"I don't think I can do this," I answered honestly. "I don't agree with your views."

"It doesn't matter what you agree with, Sydney. I thought I made that clear at the first meeting. You're part of a team now. There is no 'I' in the word team, you know. It's all for one and one for all. We stick together. And if the team decides to fight against the best friend ban, we all fight together. How you write the email is up to you, as long as you have these points included. Now you have your pen handy still, right?"

"Yes," I muttered.

"Good. Now take notes. There are some key points you simply must include."

I jotted down every reason Jackie rattled off. And while I thought she was ridiculous, I rationalized this wasn't a big deal. After all, Jackie could have insisted that I did something insane like write an email contradicting the school's ban on peanuts since Julia was allergic.

"You got it all, right?"

"Mmm, hmm."

"Excellent. Normally, I'd ask you to read back your notes, but I've got to run. Scott and I have dinner reservations in two hours and I have to get ready." She gasped. "I almost forgot. You need to have the email in everyone's inbox before six o'clock tomorrow morning. Ta ta for now!"

Click.

Craig caught my gaze. "I don't want to know what that was about, do I?"

"You sure don't." Then, in a moment of weakness, frustration, and rage, I added, "Maybe you should let Rosemary come back with Kara and her husband after all."

CHAPTER EIGHT

I RAISED MY HANDS HIGH OVER MY HEAD and stretched my tight back. I couldn't look at my computer screen one second longer. I still wasn't completely satisfied with the result of my work, but I didn't have any other ideas. I was bone tired yet determined to finish composing this cockamamie correspondence before I went to bed. I knew if I didn't complete the task, there wouldn't be a shot in hell I'd be able to sleep a wink tonight. Unlike my PTA cronies, I didn't have a secret stash of sleeping pills or tranquilizers to help me get some shut-eye.

My parents left right after we'd eaten dinner. And even though Amanda was exhausted from her afternoon with my mom, sleep was the furthest thing from her mind. She'd insisted we watch a Disney movie and play a board game before she'd even contemplate getting ready for bed. Unfortunately for her, she crashed halfway through the movie. Craig carried her to bed. She looked so peaceful I gave her a free pass on brushing her teeth tonight. I had work to do.

I glanced at my watch. It was after eleven. I had spent more than two hours staring at my laptop while eating candy, typing, and deleting. So much for never wanting to eat food again! Not only did I inhale the lasagna and cookies my mom and Amanda had prepared, I also had ice cream. And now, I was almost halfway through a bag of M&M's.

I read the email I had drafted for what felt like the thousandth time. The great thing about being married to a successful attorney was I learned how to argue both sides of any case, regardless of my opinion.

To: Parents
From: Sydney_Clayton
Date: 9/15
From: Sydney_Clayton
Date: 9/15
Subject: A little help from our friends

Dear Parents!

Friendship is an integral part of our children's lives. Friendship plays a pivotal role in developing self-confidence and social skills. Studies have shown that friendships are also known to impact academic success.

Sometimes it is hard for adults to remember how difficult it was to be a child. The world is new and scary. Having a best friend, that special someone you know who always has your back helps take away the fear.

Research shows having a best friend can help strengthen children's resistance and enhance their coping skills. Studies also show kids with best friends have higher self-esteem, cope better with transitions, and are also victimized less by their peers.

The term "best friend" has been part of our vocabulary forever. It is a part of our culture, and I am sure part of our own personal history. Also, the beauty of the phrase is its simplicity; it is so easy for first graders to understand.

Children will always have that special friend, the one they feel the most connected to. Their relationship will not change regardless if they call the other child their closest, best, or most special friend. That is why the members of the Forest River PTA feel the best friend ban is unjust. We want our children to have the freedom of speech to refer to their friends how they see fit, and we urge and encourage all parents not to let the school take away our children's first amendment rights.

Sincerely your PTA,
Jackie Martin – President
Claire Conroy, Trisha Dickens, Stacey Williams, Aimee Roberts, & Sydney Clayton

"I can't do this anymore," I muttered to myself as my fingers massaged my mouse. Like pulling off a Band-Aid, I quickly hit send. I crumpled up the stupid notes I'd made while I was on the phone with Jackie and tossed them in the trash. I was about to power off my laptop when my computer chimed, alerting me to a new email. I wanted to ignore it, but I knew it would haunt me if I didn't check to see who'd sent it. I was way too obsessive-compulsive for my own good.

"Please be an alert for a shoe sale," I prayed out loud, although I knew I wouldn't be so lucky.

The message was short and simple, and far from sweet. It also made my chest hurt. "Call me. NOW!!!!!!!!!"

I swallowed hard and paced around my office. What was wrong with me? I was thirty-six years old. Why was I allowing other grown women to manipulate me? Why did I feel like I was suddenly transported back in time to high school? I couldn't stop the bullies then, but I thought I was much stronger now.

Since Amanda was very young, I focused on making sure she had a better childhood than I did. I never wanted her to feel sad, lonely, or left out. I made sure she participated in a lot of activities, so she could meet a lot of different kids. I wanted her to find her tribe, and it seemed to work. But did I take it too far? Was I behaving the way I was so she could be friends with the cool kids, the kids she adored, or was I teaching her all the wrong lessons?

I didn't follow orders quickly enough because the house phone started to ring. Worried Amanda would wake up, I raced to answer it. I didn't even have a chance to say hello.

"Nice email." There was no emotion evident in Donna's tone, although I wasn't sure how much I expected to decipher from the two little words she'd uttered.

"Excuse me?"

"You heard me, Sydney. I'm complimenting you. Don't you like to be complimented?"

My heart started to pound in my chest. When I hit send, I had no doubt in my mind I'd upset her. After Julia's outburst, everyone knew she was behind the best friend ban and I was prepared to have an uncomfortable conversation. What I wasn't ready for was beating around the bush while she tried to play head games with me.

My silence must have irked her.

"When someone compliments you, Sydney, the appropriate and customary response is to say thank you."

"Thank you," I parroted back.

"No. Thank you." She paused and took a deep breath. "Thank you for clearing up any uncertainty I had about you. I appreciate finally being able to see your true colors firsthand. You're a hard one to judge, Sydney. I've always given you the benefit of the doubt, even when the other mothers didn't. I knew you worked. So, when you were cold or distant, or when you opted out of spending time with us, I figured you were busy. I didn't worry too much about it because you seemed nice enough. And both you and your husband are successful. That goes a long way in this town, as you must know. Your daughter is a sweet kid, and my child always enjoyed playing with her. Now, however, my eyes are open wide. I no longer have to question what kind of woman you are. I see everything crystal clear, and I don't like what I see one bit."

"Listen…"

"No, you listen to me!"

I had to hold the phone away from my ear. Her voice was deafening. "You have no idea what my life is like, what I experience on a daily basis."

"You're right." I exhaled slowly. "I learned a long time ago that you never understand what someone else is going through unless you experience the same thing." I picked up my iPad and started to play a game of Candy Crush. I needed a distraction.

She spat, "You got something. Bravo." She clapped her hands three times. "I guess I was wrong to think that you and your PTA pals would muster a smidgen of sympathy for Julia's situation."

"What situation?"

"Seriously, must I spell everything out? I can't control everything in Julia's physical world, but I can try to control how she feels emotionally. Do you know how hurt she is? And it is all your daughter's fault."

I tossed my iPad to the side. "Excuse me?"

"You heard me. This time last year, Julia and Amanda were the closest of friends. And now your daughter cast my kid off to the side to pal around with Cassidy Martin and her clan. Julia should be part of the group. Julia should be Cassidy's dearest friend, not Amanda."

I felt like I was in an episode of *Black Mirror*. "No one should or shouldn't be best friends with anyone. Our kids are people, Donna. They have the right to choose their friends and form their relationships."

"There. You used the word again! There should be no best friends!"

I didn't have the energy to engage further. I didn't feel like anything I said would matter. "I'm sorry you're upset, but it's late. I've got to go."

"You should be sorry," she hissed. "I'm not a fool, so please don't treat me like one. I know if the teacher had sent out the same note last year, Jackie and her PTA posse would have reacted differently. They would have been lobbying to declare the entire school best-friend-free. I get it. Everything is different now. I knew there would be ramifications once Jackie and I stopped speaking to each other. But I never dreamed she'd stoop so low as to take her anger and frustration out on a poor innocent child."

"I..."

"I don't want to hear it, so don't waste your breath. I have no patience to listen to your excuses or your rationalizations. I've been where you are, and I know what your future holds. Take it for what it's worth, as a friendly warning. Enjoy being part of the team, but watch your back. It doesn't take much for the ladies to turn against someone. And when they do, the one who will suffer is your child."

CHAPTER NINE

"**SYDNEY, HI!**" Kara gushed when I opened the front door to my house early Saturday afternoon.

One week had passed since my moment of weakness when I'd caved and told Craig to call Rosemary. During the past few days, I was able to breathe a bit easier. My call with Donna was the only fallout of my email against the best friend ban. According to my daughter, no one erased the word from their vocabulary. Amanda's teacher preached about the importance of being inclusive, but no one got in trouble if they slipped and used the best F word.

Kara gave me a quick hug, which was more than slightly awkward, considering I had only met her once before today. She handed me a bottle of wine. "I noticed you and Craig had a beautiful wine cellar in the basement. So, Jonathan and I wanted to introduce you to one of our favorite bottles. We discovered it a few years ago while we were on vacation in Madrid. We loved it, and now buy it by the case. Oh." She gestured to the box her husband was carrying. "We also bought cupcakes. We figured your daughter would enjoy them."

"Oh, that's so sweet of you." I took the wine and the bakery box from her. "Thanks so much, Kara. You didn't have to bring anything."

"Cupcakes?" Amanda screeched while she ran down the stairs. I was convinced my daughter had selective deafness. If I had yelled for her that it was time for school, she wouldn't have heard me. Yet, when a stranger softly said she brought a snack, Amanda came running.

Kara giggled as she studied my daughter, who was quite the

sight. Amanda was supposed to be in her room getting ready for soccer practice. She had her yellow jersey on, but it was paired with a hot pink tutu, rainbow striped knee socks, and a tiara on her head.

"Can I have one, Mommy?" Amanda begged. She bounced in place and eyed the bakery box.

"No, sweetie. You have practice in less than an hour. It's not a good idea." As soon as the words were out of my mouth, I regretted them. I knew what would come next, and I was right.

Amanda's lip began to quiver, and her eyes filled with tears. She wasn't prone to temper tantrums, but she did know how to manipulate Craig and me to get what she wanted. She didn't always succeed, but she was her father's daughter and knew how to successfully argue her case.

"Please, Mommy. Please. I..."

I squatted down. "Here's the deal. You can have half a cupcake now, and the other half after practice."

She opened her mouth to speak, but I put my finger over it. "No buts. This is the offer. You take it, or you choose to wait until after dinner. Your call."

Amanda leisurely crossed her arms over her chest. "I'll take it."

"Now, say hello to Mommy and Daddy's new friends."

Amanda extended her hand as we'd taught her to do. "Hello."

"It's so nice to meet you," Jonathan said as he shook my daughter's small hand. He was tall and slightly stocky. He appeared to be significantly older than his beautiful bride. If I had to guess, I'd say he was at least fifteen years her senior. His full head of hair was almost completely gray, but his eyes had a youthful glow, especially when he glanced at his wife. Turning his attention to Craig and me, he said, "Kara was so complimentary about both of you, and of course your house. It's funny, from what she told me already, I feel like we're already friends."

I gave him a closed mouth smile. I found his declaration of friendship annoying. After all, we'd spent less than an hour with Kara when she'd first visited. "Rosemary should be here any second," Kara announced and checked the time on her iPhone. "I spoke to her while we were in the car. Should we wait for her?"

"I don't see why. I can take you on a tour," Craig replied.

"Great," Jonathan and Kara answered in unison.

"I'm going to set Amanda up with a cupcake, then I'll wait here for Rosemary and let her in."

"I'll stay with you, Syd," Kara said.

"No." I waved my hand. "Don't be silly. Go look around with your husband."

"Honestly, I'd rather stay behind. I want Jon to check out the house on his own and form his own opinions. Besides, I'm exhausted." She placed her hand on her stomach, which was still flat as a board. "I'd so much rather sit and chat with you and Amanda than walk through the house." She tried unsuccessfully to stifle a yawn.

"I remember those days. Don't worry. The fatigue should wear off soon."

"I sure hope so. I can't stand feeling this way. I'm usually so active, hardly ever able to sit still for more than fifteen minutes at a pop. These days I feel like I'm constantly trying to walk through quicksand."

"Can I get you anything to drink? Or a cupcake?"

"A glass of water would be perfect. Thanks."

When I returned, I expected Kara to be studying our molding. Instead, she was simply sitting on the sofa, smiling and giggling with my daughter.

I handed her an icy glass and placed a cup of milk and Amanda's cupcake on the coffee table. Amanda scooted off the couch, sat down on the floor, and dug in.

Kara's eyes gleamed as she glanced at my daughter, who ate a cupcake like I did, saving the frosting for last. "She's adorable, Sydney. I'll bet you guys have a lot of amazing memories here."

"We sure do." I looked around the room. "When we moved in, I never expected to get so attached to a structure. Since Craig and I spent so much time doing renovations, how could we not be passionate?" I chuckled. "Not all the memories were great. You know the sliders that lead out to the deck?"

She nodded.

"Craig and I thought we could handle installing them on our own, even though they were huge. It was the worst decision ever!

We took out the old ones and together we managed to carry them out to the front yard because it was bulk pickup day. It was a minor miracle I didn't drop them midway. Pretty much as soon as we'd placed them on the ground the sanitation workers arrived and carted them away. When we went to install the new ones, despite all my self-confidence, I wasn't strong enough to hold them in place. When Craig leaned in to drill, the pressure and his added weight were too much for me. I dropped them. Glass shattered everywhere. It was such a mess."

"Oh, no." She gasped.

I turned to my daughter. "Do you remember?"

Amanda nodded. "Yep! Mommy said so many bad words. Grandma was so mad when I told her."

"And the worst part, besides getting yelled at from my mother because of this one," I leaned down and tickled my daughter, "we couldn't put back the old doors because they were gone. It took weeks to get replacements since they were custom ordered. We had to cover the open area with plywood. It was so dark and creepy in here. It felt like we were living in a condemned house. And Craig wasn't any help. He kept scaring the crap out of me. You'd think that after a few days I'd stop falling for his jokes, but I never did. I'm so gullible."

Amanda solemnly nodded her head in agreement. Of all the memories I could have shared with Kara, I guess this was an odd one to have picked. But it was also such a fun time in our lives. Amanda was old enough to understand and appreciate Craig's antics. And since he warned her when he was going to scare me, she was prepared for my reactions and loved to watch me squirm.

Kara giggled just as Rosemary Sanders called out, "Hello," in a singsong voice. She'd entered the house without knocking.

I was disappointed at the interruption. I was genuinely enjoying chatting with Kara. I was so relaxed with her. Usually, it was hard for me to let my guard down when I first met people. My position at work didn't help the situation since I was often involved in hiring and firing decisions; I tried not to get close to my co-workers. My only friend at work was the Director of Human Resources, Delanie Donovan, and we didn't socialize much outside of the office.

I wiped some frosting from Amanda's nose. "It's so nice outside, sweetie. Why don't you go play on the swing set for a while before soccer, okay?"

Without a backward glance, Amanda raced to the yard.

Rosemary walked over to where Kara and I sat. "I'm so sorry I was late. I scheduled an engineer's inspection at another property, which went on forever. Did I miss the tour?"

"Oh, no. Craig is taking Jonathan around the house. Kara and I were getting to know each other a little better."

"Oh, fun," Rosemary said. She sat down on the loveseat opposite Kara and me.

I squinted. "Don't you want to join the guys and walk around the house?"

"Well, unless you ladies mind, I'd rather hang with you."

"I don't mind," Kara quickly replied.

"Neither do I, although I must say I'm confused. I'd think you'd want to see the house with Jonathan."

Rosemary frowned. "I don't think I can add much, honestly, Sydney. I think Craig has it all under control. Seriously, I pray to God he doesn't decide to abandon his law practice because he'd sure give me a run for my money. He's a natural born salesman. I've never received a brochure from a homeowner before."

The other night Craig and I had been joking around, and over our second bottle of wine, decided to take a few pictures we had of our house and add some catchy taglines. He'd convinced me if we were going to make the effort to show the house again, we might as well have the best presentation possible. I was hesitant at first, but once we started, we couldn't stop. With every picture we captioned we relived our history. I was shocked we ended up with a twenty-five-page masterpiece that also included logos for all our appliances and fixtures, which Craig sent to Rosemary for Kara the following morning.

Kara picked at a cuticle and looked down toward her lap. "Sydney, you didn't send that document to anyone else, have you?"

The panic that filled Kara's eyes couldn't compare to the fear I felt at that instant.

CHAPTER TEN

"WELL, IT SURE LOOKS LIKE SOMEONE found herself two new best friends." Craig gently jabbed me in the ribcage. Rosemary, Kara, and Jonathan had left our house only a few minutes before. "I'm pretty sure Jonathan was as shocked as I was when we found you ladies giggling like a bunch of teenage girls."

"I know." I grinned. Once I'd calmed myself down, I realized that even though we'd created a dynamic presentation of our home, we were still in control of the situation. And I surprised myself by having a good time with Kara. "She was so easy to talk to, and we have a lot in common. You have no idea how I wish Kara were the head of the Forest River PTA instead of Jackie. Ever since Donna's warning, I feel like I have to watch everything I say around her." I fell back against the couch.

We'd spent three Sundays in a row together, and although I got along better with her than I imagined possible, Jackie still irked me. She was so controlling and such a drama queen. Everything with her was always an emergency. Last week she'd called an urgent impromptu meeting. She was petrified because she feared we weren't properly prepared for Halloween and was afraid we wouldn't be able to get a group costume in time.

"You seemed pretty chummy with Rosemary too." Craig sat next to me on the couch.

"She was different than I'd expected. I had her pegged for a complete work-a-holic businesswoman. I never thought she'd want to stay behind with us." I looked at my watch. I needed to get Amanda back inside soon, so she could finish getting ready for soccer. I tried to make it to most of her practices, but I was going to have to sit this one out and do laundry. I was so behind. We were all running out of clean underwear.

"Yeah, Rosemary probably knew there wasn't much of a chance she'd sell this house, so I guess she figured she had nothing to lose by sitting it out."

I shrugged. "I don't know if I agree with you. We keep giving her mixed signals. We did create that brochure, after all."

Before Craig could reply, our front door opened, and I jumped. "Sydney, Craig? Can I come back in?"

Rosemary didn't wait for an answer. She marched over to the sofa where we were sitting and plopped down in a chair opposite us. "I'm sorry to barge back in." She tucked a strand of hair behind her ear. "After speaking with Kara and Jonathan outside, I felt it was imperative I spoke to both of you, alone."

"We're listening," Craig replied and scratched the dark scruff on his chin.

She sat straight as a pencil in the chair, her head held high. "I don't want to play games. So, I'm going to cut to the chase. I know you didn't have any intention of selling this house or moving for that matter. I was surprised you humored us and allowed me to come and view your home with Kara. You're probably not aware, but I contacted all the homeowners on this block. Only you and one other family welcomed me in. Kara wasn't impressed with the other home one iota."

I leaned forward. "Whose house did she see?"

"It doesn't matter." She waved her hands. "Like you, your neighbors didn't want anyone else on the block to know they'd shown their home. They wanted to remain anonymous, and I am honoring their wishes."

Rosemary must have noticed I flinched. "I didn't intend to sound harsh, Sydney. I'm sorry if I came off that way. This isn't comfortable for me either. I hate sneaking around, keeping secrets about the homes I'm showing."

"I can understand."

"Thanks. So, while Kara didn't like the other home, she fell in love with yours."

"It's a lovely place." Craig beamed.

"Yes, it is." Rosemary nodded. "I've known Kara for years. She grew up a few blocks away from where I live. When she was in high school, she babysat my boys. And while Kara is a doll, her parents spoiled her and her sister rotten, and her husband took over where they left off. She's someone who always manages to get what she wants. And right now," she leaned over further and squeezed my knee, "she wants your house."

I swallowed hard and tried to make eye contact with my husband. He didn't meet my gaze. Instead, his eyes fixed on Rosemary's.

"That's very flattering." Craig nodded. "But not feasible. Don't get me wrong. I'm not saying it's totally out of the question for Sydney and me to consider moving; however, relocating our family isn't something we were seriously planning at the moment."

Her voice grew soft. "I know. You keep saying that, yet you continue to welcome us into your home." She smiled. "And don't get me started on the brochure. You would never have spent the time creating a masterpiece if your minds were completely made up." Her hazel eyes implored us. "I've tried to keep Kara and Jonathan's expectations realistic, but neither one of them wanted to hear it. I shouldn't say it, but Kara has her heart set on living in this house, and her husband is prepared to make her dream their reality. I told them they shouldn't get their hopes up, but I also promised them I would try to sway you guys into considering to sell."

The three of us sat in silence for a few moments. The only sound was the rapid beating of my heart.

"Sydney, Craig, listen to me," Rosemary practically pleaded. "I know you're happy here. I know this is your home, and I understand you didn't intend to sell when you first invited me in. You probably only wanted to see what your house was worth and if someone would be interested in it. Well, you got the answer to one of your questions. She's determined to call this place home. You wanted to see what your home was worth, well, here's a test for you." She took a deep breath. "Give me a number. Tell me what dollar amount you'd be willing to accept to make you sell. I don't care how outlandish you think the amount is. I want to know how much it would take for you to hand over the keys to Kara and Jon without any regrets or second thoughts."

I wished I could read my husband's mind. "Okay, Rosemary. You want a number? I'll give you a number." He licked his lips. "One point five million dollars."

I started to choke, and Craig handed me my glass of water.

Rosemary's face was unreadable. She stood up and shook both of our hands. "I'll be in touch."

I expected her to have flinched or told Craig he was insane, which he absolutely was. We'd spent hours on various real estate websites trying to gauge what our home was worth. Craig had created an elaborate spreadsheet, and while prices were escalating, the crazy number my husband had thrown out was nowhere close to what our home should value at by any stretch of the imagination. The panic I'd felt earlier returned tenfold. What was Craig thinking? Would we ever be able to kiss that kind of cash goodbye?

CHAPTER ELEVEN

I CRADLED MY CELL PHONE AGAINST my shoulder while I folded a load of laundry. I was glad I'd decided earlier in the day to skip Amanda's soccer practice. I needed to mull everything over with my sister.

"Seriously, Bethany. I think Craig was trying to kill me today. How did he even come up with an amount like that?"

"I wish I could have been a fly on your wall. Your reaction must have been priceless. You've got to give your husband an A for hutzpah." She giggled.

"He said the realtor was getting on his nerves." I tried to imitate Rosemary's nasal, high-pitched voice for my sister's benefit. "Give me a number you won't regret receiving."

"I get that she was annoying, but I bet one point five million dollars is double what your home is worth."

"I know. I'm probably crazy, but the realtor didn't seem fazed." If anything, she seemed like she'd expected an even higher number from us.

"What did you want her to do, Syd? Laugh at him? Tell him he was out of his mind?"

"I don't know. Maybe." Rosemary had mentioned that Jonathan worked for a hedge fund. Could they be so filthy, stinking rich that money was no object to them? Would they want to spend such an exorbitant amount on this house?

"Oh, come on," my sister scolded. "I know your mind is probably all over the map. You have nothing to worry about. I don't care how spoiled this Kara woman is. No one is going to pay you that much. Don't waste your time thinking about it."

I took a deep breath. I wished I could be as level-headed as my sister. "I know you're right, logically. But what if? What would we do then?" I attempted to refold the same shirt for the third time, before giving up. I couldn't focus on laundry at a time like this.

"You'll have a very difficult decision," my sister replied. "It will be hard for you to turn it down, don't you think? You'll never get that kind of offer twice."

A tear rolled down my cheek.

"Are you crying?" My sister's voice softened. "I know you don't like change, Syd. But I also know you aren't thrilled living in Forest River either."

"I know. I'm worried about Amanda. How would she handle moving? She has a lot of friends here."

"She'll make new friends wherever you guys go."

If only I shared a fraction of my sister's confidence. "How do you know?" I asked, remembering my own childhood. I was still haunted by the days of sitting in the cafeteria with only my animal crackers for company.

"Oh, now I get it. We're not talking about Amanda. We're talking about you and Kelly, aren't we?"

It took me a minute to reply. "Yes," I whispered.

When Kelly's family moved to Seattle when we were in fourth grade, I was all alone. No one accepted me. I was so sad and lonely. It wasn't until middle school that I was able to start making new friends.

"I hate to break it to you, sis, but Amanda is nothing like you were. I tried to get you out of your shell, but you wanted no part of my advice. You did turn out okay, so there's that. And if you recall, Kelly was fine once she moved. She made a lot of new friends."

It was true. Kelly needed the change of scenery to break out of our roles. In a lot of ways, I think it was much easier for her to have left town than it was for me to stay.

"Oh my God!" Bethany howled. "Do you remember Craig's drunk dream?"

I laughed too. "How could I not?"

Last year when his brother had come to visit, he and his wife had stayed with us. The boys were up practically all night joking around and drinking scotch. When they finally managed to get their sorry butts out of bed the next afternoon, my husband couldn't stop talking about his wild dream of us moving to Port Peters. Despite both having vicious hangovers, Craig and his brother wanted to look at houses there for fun. Fortunately, my sister-in-law and I were able to talk some sense into them.

"Maybe his dream was a sign," Bethany said. She was a big believer that everything happened for a reason and the universe gave us hints about what was coming up next. "Maybe for fun, you guys should take a ride to Port Peters? It's an up-and-coming area, and very laid back. They recently revamped Port Road and added a ton of new stores and restaurants. It would be a slightly shorter drive to both your offices, and you'll be closer to me and Mom and Dad."

Port Peters was less than a twenty-minute drive from my parents'. It would be wonderful to be so close to them. "Hmm, that's not a bad idea. If we ever hear back from Rosemary, we'll call Parker."

"Parker? Craig's ex-girlfriend, Parker?" My sister didn't even attempt to hide her surprise.

"Yeah, she's a real estate broker in Port Peters."

"Do I even want to know how you know this?"

Craig and Parker had dated for two years right around the time Craig started practicing law. Unfortunately for Parker, his first, second, and third priority was becoming a partner at the firm where he worked. Parker hated never getting the attention she needed from him, so she'd ended the relationship amicably, three years before Craig and I met. They still had mutual friends in common, so every now and again we'd see each other at various functions. Despite the fact that Parker had slept with my husband, we hit it off immediately. We'd never experienced any awkward moments. Parker had given Craig a cat, Simon, for his birthday. I never was a fan of felines, but Simon was special. By the time I'd realized Craig was the man I wanted to spend the rest of my life with, I was utterly in love with Simon too.

I sniffled. "Right after we had to put Simon to sleep, I became friends with her on Facebook. I figured she had a right to know.

We've stayed in contact ever since. Didn't I tell you this?"

"Probably. Let me get this straight. If you decide to look at homes in Port Peters, you're saying you'd want to work with Parker, someone who had sex with your husband?"

"Why not? Wouldn't it be better to partner with someone we know rather than a random person we find online?"

Before my sister, who had a jealous streak, could reply and tell me I was out of my mind, my house phone rang. I hung up to answer it.

I picked up without checking caller ID.

"Thank goodness you're the one who answered the phone. With everything going on, I didn't have the patience to make small talk. We have an emergency."

I exhaled slowly. I never thought I'd be so thankful to hear Jackie's voice. Not only was I relieved I didn't have a decision to make, I knew she'd provide a much-needed distraction. Initially, whenever Jackie had called me in a panic, I'd immediately assume someone was sick, hurt, or even dead. However, each time the situation wasn't even close to being cause for alarm. Well, unless of course, you were Jackie.

"Jackie, what's wrong?" I put my index finger toward my head, extended my thumb, and pretended to shoot myself, for my own amusement.

"Oh, Sydney. I didn't know where to turn or what to do." She moaned. "Then I remembered you're always a voice of reason. You have the best ideas, and I need you to put your thinking cap on right this minute! We need major damage control, immediately. I'm livid! For the life of me, I can't understand what possessed Aimee Roberts to do this."

"Do what?" It seemed like every conversation with Jackie was a riddle. Why couldn't she ever simply cut to the chase and speak her mind without my having to ask twenty questions?

Jackie let out a long sigh. "I need you to log onto Facebook right away."

"Okay, let me grab my iPad." I walked to the docking station in the kitchen where my device was charging.

"Hurry up," she shrilled.

"Okay, I'm ready."

"Good! Now go to the Forest River Mom and Dad group." Her voice quivered. "You are a member, aren't you?"

I had made the mistake of joining the group when Amanda was in nursery school. I thought it would be a fantastic way for me to connect with other moms in town. Unfortunately, it wasn't what I expected. Residents of Forest River used it to show off, rant, or prove their laziness by asking silly questions. A few months back, instead of doing a quick Google search, a mother asked the group where the closest emergency room was because she feared her daughter, who was screaming in pain, had broken her arm. Hours had passed before someone commented, and I'd prayed she hadn't left her daughter in agony while waiting for a response.

Regardless of how much the group's discussions irritated me, similar to a trashy reality television show, I was hooked and never able to turn away. "Of course I am."

As I navigated to the page, Jackie continued her rant, rambling a mile a minute. "I'm fuming. I could pummel Aimee right now. She needs to start thinking before she acts. She should know better by now. After all, Donna is watching all of us like a hawk. She's waiting for one of us to make a minor misstep so she can pounce, and make us look bad. She's out for revenge, and no one is taking my warnings seriously! I specifically told everyone at last week's meeting to be extra diligent, but Aimee obviously didn't listen. She went off the rails and did her own thing. Doesn't Aimee realize her actions affect all of us? She put the entire Forest River Valley PTA in a very poor light. Which is where you come in. I need help to right her wrong and get things back on track."

The post was at the very top of the page. I read it out loud. "'I went to Nosh A Little Bagel Shoppe this morning and was so disappointed!!! I ordered a skim latte and saw the girl prepare it with two-percent milk. When I questioned her, she told me they didn't have any skim milk! It would have been nice if she told me that little tidbit when I ordered my drink. When I asked if they planned to carry skim, she said she didn't have any idea. BUYERS BEWARE – If you go there, make sure they give you what you are ordering rather than a sneaky substitute.'"

Although I would never post something like that, I didn't find it so offensive.

"Look at the number of comments!" Jackie screamed. "It's going viral! I'll bet that witch, Donna, called everyone she knew in this town and bribed them to comment on the post. When I first saw it, there were twenty replies. When I called you, there were fifty. And now there are seventy-five! It's never going to stop!" Her voice cracked.

I took a deep breath when I read the first comment written by Donna. "'Silly-ness! Buyers beware? We should be supporting the new business in our town. Come on, it's a called a soft opening for a reason. Maybe you should be a little softer on them and yourself...'"

I realized Jackie wasn't exaggerating. All these comments couldn't be a coincidence. It took Donna almost an hour to comment on Aimee's post. When she did, the rest of the town jumped in fast and furious, with each new reply becoming angrier and more mean-spirited.

"Read the comments," Jackie begged, and I quickly scanned the page.

COMMENTER – "I get you got 2% milk instead of skim...They are a brand spanking new business. Wouldn't it be a better idea if you attempted to speak to the manager about your concerns rather than bashing them here? I know you want to warn others, but obviously, they're still getting up to speed and that's why they haven't even officially opened yet."

COMMENTER – "What's with the negativity? Talk to the NEW owners and HELP them out. Maybe they missed the importance of carrying skim milk. There is no need to destroy a business's reputation on day one. Give them a chance!!! BTW, I had a great experience there – They have almond milk!"

COMMENTER – "Seriously?!?! Unless you are counting Weight Watchers Points (lol) there is no reason for this post. Buyers beware? They have been open for 5 minutes. Give them a chance!!! I was in there this morning and had a great experience. We want them to stay open, not close!!! You sound like an entitled snob."

"These people are crazy. Everyone's temper is flaring. What do you want me to do?"

"I want you to make it stop," Jackie whined.

I threw my head back and stared at the ceiling for inspiration. "How can I do that?"

"I don't know, but you're so smart and witty. And such a talented writer! Remember the best friend email you penned for me? I know you can think of something positive to say that will end this madness. It's one thing for Donna to attack Aimee publicly, but I don't want the new business in town to get caught in the crossfire. They don't deserve all this negativity."

I bit my cuticle. "I've got it," I muttered. I began to type the hundred and first comment. *"After 'skimming' over these comments, I need to go and get a bunch of bagels with tofu cream cheese schmeared on them, because I know their bagels are the best!"*

"Okay, it's up."

"You are brilliant," Jackie gushed.

"Well, let's see if it does anything to change the tone." Jackie and I remained silent for a moment. I couldn't take my eyes away from my iPad, and I'd bet Jackie was staring just as intently at her computer.

"You did it, Syd!" Jackie exclaimed. "No one else has commented."

"*We* did it, Jackie." I was amazed her concern ran deeper than her image.

"Sydney, thank you. I know I bullied you into joining the PTA, but I'm beyond glad I did. You're something special. Hopefully we'll become real friends."

I shivered. I couldn't decide if I was ecstatic or petrified.

CHAPTER TWELVE

"GO GRAB US A TABLE, AND I'LL get the orders," Jackie said as we entered Yesterday's Yogurt, which was packed. While our daughters were at soccer practice, we gallivanted around town getting everything we needed for Halloween, which was a week and a half away.

It felt like a lifetime ago that Rosemary had badgered Craig to tell her how much we'd be willing to accept for our house. In actuality, only three weeks had passed. We hadn't heard boo from her since. Which was quite alright with me. I was up to my eyeballs at work, and I didn't need more stress. Not only was I trying to dodge a business trip to India with the other executives, related to the new software system we were implementing, my right-hand person had also given notice. There was nothing I hated more than interviewing, as it took up so much time I didn't have.

However, the stress at my office paled in comparison to the negotiations needed for the PTA to settle on group costumes for our kids. After countless brainstorming sessions, we agreed on having everyone dress up as a character from *The Wizard of Oz*. The costumes were all custom made, of course. It would be a catastrophe if another child at Forest River Elementary showed up at school wearing the same get-up as our gang.

Jackie's daughter, Cassidy, was dressing as Dorothy. There was no discussion about this; it was a demand by our queen. The rest of us did collaborate on which costumes our kids would wear. I feared Amanda would be upset she couldn't be the lead character, especially since she loved the movie. Instead, she eagerly embraced her role as the cowardly lion. She was beyond excited and wanted to perfect her character's walk and mannerisms, so she forced us to watch the movie at least five times since I'd told her the plan. The other mothers and I were dressing for the occasion, as well. I'd lie if I said I wasn't excited to be Glenda, although I was shocked that Jackie didn't save the role for herself.

Jackie handed me the three bags of costumes and candy she was carrying. "What do you want me to get you?"

"It depends." I juggled her bags along with my packages. "Are you going to eat something here or only get a bottle of water? I think after all the schlepping and lugging we've done today, you definitely deserve a snack."

I was surprised Jackie had asked me to join her today. I thought she'd pick a long-term member of her posse. Ever since I'd shut down the Facebook fiasco she and I had gotten a bit closer. We even texted about matters not related to Forest River Elementary. Although Jackie couldn't completely grasp that I had to juggle motherhood along with a full-time job, it was nice to finally have a friend in town, instead of just an acquaintance. The way she seemed to latch onto me made me wonder if, despite her apparent popularity, she was as lonely as I was.

"You're a horrible influence on me, Sydney Clayton." She giggled like a schoolgirl, and her eyes twinkled with a brightness I'd never seen before. "I like it." Her carefree attitude disappeared as quickly as it had appeared. She placed a hand across her stomach and waved her other index finger at me. "If I don't fit into the new Chanel skirt that I picked up special to wear to the penny auction, it's going to be all your fault."

I rolled my eyes. "Oh, you'll be fine. Besides the event isn't until the spring. I have utmost faith. Unlike me, you'll never struggle to fit into anything in your closet." My stomach grumbled so loudly I knew she and probably half the yogurt shop had heard it. Since today wasn't going to be the day I finally started my diet I added, "I'd love a small peanut butter cup with Heath bar crumbles." I expected her to scoff at the decadence of the added candy, but she simply strode toward the counter.

Yesterday's Yogurt was one of my favorite places in town. It was fashioned after a fifties ice cream parlor. The floor had large black and white ceramic tiles, a long, metal counter, and hot pink and bright blue vinyl stools. The walls were canary yellow, and there was a jukebox that was always blasting the best of the fifties and sixties. Every time I came in, I felt my tension drift away. It was probably the nostalgia they provided.

"Here you go." Jackie placed my yogurt in front of me.

"Who are you and what did you do to my friend?" My eyes jumped back and forth between Jackie and the medium-sized cup of double chocolate yogurt she placed in front of her. It was covered with hot fudge, sliced almonds, whipped cream, and rainbow sprinkles.

"I know this is so not me. Oh my God, this is amazing." She groaned in ecstasy after taking her first bite.

I handed her a napkin because some fudge had dribbled down her chin. "When was the last time you had something so indulgent?" I dipped my spoon into my cup.

She closed her eyes for a moment and savored the yogurt. "Seriously, I don't remember. I feel like I've been on a perpetual diet since we moved to Forest River seventeen years ago." She leaned in. "Did you know I grew up in Kansas?"

I shook my head.

"I don't talk about it much." She put her spoon down. "My parents died in a car accident, a few weeks before my sixth birthday."

"Oh my God." My breath hitched in my throat. She was in first-grade, a mere baby. I couldn't help but imagine what a nightmare it would be for Amanda to have to grow up without Craig and me. Also, the thought of not being around to see my daughter become a woman made my blood run cold. Life was often too cruel for words.

She licked her lips. "They were on their way to pick me up at a friend's house when a drunk driver crashed into them. My dad died instantly from the impact, and my mother hung on for three days, although she never regained consciousness." Jackie paused and her blue eyes filled with tears. "I was the same age as our girls, Sydney, when they died." She swallowed hard. "Forty years have passed since I saw them last and," her lip quivered, "I can barely remember them." She wiped her eyes with her index finger.

I handed her a napkin, and she blew her nose.

"I'm so sorry." The words felt so lame as they rolled off my tongue. I wished I could better comfort her, but my mind was blank. I tried to reconcile the strong, determined woman who sat in front of me with the scared child she must have been. I couldn't help but think back to my first PTA meeting when I'd been shocked at her cavalier attitude about Craig's uncle's death. I had jumped to the conclusion she'd never lost anyone important to her. Clearly, I had been wrong. Her breezy reaction must have been a self-preservation mechanism. How much more was there about Jackie that didn't meet my judgmental eyes?

She reached across the table and squeezed my hands. "My grandmother raised me. She was an amazing woman and made me the center of her universe. She did everything in her power to take care of me and make me happy. Life wasn't easy for us, but it was simple and good." She tucked a strand of long, blond hair behind her ear. "My grandmother made most of my clothes, and we never went out to dinner or a movie. We couldn't afford it. She did allow us one splurge." She took a bite of her yogurt. "Once a month, like clockwork, she'd take me into town. We'd window shop and hit the ice cream parlor. My grandmother would have a cup of tea, and I would have this very dessert." Her eyes clouded over. "Twenty years ago today, she passed away. I've been missing her a lot lately, so I figured since we were here, I'd eat this in her honor."

I dipped my spoon into my yogurt and held it out to Jackie. "To your grandmother."

She filled her spoon with yogurt, tapped mine back, and whispered, "I love you, Gammy."

I arched my eyebrows. "So Kansas, huh?"

She couldn't contain her grin. "Yeah. Bet you can't picture me living on a prairie. But I did. I came out east to go to college. I was given a full scholarship to NYU. I was petrified and excited at the same time. It was so far from home, and everyone seemed so experienced and worldly. I almost chickened out, but my grandmother wouldn't hear of it. She practically dragged me across the country by my ponytail. I was miserable at first; all the girls in the dorm were so mean to me. They—"

I cut her off. "Sorry, what's going on?" I pointed behind Jackie toward the front door.

"What's wrong?" Jackie spun her head around so fast I was shocked she didn't give herself whiplash.

We both studied a woman I didn't recognize, who'd entered the shop with six little girls all dressed in Amanda and Cassidy's soccer team uniform.

Jackie turned back around to face me and glanced at her watch. "Shouldn't they still be at practice?"

"Yes." My stomach turned, and I immediately feared the worst. "Craig didn't tell me there was any change in the schedule. He's compulsive about sticking to a plan." There was no way he'd merely switch up the team's practice schedule without giving all the parents at least two weeks' prior written notification. "Something's wrong."

Jackie pushed her yogurt to the side. "Do you think he or Amanda got sick?"

I felt the color drain from my face as I rummaged in my bag for my phone. I fired off a quick text to my husband, which thankfully he answered immediately. I breathed a sigh of relief: my loved ones were fine. I handed Jackie the phone, so she could read Craig's reply for herself.

Jackie sat up straight in her chair. "Do you want me to deal with this?"

I was already out of my seat. "Excuse me?" I called out and tapped the lady's arm. She gradually turned around after she'd successfully herded the girls into a booth.

"Yes. Can I help you?" She jumped back at my touch.

"Sorry." I flashed her what I hoped was a bright smile. I didn't want her to think I was a complete lunatic accosting her in a yogurt shop. "I didn't mean to startle you. I just got a little worried." I paused briefly. "You see, my daughter started playing soccer this year. She's also on one of the first-grade teams. I thought they all had practice now. I was here having a bite to eat with a friend when I saw you and the girls come in wearing their uniforms. I got nervous I goofed up the timing and," I placed my hand on my chest for emphasis, "well, it wouldn't be the first time I was late for pickup."

"Oh." She beamed. "Don't worry, hon. You're fine. All the teams are still in the field. My daughter's team is the only one that didn't have practice today."

"How come?" I asked even though I already knew part of the story thanks to Craig's text. My husband, who always arrived at the field at least fifteen minutes early, stood on the sidelines with Cassidy and Amanda for over half an hour as every mother of the team's members contacted him to advise their daughters would not attend practice today.

"My daughter," she pointed to a little redhead who was holding court over her friends, "had the unfortunate luck to be placed on Cassidy Martin's team. I'm sure you've heard of her. She's the most popular kid in first grade."

From the corner of my eye, I watched as Jackie put on her sunglasses. She hung onto every word we uttered. "How could I not know about her?" I asked, my voice raised several octaves. "Her birthday party was insane! My daughter couldn't stop talking about it for at least a week, maybe more."

"I know." The woman rolled her eyes. "Not only was it over the top, but it was also the first birthday party of the year. So now, no matter what anyone else does for their kids this term, every single mom will compare it to Cassidy's party. And heaven forbid anyone tries to do anything similar. They'll be condemned for copying."

I sighed deeply. "I know. I'm dreading having to plan my daughter's party this year for those very reasons." I licked my lips. "I don't understand what all this has to do with soccer, though."

She waved a hand around. "Sorry, sometimes I get carried away and ramble. So, as I was saying, Cassidy's the most popular kid in school. She already picked her best friend. The year has barely begun, and she and that Amanda kid have been completely inseparable." She shook her head. "My daughter is as special as they are, but none of the other girls in the grade are vying for her attention like they do with those two bosom buddies. When I found out one of the kids on the team had strep throat, I phoned the other moms and convinced them to call the coach and say their kids weren't feeling well, too. Instead of them spending the afternoon on the soccer field, they have an impromptu party with my daughter." She raised her fist in the air as if she'd won a gold medal in the

82 HILARY GROSSMAN

snobbery Olympics. "We're starting out here, then I'm taking them to play miniature golf. Afterward, they'll have manis and pedis followed by a pizza dinner."

I willed myself to stay calm, even though I felt my blood pressure spike. Craig had stayed up until the wee hours of the morning to work on a brief because he knew he wouldn't have time this afternoon because of his coaching duties. He had sacrificed so many days of his life for the girls on the team, and this was how a mother showed her appreciation for his dedication? Because I always had to keep confidential information to myself at work, I was an expert at hiding my true feelings. "Wow, what a wonderful day," I gushed. "The girls will all have a blast, I'm sure."

"I sure hope so! Hey, you seem like a nice lady, and I love your watch." She ran her fingers over the gold watch Craig had given me for our fifth anniversary. "I don't recognize you. Did you recently move to town?"

I shook my head. "No, but I work full-time."

"Oh dear." She placed her hand on her chest. "I'm so sorry for you. How about after your daughter finishes up with soccer practice? Do you want to have her join us? I'm always eager for my daughter to make the right new friends."

"Oh, that is so lovely, thank you," I cooed. "I'm sure she'd love to join you and the girls, but unfortunately she has plans already."

She frowned. "Oh, that's too bad. May I ask, what could your child possibly be doing that would be better than the day I have planned for the girls?"

"Oh, I don't know all the specifics, to tell you the truth." I twirled a strand of dark hair and cleared my throat to get Jackie's attention. She turned around, took off her sunglasses, and dramatically waved to the other mother. "All I do know is she had an impromptu play date with her friend, Cassidy Martin, since they were the only two kids who showed up for practice."

CHAPTER THIRTEEN

"CRAIG! AMANDA!" I called out from the hallway the second I entered my house. "Where are you guys?" Even though I'd practiced deep meditating breaths during my car ride home, I was still smarting from my conversation with that woman at the yogurt shop. "Anyone home?"

"We're in my room, Mommy!"

I ran up the stairs two at a time. I felt my body finally relax when I laid eyes on my family, who didn't seem fazed in the slightest about being dumped this afternoon. Craig sat cross-legged on my daughter's bedroom floor with a giant jigsaw puzzle spread out. Cassidy was sitting next to Amanda. I bent down and kissed both the girls' heads. Turning to my husband, in a hushed tone, I whispered, "I'm still so pissed off."

He stood up and slipped his arm around my waist. "We'll be right back, ladies. Can you finish this puzzle while we're gone?"

"You bet!" Amanda replied confidently as my husband and I headed to our room down the hall.

"What's wrong, Syd?" Craig twirled a strand of my hair around his index finger. "Why are you letting something so stupid get under your skin so much?"

"Something so stupid?" I stared at him. "Seriously, Craig! How do you always stay so calm?"

"Sorry, sweetie." He flashed me a toothy grin. "I simply don't see the major harm. So I had to cancel soccer because some mom wanted to make a power play. Big deal. You saw the girls. They didn't seem to mind the change in plans. They're having fun simply hanging out together."

I tapped my foot. "The point isn't their being happy or not."

He arched an eyebrow. "Since when?"

It took everything for me not to laugh or punch him in the eye. I sat down on the bed. "Okay, fine." I twisted my hair into a messy bun on the top of my head. "I'm glad the girls are having fun. But that's not the point. The point is you volunteered to give up almost all your Saturday afternoons to coach the stupid soccer team, and this is the thanks you get? And what was up with that mother? She's jealous the other kids like Amanda and Cassidy better than they do her daughter, so she pulls a stunt like this? Nice lesson to teach her kid! People are so messed up."

"Come on, you already know this, Syd. Why are you stooping down to their level?" He gently stroked my face. "The woman isn't worth your time or your anger."

"I know. I can't help it," I whined.

"Well, I think I may have something to put this predicament in perspective for you. In fact, I may even get you to forget about it completely for a while." His eyes clouded over, and his mouth set in a firm line.

My breath hitched. "It's not my dad, is it?" Ever since his surgery I worried about his heart and feared the worst. I spoke to him that morning, and he'd admitted to being tired. In the past, I'd assume he hadn't slept well the night before. But now, I let my imagination get the better of me, instantly jumping to worst-case scenarios.

"No, he's fine." He squeezed my thigh. "Rosemary Sanders stopped by about a half hour ago."

My chest tightened. "Why?"

Craig got up and walked over to the window. Even though he only stood there for a few seconds, it felt like an eternity had passed before he spoke again. "She wanted me to know Jonathan and Kara are willing to meet our price."

"What? That's impossible." I didn't move. I expected Craig to start laughing any second. But he didn't even crack a smile. "You're serious?"

He nodded. "Yes, I am."

I took a deep breath. "I don't get it. I love this house, and of course, I think it's perfect and priceless, but come on! There is no way in the world this home is worth one-and-a-half million dollars."

He shrugged. "I know, and frankly I agree with you. Apparently, they feel otherwise."

"How is this even possible? They'll never get a mortgage; the price is way above market value."

"They don't need a mortgage. They're going to pay cash, Sydney."

I raked my fingers through my hair. I couldn't fathom what it must be like to be able to fork over that kind of dough so easily. Craig and I were comfortable financially. However, I still worried about money. Neither my husband nor I had grown up rich. We had both put ourselves through school, and we'd worked extremely hard for everything we had. My biggest fear was that something would happen at one of our jobs, preventing us from one day making ends meet.

"Oh, and Rosemary explained they're going to handle her commission directly. If we do this, they'll pay us the full amount we asked for."

"I can't believe this. Craig, I thought you were out of your mind when you told her that preposterous amount. Now I'm wondering if you sold us too short."

He snorted. "Yeah, I know. I was thinking the same thing." He sat back down beside me. "Seriously, Sydney, what do we do now? How can we walk away from this kind of money?"

My eyes pricked with tears. "I know."

He leaned in and kissed me. "I can't believe this is happening to us. When would we ever see this kind of cash?"

I thought our showing Kara and Jon our house was one big joke. Never in my wildest dreams did I ever think we'd be faced with such an enormous dilemma.

Craig filled the silence. "This is an amazing opportunity for us."

I looked around the room and mentally replayed the last decade. Scenes of our life flashed through my mind like a movie. I saw us as newlyweds when Craig carried me over the threshold. I pictured us on that rainy afternoon so many years ago, sitting side-by-side on the bed, when I told him he was going to be a dad. "If they think it's worth this amount of money now, maybe we should hold onto it and let the house appreciate more."

He scratched his jaw. "While that's a great pipe dream, it isn't going to happen. Come on, sweetie." He reached for my hand. "Be realistic. Unless someone discovers gold underneath our garage, we're never going to see this amount of green again. The only reason we're getting this is that Kara is so adamant about living not only in this town but on this block."

I picked at my cuticle. Kara was so set on getting what she wanted we were going to have to abandon our dreams. I knew I was irrational. I should have focused on the big picture and how fortunate we were to receive an offer like this. Money didn't buy happiness, though, and until all this nonsense started Craig and I had been happy here. I was still happy here.

"I don't think we have a choice. We have to sell the house, Syd."

I lay down on the bed and curled up into the fetal position. "What about Amanda? What about school, her friends? We can't uproot her like this. She has to be able to finish the school year here. I won't pull her out mid-session, not for any amount of money. And what if we can't find a place we want to live?" I bolted up. "The money is great. Don't get me wrong. But we've been happy without the money. We'll still be happy without it. I don't want to make a rash decision. I want to make sure we consider everything." I looked at my husband with pleading eyes. "This is our life, Craig."

"Come here," he said and held open his arms. I leaned into his embrace and buried my head in his chest. "Don't worry, Sydney. I knew what your concerns were going to be. I discussed most of them with Rosemary already. She told me that Kara and Jon didn't expect us to leave before the school year ended. While they're considerate of us, the delay also works out well for Kara, too. Kara didn't want to worry about moving as soon as she gave birth to the baby. Oh, and they're also willing to wait to sign the contracts until we find a new home we're interested in buying. And if the timing works where we have to buy something before we're ready to leave here, they're willing to purchase the house as soon as we need. That way we don't have to worry about carrying two mortgages, and they'll let us stay here, rent-free."

I closed my eyes. Kara and Jon were so accommodating. I couldn't ask for more, or could I?

CHAPTER FOURTEEN

"**OKAY, MOM. I'VE GOT TO GO,**" I said as Craig parked the car in front of a two-story Colonial. "Have fun!"

We had dropped Amanda off at my mother's about a half-hour ago. It was hysterical. Whenever my mother watched my daughter, she felt the need to get my permission before taking her granddaughter on an excursion, even though she knew there was no one I trusted in the world more than her. My parents wanted to take Amanda to a local farm to go pumpkin picking and take a hayride, which was something Amanda was dying to do. She'd begged Craig and me to take her, but we weren't able to make the time.

"Is this the house?" Two weeks had passed since Rosemary had delivered the news about how bad Kara and Jon wanted our home. As far as they knew, we were still considering their offer. Our minds were pretty much made up. We'd be leaving Forest River.

"The pictures Parker sent us made it look so much bigger. And this street," I surveyed the road once more, "isn't for me. Don't you think it's way too close to the main artery? I wouldn't feel safe letting Amanda play out here alone, would you?" It was Sunday morning, and two cars had already zipped past us.

"I don't know, Syd." He drummed his fingers on the steering wheel. "Can we first go inside and walk around before you start getting all judgmental on me? If you recall, our house was a mess when we moved in, too."

"Fine," I mumbled half under my breath as an SUV pulled into the driveway. As a woman with long, light brown hair opened her door, I did the same. "Parker's here," I sang and raced out of our car.

I flung my arms around her as soon as she turned around. "Hi!

How are you? Long time no see!" I rocked gently from side to side, but she remained rigid.

Abruptly, she pulled away and cleared her throat. "Excuse me?" She glared at me. "Do I know you?"

I felt my cheeks turn crimson as I looked at her face. "You're not Parker?" I stammered.

"No, I'm not," she replied without an ounce of emotion.

"Oh, I'm so sorry," I said before I skulked back to the car where Craig sat.

He laughed. "So now you just go around and hug strangers, huh?"

I punched him in the shoulder. "I thought it was Parker. You know I only met her in person a handful of times. And from afar, she sort of looks like Parker, don't you think?"

He arched an eyebrow at me and shook his head.

"Why didn't you stop me then if you knew it wasn't her? I don't know her as intimately as you do."

His green eyes twinkled. "You have a point, but hey, where would the fun be in that?"

Before I came up with a worthy retort, another SUV pulled up behind us. Craig glanced in his rearview mirror. "This time it's really Parker. Go hug away."

"Sydney, hi!" She wrapped me into a big embrace as soon as I opened the door. "It's so great to see you both." She turned to Craig, who walked over to where we stood. She gave him a small, quick hug. Then she clapped her hands. "I'm so happy to see you guys! I was shocked when you called and told me you were considering moving up here, but I was so excited too. Thank you so much for asking me to help you."

Parker's enthusiasm was contagious. She was one of those people who lit up a room with her presence. She always made you feel special and welcome. I remember the first time I'd met her. It was so uncomfortable and awkward knowing she'd slept with my husband. My guard was way up. After a few minutes of chatting with her, I felt totally at ease. If anyone had felt like the odd man out, I'd bet it was Craig.

"As we said on the phone," Craig explained, "if we're going to consider moving to Port Peters, why work with anyone but you?"

"That means a lot to me." Parker snaked her arm in mine before she turned and faced the lady who stood in the driveway. She gave the woman a slight wave. The reserved greeting seemed so out of character for Parker. "Hey, Terri," she called out softly.

"You know her?" I asked, feeling more embarrassed than I probably should.

"Of course! She's another local broker. We've worked on several deals together. Why?" Her eyes jumped back and forth between Craig and me.

"My darling wife got a bit confused and ran over and hugged her. Apparently, she thought she was you."

Parker threw her head back and let out a belly laugh. "Oh, man! I can't even imagine. I wish you videoed it, Craig! Terri is very good at her job. She's a killer negotiator and the ultimate professional. Wow, wow, WOW! She's cold as ice. I wish I saw her face when you molested her, Sydney." Parker poked me in the ribs, and I started to laugh. "Seriously guys, let me tell you about this place. I did some more research after we spoke. I know you were adamant about seeing this house, Craig, but I honestly don't think it's right for you. First off, I'm not a huge fan of the block. It tends to get a little busy if there's traffic on the main road. Considering your daughter's age, I would rather see you in a different part of town. I'm not sure how familiar you guys are with Port Peters, but it's made up of seven different incorporated villages. They're part of the Port Peters' school district and all have unique characteristics. The other houses we're going to look at are in areas that tend to have larger plots of land, so there would be more room for your daughter to play outside. Also, in the other villages the roads are less congested."

"I think I'd like that better," I said while I wondered if I really wanted to live anywhere besides Forest River. I wished I didn't have so many reservations about this decision.

"The current owners have completely renovated this place. And while on the surface that may sound fabulous, I don't know if it's the best option for you guys." She thumbed through a stack of pages in her folder. "I know you both like to remodel. I'm always shocked when I see pictures you post of your house, Syd. I can't wrap my head around how much of it you two did yourself. Especially since neither one of you look too handy." She giggled. "Seriously, I think you may be better off in a place that you can make your own. You know, put the Sydney and Craig spin on it."

Craig nodded, reluctantly. "I'd tend to agree with you."

"Depending on what you think about this place, I have several others lined up to show you today. If you have the time, I have the keys. And Sydney, I have a ton of amazing girlfriends who I'll introduce to you. They are all totally cool and completely down to earth. You'll fit right in with them."

"Sounds great," I said and tried to imagine getting together with a new gaggle of girls. It was funny, for most of the time we'd lived in Forest River, I didn't have any local friends. When we'd first moved in, it had been impossible to meet people. And then when Amanda had started pre-school, I figured I'd make friends then. But I never invested the time to get close to anyone. Instead, I used the little free time I had to spend with our family or old friends.

It also hadn't helped that I didn't fit in with the other women. Yet practically overnight I'd become one of the "it" mothers. I'd walked into my first PTA meeting counting the minutes until I could escape the ladies, and now I looked forward to getting together with them. Sure, they still often got on my last nerve, but I did enjoy the camaraderie. And if we moved away from Forest River, I knew I'd miss them, especially Jackie. Don't get me wrong, Jackie was high maintenance and over the top most times. But when she let her guard down, she could be fun. And when I was with her, I felt strong, like I finally belonged. It was amazing that even though the pain from childhood faded, the scars always remained.

Parker reached into her giant handbag and pulled out an orange folder. I peeked over her shoulder at the multiple listings she was reviewing. "The problem is inventory is pretty limited this time of the year. If only you'd reached out to me a few months ago, it would have been a different game. Most people wait until the spring to put their houses on the market, so the sales correspond to the school term."

I opened my mouth to speak. Parker didn't give me a chance. She looked directly into my eyes, as if she'd read my thoughts.

"Don't worry, Sydney." She patted my forearm. "It may take us a bit more time, but I will make sure you find the perfect house. I'm here to help you."

***

"Craig, please promise this will be the last one we look at today," I begged as my husband parked our car in front of an ultra-contemporary house on a quiet, tree-lined street. I ran my fingers through my hair and yawned loudly. "I'm tired, cranky, and disappointed. I know Parker is trying, but seriously, each house she takes us to seems worse than the one before. And the last place she showed us? It was filthy! How can people live that way? I need a shower. And look." I angled my head down. "Do I have cobwebs in my hair? We should never have ventured down into that basement. What were we thinking?"

Craig leaned over and combed through my hair with his fingers. I knew he was only humoring me. "You're all good. There's nothing there." He opened his car door. "Come on, let's go. Parker is pacing in the driveway."

"Hey, slowpokes." She giggled as we approached. "I didn't think you two would ever get out of the car. Not that I can blame you, of course. The homes we looked at were less than stellar, and the last one was pretty much the pits. It's to be expected, though. It's only our first outing. Don't worry! And this is the last home I have to show you today. Before you know it, you'll be back home, with your feet up on the couch, sipping a glass of wine. Oh," she shook her head from side to side, "maybe that's only my plan."

"No, it's my plan too!" I massaged my neck. "Although, first I have to help Amanda with her homework, do a load of laundry, and make lunch for tomorrow, so I don't have to do it in the morning. Whoever came up with the bright idea that first-graders needed two hours of homework on the weekend should have to help them with it."

"I'm glad I'm not you," she joked. "So here's the skinny on this one: it's a short sale."

"What does that mean?" I'd heard the term tossed around over the years but didn't really understand it.

"The homeowner isn't in control over the sale, but he has an involvement."

I scrunched my face. I was too tired for riddles. "Huh?"

Parker sounded as if she'd relayed this message a million times. "It's his get-out- of-jail-free card. His last chance to get out from under this house before it goes into foreclosure. Every short sale is different." She started to tick off on her fingers. "Sometimes the homeowners are eager to be free from their debt and are extremely cooperative. Other times, they're angry and fight tooth and nail every step of the way. Ultimately, all the offers must be sent over to the bank. However, the homeowner has the right to decline the offer before it's submitted to the bank if it's below the asking price."

"Wonderful." I let out a huff as the small tension headache I'd had morphed into a full-blown migraine. "It sounds like a nightmare."

"I'm not going to lie. It isn't an easy process. Short sales aren't impossible, but they are quite difficult. The good thing about them is the prices tend to be substantially lower than the market value because the bank wants to move the property quickly to mitigate their losses. Also, most times the homes aren't in great condition. Which in your case could be a great thing since you guys love to gut and remodel."

"Got it," Craig stated with a nod of his head.

"The other broker is waiting by the front door for us. I don't know him. He's not local, but he seems nice enough. I was chatting with him a bit while I was waiting for you two to get your butts out of your car. Oh," she smacked herself in the head, "I did find an issue when I was poking around outside."

I exhaled, again. Of course, there was an issue. Every house we'd looked at today had some problem; some probably had over a hundred. Seriously, if I could have magically transported myself home this instant, it wouldn't have been soon enough for me.

***

"Come on, sweetie. Say goodbye to Grandma and Grandpa now. We have to go home."

"But Grandma is making my favorite chicken for dinner. I don't want to go home," Amanda whined as my mother beamed. It was a toss-up which of my lovely ladies wanted us to stay for dinner more.

I leaned down and kissed the top of my daughter's head. "I know, and I'd love to stay too. But tomorrow's a school day, and you still have homework to do, remember?"

"I don't have any homework." Amanda pouted.

"Yeah, right. I'm not falling for that one." I hated having to always be the one who spoiled the fun. I wish the days could be long enough to accomplish everything I had to do as well as what I wanted to. I felt like I was always compromising something.

"Are you sure we can't twist your arm, honey?" my dad asked.

"It wouldn't require much twisting, but yeah. We have to go." I kissed my father and hugged him tightly. "Thanks for spending the day with Amanda."

"Oh, don't be silly." My mother wrapped her arms around me. "Daddy and I had so much fun today."

"Love you, Mom," I said as Amanda hugged her grandparents once more.

By the time Craig entered the highway Amanda had given us the full play-by-play of her day. I knew I should have kept her chatting so she wouldn't doze off on the drive, but instead, I let her watch a movie on my iPad. It was out of character for me not to utter one word for such a stretch of time. I couldn't help it. I was too busy trying to sort out my thoughts and feelings to carry on a conversation. My emotions were all over the map while I pondered numerous what-if scenarios. Typically, in times of confusion or distress, I tended to babble, finding comfort in incessant chatter. This time, however, I couldn't find any words.

As Craig exited the highway, he reached over and ran his hand over my thigh. "I guess we should talk about it. What did you think?"

I turned and checked out the backseat. As predicted Amanda was out cold. I was relieved I didn't have to speak to Craig in code. I opened and closed my mouth, trying unsuccessfully to get my thoughts in order. There was not a doubt in my mind Craig already knew what I felt about the last house we'd seen. I struggled to keep my voice steady. "I think you already know."

"Yeah. I think I have a hunch." His smile wavered. "And if I'm right, I think I might feel the same way."

I gave him a half-hearted smile while I pulled my hair into a ponytail.

"Obviously, it needs a lot of work," Craig said. "The kitchen is in complete shambles. I never expected to walk into the master bathroom and only find piping."

I grimaced as I recalled the room. There was a hole in the tile floor where a toilet bowl should be. There was no bathtub or shower, and only about a quarter of the tiles were installed; the rest remained in boxes.

"They must have been in the process of renovating and ran out of money or something. I wonder what happened to them." I felt concerned for the people who lived there. "I saw some pictures scattered around. It looked like a family with a teenage boy. It's sad."

"I agree. But we can't worry about people we don't know. We have to think about what's best for our family."

And what was best for our family? "I guess I'm afraid of bad karma."

Craig let out a slow chuckle. "Seriously, you're spending way too much time with Jackie and your other PTA cronies. It's a house we're talking about, Syd. You can't catch bad luck from a building."

I nodded, even though I wasn't sure I agreed with him.

Craig carried on. "For starters, I liked the block. I saw a bunch of girls who looked like they were Amanda's age playing together."

"That's one for the plus column." If we did move, it was important to me that we settled in a family-friendly neighborhood.

"And I loved the layout," he continued. "It was so different than most houses, so modern. I also liked how the double-sided fireplace was in the center of the living room and the dining room. We'd be able to enjoy it from either room."

"It would make entertaining fun." I pictured hosting holidays, with our family filling the two rooms as a fire blazed. "What I thought was cool was how the kitchen was on the second floor. I could imagine, once there were working appliances, of course, cooking dinner while taking in the view of the backyard. As for a negative, carrying up groceries could be a pain."

"So, this is what my future holds? Am I reduced to being your schlepper? Nice." He snorted. "That's a job I think I can handle, doll. What I'm not so sure about is the retaining wall. It may be a big issue."

"Do you think we could it have it repaired or would we have to rebuild?"

He shrugged. "It's easy enough to find out, but do we even want to travel down that road? Could you picture us living there, Syd?"

A tear trickled down my cheek. "Oh, Craig. I can't believe I'm about to say this. But yes, I can picture us living there."

"Craig, do you think…" The ringing of my husband's cell phone interrupted my question. We both glanced at the car display to see who was calling. I swallowed hard as Craig rolled up our windows, flicked on the air-conditioning, and answered the call.

"Hello, Craig!" Rosemary practically sang out the greeting. "I hope I didn't catch you at a bad time. I'm dying to know, how was your trip to Port Peters? I think you mentioned that you were going to take a ride there last weekend."

"Hi, Rosemary." He pointed a finger gun at his head.

It infuriated me she was playing dumb. She knew our house-hunting excursion was planned for today; after all, Craig had mentioned it to her at least three times when they'd spoken a few days before.

"Oh, you must have misunderstood us. Sydney and I didn't go last weekend. We went today."

"Oh, silly me." She made a tsking sound. "I must have made a mistake in my notes. Since I have you on the line, how did it go? Did you find anything you liked?"

"We saw a bunch of places today, Rosemary."

My heart fluttered with love. I was thankful Craig had avoided her true question. We had a big decision to make, as a family, and I didn't want her or her clients rushing us.

CHAPTER FIFTEEN

"WHERE WERE YOU? I WAS STARTING to worry." Jackie grabbed my arm as I rushed up the bleachers. I hadn't even noticed her. I was lost in my own world. Our daughters had a soccer game tonight, and of course, I was late. I'd meant to leave work early enough to make it to the game and get a decent seat. But as usual, right before I was about to head out, there was an emergency I had to handle.

"Stupid work," I muttered. "Did you save me a seat?" I asked even though I already knew the answer. The entire row of the bleacher was packed.

She frowned. "I tried, but they're already in the second period."

"No worries. I'll find something." I had to continue up to the very last row before I could find a spot. Amanda's team broke from a huddle and even though I felt like I was in another zip code, she spotted me and waved. Craig was too focused on his coaching duties to look for me.

"Pass it, Jenna!" A mother screamed at the top of her lungs. "Don't hog the ball."

"Jordan, defense! Pay attention to what you're doing!" a different woman yelled.

I hated the way the parents carried on. They put so much pressure on the kids. What happened to children playing for fun? I craned my neck to check out the scoreboard. Neither team had scored a goal, so at least I hadn't missed much. Cassidy passed the ball to Amanda, as my phone started beeping. Rather than keep my eye on the field, I read the text from my boss.

Syd – sorry to bother you. Did you initiate the interest wires?

As my heart pounded, the man next to me stood up and waved his fist in the air. "What are you doing, Lindsey? Concentrate!"

I replied: No.... *You told me to send the money tomorrow.*

Then second-guessing myself, I scrolled through my emails to make sure I wasn't crazy. I'd never missed a deadline, but there was always a first time.

Syd - I made a mistake. I need you to take care of it tonight, though. TY.

I looked at my watch. Wonderful. At least I always kept the bank security token on my keychain. I pulled my laptop out of my backpack and connected to the Internet on my phone. I only had ten minutes to process before the bank's cut-off time.

"Are you insane!" someone shouted, and I tried to tune him out. I was too busy with my computer. Then the man's voice grew louder. "What is wrong with you? Are you blind? How could you say that was a goal, asshole?"

The crowd became eerily silent. I was now fully focused on the field. My jaw dropped when a man in one of the first few rows stood up and marched onto the field to where my husband was.

"No!" someone yelled. It was probably my imagination, but it sounded like Jackie.

I tossed my laptop in my bag as the man poked his finger in my husband's face. What kind of lesson was this guy trying to teach his daughter by screaming at the opposing team's coach?

"You are a moron!" the guy bellowed again.

I felt like I was watching a bad movie in slow motion. He punched Craig before the other coach could tackle him to the ground.

"Oh my God!" I yelled and ran down the bleachers.

Jackie beat me to the field, and immediately grabbed my daughter, who was hysterical. "I've got her. Go to Craig."

With my heart in my throat, I raced to where Craig stood. The other dads had escorted the lunatic off the field. Half the kids stood frozen and petrified in place, and the rest had fled to the security of their parents' sides.

"Oh my God! Are you okay?" I scanned his face and handed him my scarf so he could try and control the blood. "Is your nose broken?"

"How should I know?" he replied through gritted teeth. "But it sure as hell feels that way."

What was wrong with people? This was a first-grade girls' soccer match, not the World Cup, for goodness sake.

"Daddy!" Amanda cried. She had broken free from Jackie's clutch.

"I'm fine, baby." Craig leaned down and squeezed her shoulder, giving her a huge smile that didn't reach his eyes. "Don't be scared."

I forced myself to stay calm for my daughter's sake. "He only has a boo boo. We'll go to the ER and get him all fixed up."

"Sydney, no. There is no reason Amanda has to go to the emergency room with you. It'll cause her to worry more. Besides, who knows how long you'll be there? I'll take her home and she'll sleep over. I'll drop her off at your house in the morning.

"You sure?"

Jackie squeezed my arm. "Of course."

Amanda's sobs subsided after hearing her dad's voice. "Are you okay with spending the night with the Martins?"

She nodded. I kissed her and sent her over to where Cassidy stood with her sister. I needed a moment with Jackie. The other coaches had returned to the field and were speaking with Craig.

"Was it you who screamed?"

"Yeah. I was right behind him. When he stood up, I knew what was going to happen. He's pulled this stunt several times already."

"He's done this before?" my blood boiled.

Jackie looked up at the sky. "Way too many times to count. He's notorious at his son's soccer playoffs."

"But this was just a regular game." As the words escaped my mouth, I realized I'd almost tried to rationalize his past actions. What was wrong with me, and what was wrong with this town? At times like these, I was so happy that we'd decided to move. I didn't want Amanda to grow up surrounded by so much unneeded pressure and stress. I wanted her to enjoy her childhood. But was moving the answer? Was this town the problem or were parents, in general, the real issue? Would life somewhere else be any better?

CHAPTER SIXTEEN

"SYDNEY, HI!" Jackie exclaimed and frantically waved to me from the doorway of Bistro Baron. It was two o'clock on a Saturday afternoon, and the restaurant was packed. Amanda and Cassidy were next-door at the bowling alley for a birthday party, and clearly Jackie and I weren't the only two mommies who decide to take the opportunity to meet here for a bite. It was the first week of November a couple of days after the soccer match from hell, and it was unseasonably cold. When Jackie had insisted I make a reservation, I thought she was nuts. But I didn't want to argue with the queen. It was easier that way.

I was happy I listened because I wasn't in the mood to make small talk with the mass of women who stood by the bar. There was no way I wanted to rehash what happened on the soccer field. Word of the incident had spread through Forest River like wildfire. Someone I'd never met had posted a picture of Craig, post-punch, on the parents' Facebook page. By the time we came home from the emergency room, there were one hundred and seventy-five comments. Fortunately, Craig didn't break his nose. He was still black and blue, but his ego was more bruised than his face.

Despite Jackie's insistence, the PTA didn't draft a ban to prevent the smack-happy dad from coming to future sporting events. Craig had sent the police over to his attacker's house the night of the assault, but when push came to shove my husband decided not to press charges.

While Jackie meandered over to where I sat, she stopped by at least twenty-five ladies she knew along the way. For once, I was thankful she was so popular. While she doled out air kisses to her admirers, I was able to put the extra few minutes to good use. I finished off the long-winded email I was in the middle of writing my boss, even though I knew it was a pointless exercise. Just like Jackie, once he made up his mind, there was no changing it.

Since he'd already once put this trip to India on the back burner, I didn't want to miss the chance to try to convince him to postpone it again. I knew I wasn't the only executive in my office who dreaded the thought of having to travel across the world right before Thanksgiving. I hoped I wouldn't be the only one who spoke her mind.

I hit send and placed my phone face down on the table as Jackie approached. I stood to give her the customary air kiss. Uncharacteristically, she opened her arms wide and pulled me into a tight, sincere embrace. I'd never witnessed such a show of affection from her, especially one directed at me. "Sydney, thank you so much for agreeing to meet me today, particularly on such short notice. I needed this."

"How could I not? You sounded so upset on the phone. What happened?" It was weird. Over the last couple of months, Jackie and I had spent a lot of time together. But it was a struggle for me to put into words, accurately, what I felt about her. I didn't consider her a friend. I didn't have a high level of trust for her after she'd pretty much blackmailed me into joining the PTA. I did feel like I could rely on her.

I enjoyed her company, especially on the rare occasions she genuinely let her guard down. Oddly, I felt comfortable being myself around her and I think she appreciated it, which was probably why it seemed she turned to me first when something didn't go her way.

Craig and I had planned on going back up to Port Peters today to meet with Parker. He'd arranged for several contractors to come to the house to provide quotes on how much the retaining wall would cost us to either repair or replace. The damp chill of the November air, combined with my lack of knowledge about structural construction costs, made it an easy decision to abandon my husband in exchange for an outing with Jackie.

"Oh, Syd." She held her face in her hands. "I don't even know where to start. But I do need a glass of wine, pronto!" She waved over the waitress as her bracelets clanked loudly on her arm.

After she'd ordered a bottle of Shiraz, she gave me a play-by-play of her week.

And while I did enjoy her stories, I was exhausted and drained, both emotionally and physically. Suddenly, I regretted not joining my husband and Parker to see the house again. I felt guilty I'd left him to deal with it on his own, especially considering what he'd just gone through. Also, I was itching to check my phone to see if my boss had replied to my email yet. I felt weak in my knees thinking about the possible trip. And now I was concerned that Jackie had concocted an emergency to get me here under false pretenses. Was I so lonely for a girlfriend that I spent time with a woman who stressed me out so much?

I was never so thankful to see a waitress approach our table. In typical fashion, like practically all the ladies scattered around the room, Jackie ordered a salad with grilled chicken (sliced not cubed) and dressing on the side. From experience, I knew, except for possibly dipping one leaf of lettuce in it, she wouldn't even touch the vinaigrette. I wasn't in the mood to follow social norms. Blowing caution to the wind, I selected a cheeseburger with fries. From the look on Jackie's face, I expected her to have a coronary right there at the table. Her shock quickly turned into a small grin as soon as the waitress retreated.

"I admire you, Sydney. You follow your heart. You never worry about what other people think."

I answered without thinking. "Thanks, but that's not true. I worry plenty. How can I not, especially in a superficial town like this?" I quickly covered my mouth with my hands. How could I say something like that to Jackie? I was petrified to make eye contact with her. I mumbled, "Sorry."

She tossed her head back and laughed. "See, that's what I'm talking about. You speak your mind and beat to your own drum."

I let out the huge breath I hadn't even realized I was holding. "I guess I think it's important to know what you want and not be afraid to achieve it. It took me a lot of years to realize, but once I started worrying more about what mattered to me instead of everyone around me I became much happier. I hope Amanda can learn from my example, and not make the same mistakes I did. I want her to be comfortable in her skin and not feel like she has to live up to anyone else's expectation of perfection."

The words felt hollow. My strength seemed to evaporate when I was around Jackie. I wanted so much for Amanda to have a better childhood than I did, but I'd allowed myself to be her best friend's mother's pawn.

Jackie leaned in. "And are you comfortable in your skin now?"

"For the most part, yes. I think I am."

"I've got to say, I'm so jealous of you. I am completely the opposite. I'm constantly worried about making the right impression and saying the right things. I always agonize about making sure I always put my best foot forward, especially when my actions could negatively affect Scott or our girls."

"I get it, Jackie. I worry too. I don't ever want to hurt my family either. I do believe in picking your battles, fighting for what's important and letting the petty stuff go. After all, what difference does it make to anyone besides me what I eat for lunch? And if you count running because I'm late as exercise I manage to work out most days." I smiled. "I know I'm not as thin and fit as you, and while I admire how you look, I'm okay with having a few more curves, especially since Craig doesn't seem to mind." I felt my face flush slightly. "I want Amanda to be okay with that, too. There's enough pressure in the world. We don't have to manufacture more."

"You are a genius." She stood up with such force I thought her chair would go flying. "I'll be right back. I'm changing my order."

I stared in disbelief when she marched up to the waitress stand.

"I caught her right in time." Jackie let out a small sigh and sat back down. "Oh, Sydney, the expression on her face when I said I was going to have what you were having was priceless." She beamed.

I flashed her a small smile. I was losing patience. "Jackie, you sounded so upset on the phone, yet I'm the one doing all the talking. What's wrong?"

She took a sip of wine. "I'm sorry. You're right. I do have a problem." She tapped her nails on the glass. "I should be used to all the drama already. It seems like every month something new happens. I thought as the kids got older the drama would decrease. Man, was I wrong. So, you know, Hayley's in fifth grade. All the kids in her class have iPhones. They all received them right before the school year ended. Can you imagine the horror if the girls had to spend one second during the summer and not be in constant communication with each other?"

I snorted. "How would they have survived?"

"Exactly. I knew you'd understand. When the topic first came up with the other mothers, I was adamantly opposed. I didn't even try to hide my feelings. I told them flat out I felt the girls were too young. There was quite the debate; even my husband disagreed with me. Then, as soon as the first mother caved and bought a phone, I ran out and got one for Hayley."

Hayley was Jackie's oldest daughter, the one who'd started off the school year being ostracized from her friends. Now that I'd had the opportunity to spend some time with the child, I had no idea how the school psychologist had fallen for the shenanigans about her being mean-spirited. She was a sweet girl who, unlike her mother, tended to be on the quiet side. She always included her little sisters in her activities, and Amanda adored her.

I had a sweet spot for Hayley that ran deeper than my appreciation for her compassion for my daughter. How could I not? She reminded me a lot of myself growing up.

It took a while, but I eventually learned the full story about what had happened between Jackie and Donna. When Hayley had started school, she was painfully shy and would cry every morning before leaving the house. Donna's daughter, Christie, had a terrible stutter and the other kids, except for Hayley, teased her mercilessly. Jackie convinced Donna they should team up and join the PTA together to try to help the girls by having a say in the school's activities. They planned parties and outings for the other kindergarteners, so Hayley and Christie could interact with the other children. Their plan worked, and the girls made friends. Jackie and Donna promised to always look out for each other's daughter, but Donna didn't take her vow seriously.

The waitress dropped off our lunches, and I quickly popped a fry into my mouth.

"Hayley has been so responsible with her phone. Then last week, I was bombarded with texts from the mother of one of her classmates." She pulled her phone out of her Hermes bag and handed it to me. "See?"

I quickly scrolled through the tirade of texts. It would be impossible for me to read through all of them and still get home before dark. "There sure are a lot of words here. Can you please give me a reader's digest?"

Jackie took back her phone and I cut my cheeseburger in half. "Sure. It appears this woman's daughter sent Hayley a text about who she wanted to sit next to at a birthday party and Hayley showed the text to her friends."

"What's wrong with that?"

"Apparently, everything!" Jackie exclaimed. "The mother went berserk. She kept carrying on how Hayley had violated her daughter's privacy, and how her kid is now traumatized and considered an outcast."

I raised a brow. "You've got to be kidding."

"No, I wish I was. I spoke to Hayley about the incident. She admitted she showed the text to her friends. There wasn't anything personal or private about the message, and Hayley didn't have any malicious intent. It was completely innocent. Regardless," she waved her hand in the air, "I told Hayley to apologize to the girl for hurting her feelings, which she reluctantly did."

"That was very reasonable of you."

"Yeah, well, Hayley's had enough drama this year, and she didn't need anymore. Not that her apology made a difference. The mother told me saying sorry wasn't good enough."

I took a slug of my wine. "What?"

"You heard me. The crazy woman kept saying I was condoning cutthroat behavior to exclude her daughter from the group. She claimed that Hayley was a bully and she purposely passed her phone around to her friends to hurt her daughter. She then went on to say all the other girls ganged up on her daughter to make her feel unwelcome in the group. Somehow, she conveniently forgot the fact that her daughter ended up sitting next to Hayley and her best friend at the party."

I shook my head. "I have no words. This is ridiculous."

"I know! When I tried to defend Hayley, the woman sent me links to at least fifteen articles defining the various forms of bullying."

Jackie once again thrust her iPhone into my hand, so I could scan the texts.

"This is insane." As a victim of bullying as a child I was sensitive to the matter, but this mother was clearly blowing the situation out of proportion.

"I figured after the party all the hard feelings would be forgotten, and life would return to normal. Of course, I couldn't be so lucky. The party was four days ago, yet the woman continues to text me incessantly. She simply won't stop! She is still insisting her daughter is hysterical every morning and night because of what happened."

I pushed my plate to the side. "You need to stop engaging with her. You've already said everything you need to say. You aren't going to be able to change this lady's mind, no matter how hard you try. She's the one with the issues, and she's the one who needs massive help. Maybe Hayley shouldn't have shown the texts to the other girls, but it's history. She can't change what took place. You had her handle the situation afterward perfectly. The girls have moved on. It's the mother who can't."

"Do you think Hayley hurt the girl? I don't want another child to go through what I did."

I did a double take. I had to have heard Jackie wrong. Given her confidence and the way she carried herself, there was no way that she could have been anything but the queen of her schools. Right?

"Jackie, tell me more about your childhood." I desperately wondered if we had more in common than I'd ever imagined.

"No, it's not relevant." She shook her head. "This is all about Haley. So do you think she hurt this other kid?"

"Possibly. But she didn't mean to. She worked it out with the other girl. They've moved on, and it seems like she probably understands how her actions cause reactions. At the end of the day, it doesn't matter what you try to teach her. She learns the most by watching your behavior."

CHAPTER SEVENTEEN

SPOKEN WORDS NEVER WORRIED ME. It was the words that went unsaid that haunted me and kept me up at night. I'd seen a completely different side of Jackie the other day at lunch, a vulnerable side. I tried to get her to elaborate on what had happened to her as a kid. But as quickly as she'd let her guard down, she'd pulled it right back up. She clammed up and refused to speak any further about her childhood. But who was I to judge? I'd never once confided in her how isolated and lonely I'd been as a child. Unfortunately, neither one of us, it seemed, let our guards down easily.

Like Jackie, I put on an act every single day of my life. I created a persona and tried to portray myself the way I wanted others to perceive me. How much of what we saw in life was real? How well did we know those closest to us? And were we ever one hundred percent honest with ourselves?

"Are you okay?" Craig asked me when I joined him and Amanda in the den after finishing the dishes.

Like my friend, I lied to my husband and myself. I suppressed the constant conflicting thoughts that had plagued my mind and focused solely on the superficial instead. It was so much easier to pretend everything was okay instead of trying to fix what wasn't. "Yeah, I'm fine." I put the steaming cup of herbal tea I'd made myself on the coffee table and curled up on the couch next to my husband. I reached for the remote and turned down the volume, slightly.

"Mom," Amanda whined from the floor. She, like Craig, loved to blast the television.

"Jane down the block could probably hear your show, silly. This is plenty loud for you, but when Mommy and Daddy's friends come over to talk, you can make it louder again, okay?"

Amanda hugged her stuffed rabbit tightly against her chest. "Deal." When a commercial came on, she scratched her head. "Mommy, why do grownups talk so much?"

"What do you mean?" I asked.

"You know. You and Daddy are always talking. Why?"

I was stumped. "Why do you talk, Amanda?"

"Because I love the sound of my voice. It's beautiful."

I giggled. Some of the tension I felt eased slightly. I studied my husband. I was so tired. "You have no idea how much I wish you hadn't agreed to let the dynamic duo and their bosom buddy come over tonight. I think I'd rather sit through a double root canal than have another play date with them this evening."

Craig kissed the top of my head. "Don't worry." Even though Amanda was totally engrossed in her show, he lowered his voice to a whisper. "They won't be here for long. I'm sorry. I didn't feel like I had a choice. Rosemary has been hunting me down like a rabid dog. According to her, Jon is desperate to speak with me."

"Maybe they changed their minds?" I didn't mean for my statement to sound like a question, but it came out that way. Part of me hoped that would be the case. It would be such a relief for the decision to be taken out of our hands. I was exhausted from lying awake night after night, constantly weighing the pros and cons of this move.

If it were only Craig and me, the choice would be a no-brainer. We'd pick up, leave, and start over. But we had our daughter to consider.

Before Craig could reply to my question, our doorbell rang. Amanda didn't even wait until we were out of the room to raise the volume of the television. Clearly, she didn't feel the same way about our voices as she did hers.

"Sydney, hi!" Kara exclaimed and wrapped her arms around me.

Feeling a bit vulnerable and confused, I returned her embrace with more gusto than I had ever done before. Somehow, her enthusiasm and positive energy had either worn me down or won me over.

Jon handed Craig the customary bakery box that they always brought. Rosemary picked up the rear, hobbling behind the group.

"What happened to you?"

Rosemary sported a fluorescent blue air cast on her left ankle. Between her foot and my husband's battered nose, I felt as if I was standing in the waiting room of an urgent care clinic.

Rosemary shot a knowing glance Kara's way before smirking. "By now I should have concocted a better story, but I'm not creative. So, I'll stick to the truth. " She giggled. "So, there is one step in front of my house." She raised her index finger and repeated, "One step. The other day, I was late for a showing. When I raced out my front door, my neighbor called my name and distracted me. Somehow, I missed the step and went down, hard. Thank goodness the house I was showing after was a ranch. As soon as the offer was accepted, I headed over to the orthopedist."

"Did you break it?" I asked.

"Of course I did. No simple sprain for me."

"Oh no. But if it makes you feel better, Rosemary, I broke my arm when I went to sit down on a run-a-way conference room chair." Almost five years after the fact, my co-workers refused to let me live the moment down.

Rosemary smiled.

"I told you, Ro, we all do this stuff." Kara held out her left palm and showed me a huge, red, jagged line that started from between her thumb and index finger to the corner of her wrist. "I was on the phone with my sister, drying off a knife. Our conversation was obviously more important than my keeping track of where the dishtowel was."

"We're sure hot messes. Come on, let's sit down." I gestured toward the kitchen. "Do you want anything to drink?"

Both ladies declined, and we silently joined the men, who sat at the kitchen table deep in conversation, the opened bakery box of black-and-white cookies untouched. I prayed Amanda wasn't catching a cold, as it wasn't like her to miss the smell of chocolate or cookie. Rosemary and Kara sat down next to the men, and I leaned against the counter.

Jon's leg bounced a fast and furious pace as beads of sweat framed his brows. "Craig, I'm sorry, but I'm very worried. We agreed over a month ago, yet you still refuse to sign a contract."

Craig leaned in. "Jon, we've gone over this before. Until Sydney and I find a place we're interested in living, we won't sign anything. I'm not going to risk losing our home unless I have someplace set for my family. If it were just Syd and me, it would be a different story. We have our daughter and her schooling to think of." He pointed at Kara's swollen stomach. "I'm sure you can appreciate we have to put our child's needs first."

"Yes, I can." He ran his fingers through his salt and pepper hair. "You need to understand our position too." He reached across the table and took hold of his wife's hands. "Like you, I have my own family to look after. My wife and I stopped looking for houses once you accepted our offer. Kara fell in love with your house the moment she set foot inside. It is here, inside these four walls, where we want to raise our family, where we want to make our memories. We are no further now than we were weeks ago, and I'm tired of being jerked around."

I gulped air; I didn't appreciate Jon's attitude. We were on the precipice of making a huge decision, and I didn't need the added pressure. Sure, they'd waved a wad of money in our faces, but we hadn't accepted one penny yet.

"Jerking you around, Jon? Really?" Craig's face reddened. "From day one, I told you this deal was contingent upon us finding a new home. You, of all people, should know the process takes some time."

"I'm fine with giving you time. I'm not fine without a firm commitment. Craig, I worry day and every night you and Sydney are going to change your mind about selling us the house. I'm worried someone else will approach you about this place. What happens to us if someone else wants to buy? We have no protection here."

Craig looked him square in the eye. "Jon, you have my word."

Jon frowned and crossed his arms.

"Sydney and I aren't going to sell our house to anyone else. We need to make sure we'll have a home, too. Don't worry. We're getting very close." He faced me and smiled. "We found a place we both fell in love with."

Kara and Jon sat up a bit straighter in their seats. Rosemary practically bounced off her chair with glee. "You did?" Rosemary glowed.

Craig faced the real estate broker. "Yes, remember the house in Port Peters I mentioned to you? We've had it inspected, and I'm working with several structural architects to determine how much the retaining wall will cost us. Once I get a handle on everything we'll put in a bid to the bank."

Rosemary frowned. "Oh, you're talking about the short sale, right? Remember, it may not be such a quick and easy process."

"I know," Craig said.

Parker kept repeating the same message to us. I knew she meant well, and her only goal was to prepare us. However, her constant dosages of reality fueled my anxiety. I hated living with so much uncertainty. I hated not being in control.

I felt the walls close in around me. A silent tear ran down my cheek. I didn't even bother to wipe it away. I couldn't stay here anymore. I was suffocating. I had to get out of the house. So I did.

"I'll go to her," I heard Kara say as I descended the deck steps.

Although I had enough adrenaline pumping through my veins to power a run to the next county, I only made it as far as Amanda's swing set. Kara sat down next to me and handed me a tissue. "Are you okay?"

"Yeah." I rolled my eyes. "Never been better."

"Liar. What's wrong?"

I sighed deeply. "Nothing. Everything." I let out a huge sob.

"Come on, Sydney, talk to me, please," she cooed.

I sniffled. "Sorry, I should be able to hold it all together, but I can't. It's all too much. I never thought leaving our home would be this difficult."

"Tell me what's bothering you."

I started to swing, slowly. "In my head, I know we're making the right decision to move and to sell you the house."

"You're having second thoughts?"

I struggled to put my thoughts in some semblance of order. "No, it's not that." If Craig and I had come to the conclusion relocation was the best move for our family independently, I'd probably have been coping better. But the way this deal had gone down, I didn't have time to prepare myself mentally. People said that moving was one of the most stressful events in life. Now I believed them.

"Are you sure? Because if you've had a change of heart, let me know. I can stop this."

"That's sweet of you to say, but come on, Kara. You're dying to live here."

She grabbed hold of my arm. "I want nothing more than to move into your house. But I wouldn't feel comfortable if I felt like I forced you and your family out of it. I know we offered you guys a lot of money. I don't want you to feel bullied into moving."

"I don't feel that way," I lied. Between this and the pressure Jackie had put on me to join the PTA, I felt as if I'd lost all my free will. Sure, I'd ultimately made both decisions, but neither was one I would have contemplated on my own. I decided to go along with both plans because I knew how happy they would make the two people I loved the most in the entire world. I always put my family's happiness ahead of my own.

She gave me a curt nod. "Seriously, Sydney. If you don't want to move, tell me." Her fists tightened, and she stared at me with unblinking eyes. "Give me the word, and I will tell Jon I changed my mind. I'll say I realized I didn't want to live so close to my friend's mother because I was worried she'd be overbearing because she doesn't have grandchildren of her own. Jon won't question me. He'll call Rosemary and rescind the offer. Neither of the men will ever have to know we had this conversation. It could be our little secret."

Thoughts ran through my mind a mile a minute. Could Kara be serious? "You'd do that?"

She nodded. "Yeah, I would. I wouldn't want to, but yes, I'd end this all right now if I had to. I want all of us to feel good about this decision."

"Wow. Thanks. I'm speechless." I stopped swinging.

She winked. "I'm not totally selfless, mind you. I'd rather learn now this is a no-go than waste any more time." She put her hand on her stomach. "You and I both have a lot to deal with."

I nodded. "Thank you. We made our decision, and we are going to stand by it." I didn't doubt for one second we'd made the right choice. I longed to live closer to my family and office and having the added cash would alleviate a lot of stress. More than anything it would be a relief to leave Forest River while Amanda was still young enough not to be too affected by the superficiality of this town. "I guess I'm sad about leaving our home and the life we lived here. I feel like the house is part of our souls. I can't fathom leaving here and never coming back."

"Sydney, this is your home." She squeezed my arm. "You made it what it is. From the first moment I walked through the front door, it was apparent to me this place was built with love. The house has so much heart, and it's because of that vibe Jon and I fell in love with it. As long as Jon and I live here, this house will always be your home too. You, Craig, and Amanda will always be welcome here, anytime. The three of you have roots here. Those roots will continue to grow and thrive. I know you'll be back to see your friends, and when you do return, I want you to visit us."

I closed my eyes as relief washed over me. "Really?"

"Yes. I mean every word I'm saying. Jon and I will fill this house with laughter and love, the same way you and Craig have done. We will entertain often, and host holidays here. And while I know you have your own family to contend with, if you want a break from your relatives, you'll always be welcome to celebrate any occasion with us."

"Can I send my mother-in-law over instead?"

CHAPTER EIGHTEEN

"LADIES, LADIES. CAN YOU ALL MANAGE to be quiet for a moment?" Jackie's words fell on deaf ears, so she picked up a chopstick and clinked it against her wine glass in rapid succession. "Please can I have your attention?" Even though she'd practically begged, it still took several moments for all of us to focus our attention solely on our queen.

Satisfied with the silence, she dramatically sat down on one of her large wing chairs. "Thank you." She placed her hand on her chest. "I'm sorry to have to come down so strongly on all of you. I understand it's been a while since we met. I get it that you all have a lot of catching up to do, which is fabulous!" She glanced at me and winked. "I love how you've all become fast friends. Let's not forget why we're here tonight. We have important matters to tend to before we can kick back and relax. You all know very well by now, when it comes to the Forest River PTA, work always comes first!" She beamed and batted her baby blues.

"Unless work interferes with a manicure appointment, of course," Trisha Dickens muttered under her breath, loud enough for only me to hear since I sat next to her on the sofa.

I stifled my laughter by biting down on my lip while Trisha innocently popped a piece of Rainbow Roll into her mouth.

"Aimee, please be a plum and pass out these pamphlets." Jackie reached down and picked up a small-corrugated box, fresh from the printer, which she handed to Aimee. The poor woman was still struggling to regain our majesty's respect after the great bagel shop debacle of September, even though almost two months had passed.

As usual, Jackie didn't spare any time or expense; the pamphlets were thick, glossy, and filled with pictures.

"Why do you go to all this trouble year after year, Jackie?" Claire asked. She placed her pamphlet face down on the glass coffee table, without so much as glimpsing at it. She picked up her wine glass but didn't take a sip. "Look around. We're all pretty bright ladies. Between us, I'm sure we could figure out how to make sure we celebrate the holidays in proper Forest River fashion." She rolled her eyes before continuing. "We don't need to have most of November through January charted out for us, like a map to a newly undiscovered continent."

Aimee gasped. This was only my third PTA meeting, and the first time anyone had ever questioned the actions of our fearless leader. I felt more comfortable today than I did at previous gatherings. Since I already knew the members a bit better, I was less nervous about being the newbie. Also, Jackie had called the meeting earlier than usual and invited all the kids over for organic pizza. It was such a relief not to have to rush home from work to feed Amanda before heading over here. The kids' laughter from the kitchen almost provided background music.

"What's going on?" I whispered to Trisha.

"Hopefully nothing but be on the lookout. Sparks may very well soon fly."

Stacey leaned over toward Trisha and me. "I was afraid something like this might happen. I warned Claire on the phone to keep her tongue in check. She assured me she'd stay quiet, but I should have known better. She always takes her frustrations out on the wrong person. She needs a hard look in the mirror. She should know that no good comes from giving Jackie an attitude."

Jackie put her hands on her hips. "Claire, if you don't feel the need to refer to your pamphlet, you don't have to. I'm not forcing you, or anyone else, to take it home to hang on your refrigerator. My only concern is for Forest River Elementary. My only goal is to make this school year a success for every child, parent, and faculty member. To accomplish that, I feel it's important we all stay focused. What better way to keep us on the same course than to chart everything out? If we spend the time now to square everything away, we'll have fewer issues and uncertainty to deal with later. You all should know by now that I'm a firm believer in the adage, 'Proper planning prevents poor performance.'"

"What's going on with Claire?" I asked Stacey who apparently was in the know.

"She was busted," whispered Stacey as Trisha gasped.

"Doing what?" I'd overheard a rumor about her the other day while I was standing in line at the deli counter. I couldn't believe it might be true.

My question went unanswered until Trisha spoke. "You're kidding, Stacey. How did Kevin find out?"

"She's having an affair?" I guess the gossip in the supermarket knew her stuff.

Trisha whispered in my ear, "For years! You didn't know? I thought everyone knew by now."

I often wondered if I lived under a rock or something. I felt like I was always the last to find out when something happened in my hometown, although maybe I was better off being in the dark.

Claire and Jackie were oblivious to our side conversation; they were too focused on bickering.

Stacey leaned in. "Well, it was just a matter of time, wasn't it? For the life of me, I can't figure out how Kevin didn't figure out something was going on between them sooner. After all, the first time I saw them together, I knew instantly. Our girl Claire convinced herself hiding out in plain sight was the way to go." She turned to me. "You probably don't know. Jake is Kevin's best friend."

My mouth fell open. I couldn't fathom being unfaithful to Craig, especially with someone he considered a friend. It was a double insult.

"*Was* his best friend is probably a better description at this point," Trisha interjected.

"True that!" Stacey smirked. "So anyway, here's how it all went down. Kevin and Jake were supposed to play golf last Saturday. Claire was on the phone with her cousin in Kentucky. She decided to confide all the details about her affair. Apparently, she was finally contemplating leaving Kevin for Jake. Her cousin is a relationship maven, with a popular blog or something. The guys ended up not playing because Kevin's knee started to bother him. He didn't realize

Claire was home since she was supposed to have gone shopping with his sister. Always hungry, he picked up the telephone to order a pizza. Well, instead of getting a pie he got an earful. He stayed on the line for pretty much the entire conversation."

"Oh my God!" I gasped as my heart went out to the guy. I couldn't even grasp what he must have felt.

"Why in the world would she have a conversation like that at home, on a landline, no less?" Trisha questioned.

Stacey shrugged. "She probably never thought they'd cancel their game. They're both obsessed with the sport. Still, she's an idiot. I guess it makes sense she's questioning Jackie's faith in her intelligence."

Jackie once again clinked her wine glass with a chopstick. "Guys, come on. I don't know what's going on here tonight, but we have work to do." She glared first at Claire. "Keep or toss your pamphlet, I don't care." Then she turned to face my group. "We do need to stop the chatter and get back on track. Time is flying." Then, she patted Aimee on her thigh. "Fortunately, one of the members of the Forest River Elementary PTA is properly focused tonight."

Aimee grinned from ear to ear as Trisha elbowed me and muttered, "Kiss ass," under her breath.

"The next few months are going to be especially busy for us. Everyone is going to have to pitch in and step up their game for us to get everything finished." Jackie picked up her pamphlet and glanced down at it, although I'd bet my life savings the action was only for show. I was sure she had all the dates and times committed to memory. "Our biggest event, of course, will be the penny auction in March. Thank goodness we're in great shape!" She started to clap her hands and, like trained monkeys, we all joined in the applause.

I looked around the room. Was I the only one who found our actions ridiculous? Or was I too wound up to find pleasure in planning events for my daughter's school?

"The big-ticket items on our agenda before the big day are Snack with Santa and the Thanksgiving feast. I've been working very closely with the principal to pick the perfect day in between Christmas and Hanukah for the snack. I wanted to make sure all the kids, regardless of their religious backgrounds, feel comfortable. We settled on December eighteenth." With an evil grin, she turned her attention to Claire. "You'll be able to get that hunky friend of yours, Jake, to play the role of Santa this year again, won't you?"

Claire turned crimson and nodded. "I'll try."

"Very well." Jackie smiled. "Keep me informed about the status of the situation." Then looking at all her loyal subjects, she continued. "Since Claire is doing Santa, it makes sense for her to be part of the snack committee."

Claire opened her mouth to speak, and Stacey shoved a plate of sushi her way. I was shocked at how Jackie's comment was met with silence. Yes, it was uncalled for, but it was funny. I covered my mouth with my hand, not wanting to laugh and insult Claire. The other ladies must have been concerned about her feelings, too. It was nice to see they had compassion for their comrade.

As Claire chewed and stewed, Jackie kept going. "Aimee and Stacey, I have assigned you to this event, as well. In your pamphlets, you'll find I've already outlined everything that must be accomplished to make the event successful. Of course, if you have any questions, ask."

"As for the holiday feast, it's right around the corner, the Monday before Thanksgiving. I'm not expecting this event to go smoothly since it never does. As a result, I'm going to be taking the lead on it along with Sydney and Trisha." She started passing out hot pink pieces of paper. "Here is a typed copy of the sign-up sheet for the event. During this year's orientation, I had all the parents commit to what they were going to prepare for the party. History shows, at least one-third of them will either change their minds about what they're making or flake out completely. It is our job to make sure every kid present brings something appropriate to share at the event, even if it means we have to bring it ourselves."

I glanced at my pamphlet as a pit formed in my stomach. "Jackie, I'm sorry. I'm not going to be able to help with this event."

"Don't be silly, Syd. If you don't have time to cook extra meals, you can always run out and buy what you need."

"No, it's not that." I swallowed hard. "I'm not going to be in the country that week."

"Oh, you're going on vacation? I hope it's somewhere warm and sunny," Claire commented. "I sure could use some time away from this town right about now."

"I'm going somewhere warm, alright," I said. I ran my fingers through my hair. "It's far from a vacation."

"What?" the ladies all asked in unison.

I grimaced. "I have to go to India for four days for work." No matter how hard I tried, I couldn't manage to get out of going on this trip. My boss wouldn't budge. Part of me blamed Craig for putting me in this predicament.

He had spent so much time dissecting every contract we'd received that my boss changed his mind and decided to build a system from scratch using a firm based in India. The vendor who was in the lead to get this project, prior to this change of plan, continued to contact our IT department to try to convince them to change their minds. If only we had selected his firm, I'd have one fewer worry right now.

"India?" Aimee asked and scrunched her face. "I hate Indian food."

"Aimee, you are unbelievable. She tells you she's going to India and all you can think of is the food?" Trisha rolled her eyes. "Not like you ever eat anything anyway." Then she turned to me. "Sydney, I'm so jealous of you. You're going on a trip of a lifetime. India is the number one destination on my travel bucket list. Will you see the Taj Mahal?"

"I doubt it. I'm going to be in the complete opposite direction, by the southern tip."

"Ridiculous." Jackie shook her head from side to side and folded her arms across her chest. "All that traveling for nothing worthwhile?"

Like Trisha, I'd always dreamt of going to India. However, when push came to shove, I wanted no part of this journey. The thought of spending over twenty-four hours traveling to the other side of the world with my co-workers made my head spin. I feared I wouldn't be able to perform properly in a business environment with a ten-and-a-half-hour time difference. And while Indian food was one of my favorites, I was petrified I'd get sick.

I could have brushed all those fears aside and embraced this excursion if I didn't have a first-grade daughter at home to worry about. Yes, my husband would care for Amanda while I was gone, so I knew she'd be in good hands, for the most part. But a father wasn't a mother. If she fought with a friend, would he be able to properly comfort her? Craig needed constant reminding about domestic duties. I didn't even want to consider how many times he'd forget to make her brush her teeth before bed. I'd already jotted down enough notes to fill half a composition notebook for him, and Sally, our babysitter, to consult. But the part of the trip that filled my stomach with dread was the distance; I'd be so far away. If Amanda got sick or hurt, there would be no way that I could race home and be with her.

My face flushed as my blood boiled. "Nothing worthwhile?" My eyes met hers as my heart pounded hard in my chest. "I'd hardly say that, Jackie. In fact, I honestly find your comment incredibly insulting."

Trisha whispered to no one in particular, "This is going to be good."

Aimee let out a sigh." Totally the best PTA meeting ever, right, Trish?"

I didn't give Jackie a chance to comment. "The company I work for is investing a lot of money designing a new computer system to run our entire business. After almost a year of careful consideration, we decided to partner with an Indian based company. Even though we started working together a few months ago, we decided it was best for all our executives to travel there to meet their executives face-to-face to kick off this project properly and set everyone's expectations for the deliverables."

I shouldn't have had to explain or defend myself to Jackie, or anyone else in the room. But I was so angry. I felt like all the other mothers were always so disrespectful and dismissive of my career. I was sick of feeling judged because I worked outside of the house. No one bothered to try to understand how hard it was for me to juggle my obligations each and every day. And no one even stopped to consider that I was trying to teach my daughter how important it was to be self-sufficient.

"Oh, Sydney." Jackie walked over to where I sat and kneeled.

"Sweetie, I'm sorry. I didn't mean to hurt your feelings. You misunderstood my comment. I think it's wonderful you have such an important job, one where they need you across the world. I admire that. I only meant it was sad you had to travel so far and not enjoy the sights. Scott and I spent three weeks in India right after we were first married. It was one of my best experiences ever. It was so humbling. The disparity between utter wealth and utmost poverty in the country is outstanding. And if you're anything like me, you'll love the food. It took me years to be able to eat Indian in this country because it paled in comparison. I guess what I'm trying to say is I'm sad for you it's going to be all work and no play. You're missing out on such an opportunity."

I smiled at Jackie. I saw her and the other ladies in a different light. I always assumed they judged me for being different. But did they ever say or do anything to justify my beliefs? Or did I simply allow my own guilt and insecurities to cloud my perception of them?

CHAPTER NINETEEN

"GET THE HELL OFF MY DRIVEWAY!" The fiftyish-year-old man charged out of his house as soon as his real estate agent pulled away. The man's jet-black hair was wild, and he was dressed only in boxer shorts, despite it being thirty-five degrees outside.

"We'll be out of your hair in a minute," Craig replied calmly and gave the man a curt nod.

Along with Parker, we had just finished meeting with another structural engineer to discuss the retaining wall. It was early Saturday afternoon, and Amanda was attending a birthday party, again. Only in first-grade, my daughter had a social calendar that could put a supermodel's to shame. This was her third birthday party this week, and she had another tomorrow. Over the last few months, I had spent so much time shopping for and wrapping birthday presents for her friends. Fortunately, I finally came to my senses and bought gift cards by the stack. I had them ready to go, along with a pre-printed birthday message. It wasn't personal, but I didn't have time to do anything more.

"No!" the man bellowed. "Get off my property now! I'm expecting company, and I don't want you people standing in my driveway when they get here." He glanced at his watch. "If you're not gone in two minutes, I'm calling the police." He flipped us the bird before he turned around and walked toward his front door.

"Come on." Parker tapped Craig's arm. "We can finish this by the cars."

I'd exhausted my patience level. Today's visit would probably set us back another five hundred dollars. We kept throwing good money after bad evaluating this stupid retaining wall. Every architect and engineer we'd spoken to held a different opinion on the severity of the situation. I had no idea who we should trust, and I worried if we managed to buy this house, all the profit we made by selling our house in Forest River would be sucked into the wall.

"Thanks again, Jack." Craig shook the guy's hand. "I'm eager to receive your proposal."

I had my seatbelt buckled before Craig and Parker even descended the driveway. "Remind me again why we're doing this." I didn't bother to face my husband, who pulled away from the curb and began to follow Parker's SUV.

He exhaled. "You know why we're doing this. We can't stall Jon and Kara forever, and we need a backup plan."

I leaned against the car window and admired the autumn foliage as we entered Shells Point, a village located at the furthest end of Port Peters.

"I know that. But why do we have to do it today, of all days?"

"Sydney, I don't know what you want from me." He punched the steering wheel and stopped abruptly at a yellow light behind Parker. "You're the one who kept carrying on how it was a mistake to plan our future around a house we may not be able to buy. Now Parker and I found another one to look at and you don't want to be bothered to see it?"

I looked down at my lap.

"I thought we made a decision. If you're having second thoughts, say the word, and I'll call Rosemary and put this all to bed."

"No, it's not that." I clenched my fists. Sometimes my husband was so dense.

"Then what is it? The other day you seemed gung-ho to check out this place, and now that we've made the drive all the way here you no longer want to see it?"

"I want to see it. But I don't understand why we're doing all of this today. I have to leave for India first thing tomorrow morning. I should be spending what little free time I have left at home with Amanda."

"Amanda isn't even home. She's at a birthday party. You already have all your bags packed. You aren't missing out on anything."

"I guess so." I should never have let Amanda go to the party. I tried to convince her to skip it and spend the day with me. I even tried to bribe her with a new Alex and Ani bracelet, but she wanted to be with her friends.

I raised the volume of the radio and closed my eyes. We spent so much time mentally masturbating over the other house and had nothing to show for our time or money. I had a sinking feeling in my stomach this place would be another waste.

I pulled down my sun visor and checked my makeup in the mirror, as Craig turned right and drove down a tree-lined cul-de-sac. He stopped the car right behind Parker's vehicle.

"I forgot to ask you before, Syd," Parker said. "You did go and get all the shots you need, right?"

I smiled and thought of the scene at passport health where three of my co-workers and I had lined up like soldiers to receive rapid-fire inoculations. "I've had so many shots that I could lick a toilet in the airport tomorrow and not worry about catching a disease."

"Good. Because you may need those vaccinations to look at this place." Parker gestured to the house. "Craig, Sydney's safe, but you and I probably shouldn't touch anything inside."

For the first time since we'd stopped the car, I seriously took in my surroundings. There were humongous oak trees, surrounded by scattered leaves the color of a beautiful autumn rainbow. The ground had far more patches of dirt than grass. The structure was incredibly dilapidated. The white shingles were filthy, looking more like a gloomy shade of gray.

Walking on a cracked cement pathway, we followed Parker to the front of the house. I almost tripped twice. Parker bent down and removed a key from the lockbox. Before she opened the door, she explained, "Shells Point is the most exclusive village in Port Peters. The elementary school is only a couple of blocks away. The village has the highest tax rates and the asking price of this house is much more than the one you're looking at, and I'm afraid in far worse condition. While it looks beautiful in the pictures on the Internet, the condition inside is far from pretty."

I swallowed hard. Once again, my fears had become reality. I felt like the real estate gods had put a curse on Craig and me. We were never going to find a suitable house.

"Don't look so down, Syd. The crappy conditions could be a blessing in disguise. Most people who want to move to this part of town don't want to do a complete renovation project. Then again, most people aren't like you guys. I could see you putting the Craig and Sydney touch on this place. You could make it spectacular. I don't know all the details, but I do know the owners haven't lived here for many years. They've been renting the house out. And, I don't need to tell you how renters typically treat a home. They've had it on and off the market for years. I spoke to the listing broker this morning to get the skinny, and it seems like they finally made up their mind to sell."

Parker ran her fingers through her hair. "Don't let the sticker price shock you. It's pretty steep despite the current condition. But you need to look at the whole picture. When you take in the location and size of the property," she glanced down at a sheet of paper she was holding, "which is one and a half acres, this house is priced properly for this neighborhood. If you guys are interested, you'll have to move fast because I know this place won't be on the market long. Are you ready to see it?"

Craig looked like he was doing long division in his head as his eyes scanned the front lawn.

"Let's do it."

All I wanted to do was get Amanda from the party and take her home.

Parker fumbled a bit with the keys but finally managed to open the door. We all entered the tiny hallway.

On Zillow, they said the ranch was over four thousand square feet, but due to all the walls and closets, it felt much smaller, almost claustrophobic.

I walked toward the rear of the house where Craig stood. "What is that?" I tugged at a sliding glass door, which refused to budge.

"They call it a Florida room." Parker gestured to the glass-enclosed porch. "I call it a hazard. The structure was built so poorly it could probably collapse any second."

The windows were all crooked. The floor sloped, and there were holes in the roof.

"I'll bet there isn't even foundation under there," Craig interjected.

"Whoa. Is this the kitchen?" I walked over to the stove that looked far older than I was. I reached for the knobs but didn't dare try to turn them on.

"Got to love the tiles." Parker pointed down to the ceramic floor. More than two-thirds of the tiles were cracked.

I spotted a large picture window in the center of the living room. The afternoon sun brightened up the dingy room. And while the view outside was horrible, in my mind's eye I could picture sitting curled up by this window with a cup of coffee and a good book looking out on what could one day be a lush, green lawn.

I sagged against the wall as my legs wobbled slightly. I felt lightheaded as the tension I'd carried around all day began to melt away. I closed my eyes and saw what this house could look like if it received some tender loving care.

Despite all the things wrong with this place, I knew I was home.

CHAPTER TWENTY

"I LOVE YOU, BABY," I whispered into Amanda's ear. I carefully untangled myself from her covers. She didn't stir. She had fallen asleep at least a half-hour ago, and I took the opportunity to snuggle up next to her. Usually, Amanda begged me to stay in her room longer at night, as she tried to prolong her bedtime. But tonight, I was the one who insisted on more time with her. I wanted to cherish every second with her. I knew once I left for the airport tomorrow, it would be hard for me to communicate with my daughter.

I took a deep breath as I entered my bedroom. Craig and I had unfinished business to attend. "Come on, Craig, hear me out," I said as I sat down on our bed next to him. I was bone tired.

On any other night, I would have probably dozed while cuddled up with Amanda, but not tonight. There was no way I'd be able to get a wink of sleep until I got him to see things my way. It took all my willpower not to strangle my husband.

Craig closed his laptop and placed it on his night table. "Sydney, how many times do we have to rehash this?" He looked as exhausted as I felt. His eyes were bloodshot, and his hair was disheveled.

"As many times as we need until you come to your senses." I folded my arms across my chest.

He stood up and paced the room. "I'm not the one who needs to come to their senses. You're completely irrational."

I pointed at my chest and tried to steady my voice. "I am? How could you say that? You one hundred percent agreed with me how much potential the house in Shells Point had. Hell, you and I had the same vision of how we could remodel it."

On the drive home, we had discussed how amazing the place would look if all the little rooms on the main floor were knocked down and replaced with a window-filled great room and a state-of-the-art kitchen. We'd both pictured transforming the dilapidated Florida room into a deck. We also loved the idea of converting the maid's room, which was off the kitchen, into a walk-in pantry.

Craig pursed his lips, probably silently counting to ten. "Yes, I can picture the house fully renovated, the same way you can. But there is no way you and I can take on a project of this magnitude."

"We love to remodel." I waved my arms around. "Look what we did here."

"Sydney, we did this years ago. Forget the fact we had a lot more free time on our hands to putter around. We didn't have a child to think about. We need a home where we can live. We can't expect Amanda to live in a construction zone."

My thoughts danced. "Kara and Jon are flexible. They're in no rush to move in. Kara told me she'd prefer to move when the baby was a few months old. She wants to have a chance to adjust to motherhood before she settles in a new home. They're not worried about timing. They are only worried about getting this house. I'm sure they'd let us stay here as long as we need. So we'd be able to get the house in working condition."

Craig sat back down on the bed and gave me a closed-mouth smile. I prayed he was finally coming to his senses. "That only solves one issue. We have to look at the whole package. The house sits on an acre and a half of property. Do you have any idea how much it will cost to maintain a yard that size?"

"Big deal. We're making a lot of money on the sale of this place. So, we spend some on yard work."

"And what about the pool? Did you even look at it?" His eyes bulged. "I think the last time it was cleaned was during the Kennedy administration. God only knows what's lurking in those murky waters."

"So we clean it." Considering how wishy-washy I had been during this entire experience, I couldn't believe how hard I was fighting for this house. He was probably caught off guard as well.

He shook his head. "You're making everything sound simple."

I snuggled up next to him and nuzzled his neck. "It could be."

He jerked away and sat up straight. "And it could be a complete disaster, Sydney. Even if Jon and Kara are willing to let us start construction before we move, they are not going to wait around for us to finish the work. Are you prepared to live in shambles for a year, or more?"

I nodded as a smile crept across my face.

"Are you prepared to risk having to invest all the profit we're making, plus more, into that house?"

Our decision to move might have resulted from the offer we'd received, but the thought of being closer to my family was worth far more to me. My voice was a whisper. "I am."

"I'm sorry, Sydney, but I'm not."

***

I'd learned a lot about myself recently. I'd believed I was someone who embraced new challenges head-on. Unfortunately, during the past few months, I had come to the sad realization my perception of myself didn't match my personality in the slightest. I was shocked how emotional I had allowed myself to become at the prospect of moving. I also couldn't believe how I let my, mostly irrational, fears about a trip to the other side of the world consume me. I had been a nervous wreck.

I wandered through the airport and waited for my colleagues to arrive. I reflected on my recent thoughts and actions. I had wasted so many hours and days of my life worried about this trip, and for what? No matter how anyone looked at it, dashing off to India was a once in a lifetime experience. I was extremely fortunate to have this opportunity, the same way I was incredibly lucky to be in a position where someone was offering to pay us so far above market value for our home.

I wasn't over the fight Craig and I'd had last night. And while intellectually I could understand his concerns, my heart didn't want to hear them. I was up for the challenge the house at Shells Point offered and so disappointed he didn't feel the same way. I could continue to try to persuade him, but I knew from past experience it would be a futile exercise. Once that man made up his mind, there was no changing it.

Saying goodbye to Amanda was so difficult for me, and annoying to her. All I wanted to do was cuddle her and have her sit on my lap. She wanted no part. In fact, she looked me square in the eye and said, "I can't do this right now." Then pointing to the chair opposite from where she sat, "You have your space. I have mine. You sit there. I sit here."

My phone beeped, alerting me to a new text. I hoped it would be from Craig telling me how much Amanda missed me. Instead the text was from Jackie. I scanned it and fired off a short reply. Before I could even put the device back in my bag, it rang.

"Don't worry. Craig has it covered," I replied, impatiently, without even bothering to glance at the display first.

"Oh really." Craig chuckled. "What do I have covered?"

"Oh, sorry." My voice softened. I didn't want to board my plane with us both harboring hard feelings. "I thought you were Jackie. She texted a second ago to triple check I reminded you to bring food to school tomorrow for the Thanksgiving feast."

"What is it with you two anyway?"

"What do you mean?" I gazed at a gold bracelet in a duty-free store window.

"Well, it sure seems neither of you has any faith in me."

"Huh?" I scrunched my nose. "What do you mean?"

"You're adorable when you're in denial. Come on, Syd, how many times did you remind me of the feast over the past few days?"

"Um, maybe once or twice." My voice raised a few octaves as my lies continued. "Three times, tops."

"Yeah, something like that. All's forgiven. After all, it does make my heart swell with pride you had the confidence to tell your gal pal I had it all under control. Hopefully, you put her obsessive-compulsive mind at ease. Especially since neither of you lovely ladies have a reason to worry. Have faith. I'm not nearly as dumb as I look. I did pass the bar. So I think bringing a box of brownies to school is a task I could accomplish."

I rolled my eyes. "Yes, I know. You're quite capable."

"Finally!" He laughed. "You ladies are appreciating my talents." His tone turned serious. "All joking aside, I don't want you to worry about this trip."

I didn't reply.

"Sydney, listen to me. I know what you're doing. You're trying to blame your anxiety on a lot of different things. I know what's bothering you the most. You're scared of being so far away from Amanda for so many days."

A tear rolled down my cheek. "No, I'm not."

"Don't lie to me. And don't lie to yourself. It's okay for you to be nervous. You have every right to be."

"But you're her dad."

"Yes, I know. But this is not a normal trip. Every other time you had to travel for work you were in the States and could get home fairly quickly if you needed to. This time, it would take you over twenty hours by plane to get home. Just talking to her on the phone will be difficult, thanks to the time difference and your work schedule."

Tears stung my eyes. If he'd intended to make me feel better, he failed miserably. "You're right. I feel horrible being so far from her. What if she needs me?"

"She'll have me. She's going to be fine. I can handle anything that comes our way. Don't worry about her. Please."

My lip quivered. "I'll try, but it won't be easy."

"I know because I'm always right." He laughed. "I know right now it feels like you're going to be away forever. And yes, a week is a long time. But two of the days are going to be spent in the air. The other few you're going to be working your butt off. Trust me, time will fly. Before you know it, you'll be back home. Try not to waste the time you're away worrying. Enjoy some of this trip. What are the chances you'll ever go to India again?"

I walked into a shop to buy a bottle of water. I suddenly felt better than I had in weeks. "I love you," I whispered as my voice cracked.

"I love you, too."

I took a deep breath and handed the cashier some money. "So, when do you think you'll hear back from the structural engineer?"

"I don't know, and I don't care."

I almost choked on the water. "What do you mean you don't care?"

"I'm over that house. I have no desire to live there anymore."

My stomach did a somersault. "Why?"

"I found a house I like much better."

"When? How? I don't understand. I left for the airport less than two hours ago. How could you and Parker have possibly found another house so quickly?"

"You're silly, Syd. I'm talking about the house in Shells Point. That's the house I want to focus my efforts on."

"You do? Since when?" I gasped as another tear rolled down my cheek. I was so relieved and incredibly happy.

"Since I realized how much my wife wanted to live there.

CHAPTER TWENTY-ONE

THE LAST FEW WEEKS HAD BEEN ONE CRAZY, stressful blur. Craig was right. My trip to India had flown by at record speed. It was an incredibly humbling experience to see how differently people lived in that part of the world. The discrepancy between poverty and riches was immense, and my time overseas really helped me appreciate how fortunate I was in so many ways. I prayed I'd be able to hold onto my new perspective.

Most of my colleagues had struggled with the spice level of the food, but not me. Our hosts were shocked at how eager I was to try the local cuisine. My co-workers were still teasing me how I was the only white girl in history who went to India and gained weight.

Unfortunately, except for a quick excursion to the local shopping mall, which was practically identical to any you'd find in the United States, where I'd bought Amanda a hot pink sari, my time in the country had been spent exclusively in a conference room. We worked twelve-hour days. Between the long hours and the jet lag, I was constantly exhausted. Despite my fatigue, I'd found it nearly impossible to fall asleep, and when I finally had, I'd tossed and turned all night long.

Craig, true to his word, focused on the house in Shells Point while I was on the other side of the globe. He gave me daily progress reports, but unfortunately, since the Internet connection was usually very spotty at my hotel, I didn't catch every single word he said on FaceTime. So, I was shocked when two days after I'd returned home, Craig insisted I accompany him to the house for an inspection. I couldn't understand why he was so adamant about clearing my calendar to commit to spending a few hours at the house with him. I was too tired to question him. It wasn't until I'd sat on the sofa, staring out the window looking at the trees I'd fallen in love with during our first visit, that all the pieces finally fell into place.

In conversation, Parker had mentioned how amazing it was that the homeowners had accepted our offer so quickly. I was too embarrassed to admit I'd missed that part of the story while traveling, so I didn't.

Now here I was, at a spa, gearing up to purchase and remodel a new house.

"Oh, that feels so good." I shifted my position ever so slightly.

"You are very relaxed now," the technician commented and placed another warm towel on my face.

I usually didn't pamper myself. But it was early December, and I felt like I deserved an early holiday treat. I hardly ever went for manicures. Instead, I typically chose to quickly polish my nails at home, moments before I dashed out the door to drive to work. My master plan was always to allow my nails time to air-dry while I sat in bumper-to-bumper traffic. In concept, it sounded perfect. In actuality, without fail, I managed to smudge my nails before I even pulled out of my driveway, regardless of how careful I tried to be.

Today, however, I decided to splurge. I needed a quiet, peaceful break. I started off with a manicure and pedicure followed by a facial and massage. Between the soft music and my technician's magical fingers, I felt like a different woman than the one who'd walked through the door a couple of hours before.

"Here you are." The masseuse handed me an ice-cold glass of water, complete with sliced cucumbers and lime. "Stay here as long as you like."

"Thanks." I took a small sip. I lay back down and closed my eyes. I was happy I had already paid my bill, so I didn't have to bother with anything when it was time to go. I felt utterly at peace. Uncharacteristically, I'd even shut off my cell phone, so I could fully enjoy my afternoon of solitude.

I looked at the clock on the wall. I knew I shouldn't lounge here too much longer. I should get up and get dressed, but I wanted to take in the quiet alone time for as long as possible.

"Oh my God! What is wrong with you?" someone screamed, instantly terminating my tranquility.

I bolted up to get a better listen.

"She CUT me. THREE times. SEE!" The woman's familiar voice increased in both pitch and volume with every word she uttered.

"Oh man." I put my hand on my forehead. "What is it this time?" I got off the massage table and quickly pulled on my jeans.

My curiosity continued to pique while the commotion outside persisted. How could one woman cause so much drama? I opened the door and walked into the central area of the salon.

I immediately spotted Donna, in a state of panic, standing at the cash register and frantically waving her hand. I was glad Jackie wasn't here to witness this scene, given their rift, although she'd learn about it soon enough. Every patron in the pedicure chairs had their eyes fixed on Donna as their mouths all hung open in shock. The ladies getting their manicures were all equally nosy. They had their necks craned so they could get a better view of the unfolding action through the mirrors. A few were even recording the incident on their cell phones. I was sure the Forest River Mom's Facebook page would explode later with this footage.

"No!" Donna slammed her fist onto the desk. She pointed at the man behind the register. "There is no way you are charging me for this. I demand you give me back my credit card this instant!"

"You got a manicure, you pay for a manicure," the owner said calmly, avoiding eye contact.

"I didn't get a manicure. I got MUTILATED!" She turned and pointed her index finger at a petite manicurist who cowered by the nail polish display. "She cut me not once, not twice, but THREE times. With CLIPPERS!" She thrust her fingers into the owner's face.

"I only see one little cut. No blood! No three cuts! You lie."

"How dare you call me a liar? They were all bleeding moments ago. Do you want me to make them bleed again?"

He smirked at her. "Yes. You crazy lady."

She reached over for the bowl of lollipops they kept by the register. Fearing she'd take the bowl and hurl it at the owner, I raced up to the counter and grabbed hold of her arm before she could do anything she'd later regret. "Stop it, Donna," I said.

She glared at me. "What are you doing, Sydney? I can handle this myself."

"Yeah." I shook my head. "I can see how well you're handling it so far. Why don't you try and calm down?"

"Calm down? How can I calm down?" Tears filled her eyes. "First, she decimated my fingers, and now he's calling me demented. This has been a horrible experience, and he wants me to pay good money for this type of treatment? It's all wrong!"

"I agree," I spoke quietly. "If the manicurist did cut your fingers, you're right. You shouldn't have to pay anything. Let me see your hands." I felt like I was speaking with my daughter instead of a grown woman.

She sniffed and handed them to me, and I saw she was telling the truth. I faced the owner. "She was cut. I agree that she didn't handle the situation properly, but she was injured."

Donna opened her mouth to speak, and I glared at her. She got my silent message loud and clear.

He crossed his arms and gave her the stink eye.

"I can understand her frustration. I'm sure if you were in her position and you were all cut up, you wouldn't be too happy, either." He didn't reply, so I continued. "Take a look around. Your salon is full of people, and everyone here is watching you. They're waiting to see how you handle this situation. You can demand that she pay you twelve dollars for her manicure or you can give back her credit card and let her walk out the door. It's your call. How you decide to play this game will influence how I, and everyone in this place, will think of you as a businessman. There are a lot of different salons in this town. I am sure they'd all appreciate the added business we could bring."

He stared long and hard at Donna and me. Then he looked around the room. Like I'd predicted, even more people held up their cell phones to videotape the action. "Fine!" he said, his eyes blazing. "You no pay. You go. Goodbye!"

Thankful I had prepaid for my services, I ushered Donna out the door and away from the salon's windows.

"Thank you, Sydney." She flung her arms around me and clutched so tightly I struggled to breathe. "I don't know what I would have done without you in there. He upset me so much."

"I can see." I understood her outrage. If I didn't, I wouldn't have stuck up for her. However, it was unfathomable to me that a grown woman would have a temper tantrum in public like Donna had. If Amanda ever behaved that way, she'd lose all her television and Internet privileges for a week. Sadly, this wasn't the first incident I had witnessed in Forest River. So many of the residents had a very high-level of expectation and entitlement without a corresponding sense of appreciation. It was mind-blowing to think what lessons they were teaching their children.

She nodded. "I know I overreacted. There has been so much going on this year. I can't handle it all. I think I'm losing it."

I was shocked she'd admitted that her behavior was out of line. And I knew I should probably ask how Julia's allergies were doing, but I didn't want to prolong our conversation. Ever since the time we'd spoken after I'd sent the email about the best friend ban, she'd made me nervous.

"I know. Don't worry about it." With a smile, I added, "Please don't go back there again, okay?"

"You don't have to worry about that. Hey, listen, Sydney, a few of my friends are getting together this week on Thursday for an early holiday dinner. I would love if you'd join us."

"Oh, thanks, Donna, that's very sweet of you, but I'm not sure. I've got a lot going on."

Donna cracked her knuckles. "I know we've had our ups and downs this year, but we're mature mothers. We can move on. Please come." A bit of crazy flashed in her eyes. "You really don't want to insult me now, do you?"

Fearing there was only one way to handle the situation, I replied, "Okay." I wrapped my arms around myself and shuddered. More than the bitter cold, the thought of spending time with Donna and her friends sent a shiver down my spine.

CHAPTER TWENTY-TWO

"WHAT'S WRONG, SWEETIE?" I asked Amanda. She sat on the living room floor. Her markers and crayons were scattered all about, but her pad of paper was blank.

"My heart is breaking, Mommy," she said solemnly.

Clearly, she'd overheard one too many conversations about my father. "Why is your heart breaking?"

She folded her hands across her chest. "Well, my heart is connected to my ear, and Daddy is making my ear hurt, so my heart is breaking."

I leaned down and kissed her head. I was about to ask her what her father was doing when I heard for myself.

I followed the sounds of his screams. "Parker, you saw the inspector's report!" Craig bellowed into the phone as he paced around the kitchen. He ran his fingers through his already wild hair.

When he realized I'd walked into the room, he gave me a half-hearted smile and a small wave. Between Donna's dramatics and now whatever had gotten Craig up in arms, I'd wasted my time and money at the salon. I was a bundle of tension and stress.

I sat down at the kitchen table and began to weed through the numerous printouts he had strewn all over. I struggled to make sense of the conversation.

He picked up a folder full of papers. "Let's see." He scanned the papers. "First off, the sunroom is in complete disrepair and is unusable. The inspector found the platform's base had numerous cracks, which is what you get when you build without a proper structural foundation. Almost all the windows and doors do not open, which granted, we knew. But we didn't know the roof in the sunroom wasn't safe because of insufficient support. The room is completely useless as it is, and it will have to be fully removed or replaced." He paused, and listened to something Parker said. "Yeah, I know we thought about converting it to a deck." He frowned.

"Put her on speaker," I mouthed. I hated that I had no clue what they were discussing.

He nodded, sat down at the table next to me, and pressed the appropriate button on the phone. Without missing a beat, he continued to read. "The leaders are too close to the house, which is causing water to enter through the foundation. There's already mold in the basement. In the backyard, there are several areas of steel protruding from the ground, which is very dangerous. Forget the fact my wife is accident-prone, and she twisted her ankle last week falling up the stairs, we have a little girl to think about, Parker! I don't need Amanda tripping over a piece of metal and mangling her face or breaking her arm."

"I know, but—"

He didn't give Parker a chance to finish her thought. He continued to ramble. "The brick chimney is shot!" He waved the papers in the air like a lunatic. "It says right here there are broken and separated bricks with missing mortar. As a result, we can't use the fireplace. It would be extremely dangerous unless it's repaired or replaced." He took a sip of water. "The ejection pump in the bathroom in the basement isn't working, which means any water from the bathroom drains will not go to the cesspool. So, we're looking at a flooding situation, unless we don't want to use the bathroom down there, of course." He shook his head from side to side. "And this one is my favorite, Parker." His eyes met mine. "The house is infested with mice."

"Mice?" I gasped and instinctively brought my knees up to my chest, even though I was sitting at my kitchen table, in my immaculate home, one hundred percent safe from vermin.

"You should see Sydney's face right now. She looks like she's going to die at the thought of living with rodents." He placed a comforting hand on my shoulder, and my nausea subsided slightly. "The inspector found several hidden traps and numerous dead mice with a distinct odor. The entire house will require a sanitary cleanup and a full interior and exterior extermination." He fell back against his chair. "And all this is only on the first page. There are five pages of issues here, Parker. Five."

"I know, Craig. I know." The desperation in her voice was crystal clear. "I have a copy of the report, too. Please, try to calm down. You and Sydney knew the house wasn't in good continuation from the first time we saw it."

"Yes, but I thought at least it had good bones. I believed it was a sound structure."

"You and Sydney were planning on doing major work anyway, so the project will be a bit more involved. That's all."

"You say that so calmly. I wish I felt the same way you do. When I placed our offer, I took into account how much money we'd have to sink into the dump to transform it into a habitable home. I didn't account for all this extra work or expense."

"I know, Craig."

He sighed deeply. "I'm fine with doing the work. You know that. In fact, in a way, it may be a blessing in disguise for us." He flashed me a small, sad smile. "At least now we know all the issues before we begin to restore the place, which is much better than finding them later. By the same token, I don't want to pay full price for the house, when I know how much more these added repairs would cost me."

"I understand, Craig, but—"

I felt sorry for Parker. Every time she tried to speak, Craig cut her off. I wanted to hear what she had to say. She knew more about these dealings than we did.

"When you tell me the seller isn't willing to negotiate further, I don't know how to react. On the one hand, I don't want to lose the house. You know how much Sydney and I love it. I also don't want to be screwed over. And I have this place to worry about too. Every fifteen seconds I'm getting harassed by the buyer's agent, pestering me to sign the contract. They're losing patience with me because I refuse to sign anything here until I know we have a place to go."

"They won't negotiate?" I asked Craig in a hushed voice when he finally closed his mouth.

He shook his head.

"Can you give me a chance to speak, Craig? Please? My God! How does Sydney put up with you, anyway?"

"It's not easy," I interjected, with a giggle.

"Hey, Syd! What's up? I didn't realize you were on speaker. I meant to text you. I loved the picture you posted the other day of Amanda and her friend next to the huge gingerbread house in the mall. The shots came out amazing. Amanda is one lucky girl. She looks exactly like you."

"Thanks, she—"

"Seriously, Parker? You said *I* couldn't stop talking?" Craig tried to sound angry, but his eyes twinkled while he scolded her. "Can you and my wife please carry on your love fest some other time? We have more important matters to discuss than social media snapshots, you know."

"Fine," Parker muttered with a huff. "Do me a favor first, Syd. Pour him a glass of wine or better yet get him a tumbler of scotch. He sure needs something to calm him down. Oh, and you probably do, too, since you're stuck in the same room with him." She laughed. "I'm all the way over here, and I poured myself a glass of pinot grigio, to help me cope with him." Without missing a beat, she continued, "Now grouchy, can I please get some words in?"

"Yes," we answered in unison.

"Thank you! So, here's the deal and I don't know what to make of it, honestly. It's truly a first for me. I reached out to the seller's broker right after you and I hung up this morning. I went over everything mentioned in the report, in painstaking detail, by the way. I told her you were looking for a further discount on the accepted price as a result of the inspector's findings. I provided her with the amount of the discount we'd discussed. She told me she'd speak to her client and get back to me."

"I know. You told me this already."

"Calm down, killer. I'm repeating all of this for Sydney's benefit, not yours. She deserves to be brought up to speed, don't you think?"

I placed a glass of California cabernet in front of him. He grunted before taking a much-needed slug.

"When she called me back a few hours later, she said he refused to negotiate with her."

"I know!" He leaped out of his chair. "That's why I'm freaking out. How can they not negotiate at all?"

She took a deep breath. "Again, Craig," she whined, "if you'd allowed me to finish the first time around, all of our blood pressures would be a hell of a lot lower. So, this is the weird part. The seller refused to negotiate with his agent. He said he'd speak to you directly, Craig."

"What? Why?" he asked and puckered his lips.

"You've got me. In my twenty-something years of selling real estate, I've never seen this happen. People like to have all the dirty work handled by their brokers. Apparently, the owner knows you both. He told her that he felt if you guys spoke directly, you'd be able to find an amicable solution."

Craig and I stared at each other with puzzled expressions.

"He knows us both?" I asked. "Who is he?" The home was owned by a family trust, and all the title reports, public records, and drafted contracts were all in the name of the trust. Craig and I had no way of knowing who was in control. However, that person was privy to our names, current address, and a host of other telling information including copies of our tax returns and credit reports.

"His name is Andrew Gottley." She raised her voice an octave or two as if she were expecting an a-ha moment from us.

"I don't know anyone by that name," I immediately replied. "Do you, Craig?"

"Nope."

"That's so weird," Parker replied, sounding deflated. "The other broker told me he was very adamant about knowing both of you. He flat out refused to speak to anyone but you, Craig, regarding further negotiations. I'm going to text you his contact information as soon as we hang up. Maybe that'll jog your memories." She paused briefly. "Oh yeah. Duh, I almost forgot. The other agent said he sent you both LinkedIn requests a few days after his attorney drafted the contracts. Does that ring any bells?"

"I never use the site." Craig was completely anti-social media and was probably the only attorney in the world who never logged on to LinkedIn. "I'm not sure I even remember how to get into my account."

"Me neither," I added with a frown. "I can't handle one more social media site to maintain. Seriously, if it weren't for my Forest River PTA obligations, I'd delete all my accounts in a heartbeat."
***

Craig hovered over my shoulder, his breath hot against my neck. "Are you in yet?" he asked, impatiently, for what felt like the millionth time.

"No. Calm down. You're making me very nervous." The blasting television Amanda was watching didn't help the situation. "I can't remember what email account I used for this stupid site, let alone what password I chose."

"Why don't you keep a log of all your usernames and passwords, Sydney? It would make everything much easier for you."

"Oh, the expert has spoken, huh? Maybe if you followed your advice, we'd already be logged into your LinkedIn account, big shot. Then we'd already know who this mystery man was. Parker said he connected with you too. Damn it!" I banged my fist on the kitchen table. I failed again to log into the site. "This is my last try, Craig. I've got to figure out something to feed your daughter." I probably should have ordered a pizza at this point, but I really wanted Amanda to eat healthily.

I typed my usual social media password in for the thousandth time, capitalizing the first and second letter. "Yes!" I exclaimed. "I'm in."

"Finally!" He peered over my shoulder. "So who is he?"

"I'm working on it." I scrolled through numerous requests to connect before I spotted his name and profile picture. I stared at the photograph. The man was very handsome, but he didn't have any distinguishing characteristics. He was neither heavy nor thin. His brown hair was cut short; he had no facial hair and didn't wear glasses. "He doesn't look familiar to me. Do you recognize him?"

Craig squinted at the screen. My husband needed to get reading glasses. I nagged him about it all the time, but I decided to keep my mouth shut.

"I don't recognize him either." I clicked on his profile to get more information. We both read it in silence. "Oh my God, it's the computer guy," I muttered.

"You're right," Craig replied and scanned his full profile. "I'll be damned."

Andrew Gottley. The head of the IT firm we'd turned down, in favor of the one in India.

"Now that I know where he's from, I guess he looks sort of familiar to me." I'd met him only once when he'd come with his sales team to make the initial presentation. After that, I didn't participate in the other meetings. I wasn't sure if he even came back again.

"Well, I never even met him," Craig commented and examined his profile picture more closely. "Why doesn't anyone ever look like they sound on the phone? I pictured him much older. He's a nice-looking guy."

"Yep." I smiled. "The ladies at the front desk were sad when he left and never returned. He completely charmed them."

For a period, it seemed like my company was going to select the system he was selling. He and his team had made an impressive presentation. He'd brought a few programmers with him, and I thought they'd be the perfect partners for our technical staff. Even the price seemed fair to me. However, as always, Craig had reviewed the contracts. He'd ripped all the vendors' terms to shreds. He'd found many loopholes he didn't like in all of them. Andrew, in his defense, made almost all the changes Craig had requested. The whole process took much longer than anyone had expected. My boss used the time to contemplate what he wanted to accomplish. In the end, he decided he'd prefer to create a system from scratch rather than use an established one that could be customized, hence the Indian vendor.

"You know, he recently emailed the entire executive team. He tried to set up one more meeting. I know for a fact Steve told him we selected and started working with another software company months ago. He didn't give up. I wonder if he thinks there's a shot that we'll scrap all the work we've already done and simply switch to his software?"

"Sydney, I think you're missing the point. He probably contacted you guys when he realized we were the ones trying to buy the house. I'm sure he had a laugh or two at his private joke."

I rolled my eyes. "Maybe." Then a realization hit me. "What if he's angry at us about not getting the deal? Maybe he feels like you sabotaged his chances. I know how you get when you negotiate and review contracts. You were probably a royal pain in the ass to his attorneys."

"Yep. That's how I roll, kid." Craig winked at me.

I wasn't amused. "What if Andrew wants revenge? Payback is a bitch, you know. We're in a very vulnerable spot."

"What's the worst thing that can happen, Sydney? He and I can't come to terms, and we'll have Parker find us another house."

I slumped down in my seat, and my eyes burned with tears I didn't want to shed. "No, Craig. I love the place. If we're going to leave here," I dramatically looked around the room, "I want to live there."

He placed his hand on my shoulder. "I know you do. And believe me, I don't want this to turn into a complete nightmare either. I guess the worst-case scenario would be for us to pay the accepted price and move on. I hate to throw out money. We're making a nice profit on this place, so financially we'll still be okay."

"Who are you and what did you do to my husband?" I arched my eyebrows. "Come on, Craig. Who do you think you're fooling? You love to fight."

"Yes, I do. But I love you more."

CHAPTER TWENTY-THREE

"PUT THE CALL ON SPEAKER." I sat down on the den sofa next to Craig after putting Amanda to sleep. Despite our eagerness to have all these negotiations behind us and move on, we'd decided to wait a few days before calling Andrew. If it were up to me, I'd have placed the call immediately. Craig, on the other hand, was all about playing head games. I guessed that was why he'd always been a successful lawyer.

Craig keyed in the number. "Of course."

I wrapped myself in the multi-colored afghan and grabbed a handful of freshly made popcorn. Call me corny, but I was ready for the show.

Andrew didn't rush to answer the phone. He let it ring four times. Right as Craig was about to leave a voicemail, he picked up. "Andrew Gottley."

"Hi, Andrew, it's Craig Clayton. How are you?"

"Craig. Good to hear from you, my man. I have to admit, I'm a little surprised you're calling now. I would've thought you'd wait at least one more day before reaching out. But I'm eager to put this whole business behind us and move forward, pun intended."

Craig grinned. "Me too."

"Can you even imagine my shock when I learned you and your wife wanted to buy the house? Speaking of your wife, how is Sydney?"

"She's doing well, thank you."

"And the project at her office? Is that going well too? Or does my company have a chance to come in again? I have to say, I think they made a mistake choosing the other group. I'd love to talk more to her about it."

I rolled my eyes.

"Andrew, listen. Sydney had no say in the decision her company made. Even if she agreed with you and felt your firm would be a better fit, the situation is out of her hands. So please, can we move on?"

"Okay, fine. You can't blame a guy for trying now, can you? Seriously though, it was a shocker to find out people I knew wanted to buy this house. What are the odds of that?"

"Pretty slim, I'd bet."

"Yeah." His voice softened. "My Missy would have been pleased."

I raised my eyebrows and jabbed Craig in the ribs as I mouthed the name.

Picking up on my hint, Craig took the bait. "Missy?"

"Yes, Melissa. My late wife. The house was hers."

"Oh?"

"Yes." Andrew sighed heavily. "Her dad was big into real estate in his day. Missy was a Shells Point girl, born and raised there. When she was about ten years old, her father purchased homes in the various villages of Port Peters for each of his three children. He made sure that Missy's was the nicest, and of course located in Shells Point. No matter how much the old man may have denied it, she was his favorite child. And who could blame him, she was remarkable." Andrew sniffed. "Her father had it set up so that he'd rent out the houses until his children reached the age of thirty. On their birthday, he'd change the title over to them. They'd be able to either move into the house, continue to rent it out, or sell it all together and keep the proceeds."

"Oh, so you guys lived in the house?" Craig asked.

Why was he revealing such personal information? Was he trying to play on our emotions to get more money from us than the house was worth?

"Unfortunately, no." Andrew paused. "Missy loved the house. She couldn't wait for her thirtieth birthday, so we'd finally be able to move in. Missy begged and pleaded with her father to give us the house earlier, but he held his ground. She even got our daughter into the act to try and get him to change his mind. The old man was as stubborn as the day was long. So, we waited while Missy planned on how she'd fix up the place. Unfortunately, three months before her thirtieth birthday, she got diagnosed with stage-four breast cancer. My poor, beautiful wife didn't last long after."

"I'm so sorry for your loss," Craig said, as my eyes filled with tears. Bethany's best friend had recently received the same news, and her prognosis was also grim.

"Thank you. After Missy passed, my daughter and I became the beneficiaries of the trust. At first, I thought Jenna and I would move into the house, but I couldn't do it. I felt like we'd be hurting Missy by living her dream without her. As Jenna got older, I worried that I'd made a mistake. I felt as if I was protecting my deceased wife at the expense of our daughter. Jenna had loved the house all her life, too. She, like her mom, dreamt of the day we'd call it home. So, when Jenna was about ten years old, we decided we'd give the new house a try. We rented our house out, and we moved to Shells Point for about a year. It didn't feel right for either of us. Jenna missed all her friends, and I missed Missy way too much. It was a very trying time for me. Missy truly was the love of my life. Even now, all these years later, I still can't believe she's gone."

Once again, Andrew sniffed. He was crying on the other end of the phone, and my heart broke for him

"Time is an extraordinary thing," Andrew continued. "In some ways, it feels like an eternity since I last held Missy in my arms. Other times it feels like yesterday I had to tell Jenna that her mommy wasn't coming home again. Jenna's nineteen now, and she's given me her blessing to sell the house. She has big dreams of city life. She has no intention of living in the suburbs any time soon. And I certainly don't need to live in such a huge house, alone."

"He's single," I whispered to Craig. "Maybe we should set him up with Parker?"

Craig shook his head and rolled his eyes. He covered the phone with his hand and hissed, "What's wrong with you? Now you want to play matchmaker? Have you completely lost your mind?"

I knew it was silly to want to set up my husband's ex with Andrew. However, listening to him talk about his wife, I wanted him to feel the love he'd had for her once again. And Parker was a perfect girl who needed a good guy in her life. I couldn't help it. I was a hopeless romantic.

"Well, there you have it," Andrew said. His tone changed. Suddenly sounding very businesslike. "I'm sorry. I shouldn't have bored you with the details of my life. It's not relevant to the situation."

"You weren't a bore." Craig squeezed my leg. "Honestly, I'm thankful you shared the history of the house. I know a house is more than four walls. It's more than only a place. It's also a feeling."

"It sure is. But we can't get hung up on romantic mumbo-jumbo. A house is also a valuable asset. And in this case, as you are fully aware, you're getting a good buy. Between the emotions I have invested in the place, and the discounted price we've already agreed to, I find it rather unsavory that now, at this point, you're looking for a further price reduction."

"I'm sorry you feel that way, but Andrew, look at the facts. At the time I made my offer I wasn't aware of all the structural defects. I specifically made sure to state that my offer was contingent on the inspector's findings."

"Do I look like a fool to you? Come on, Craig. Cut the crap! First off, no other house in Shells Point has sold at this low a price in the past five years. You're buying more than a building; you're buying property in a very desirable town. Secondly, you may not have known the full details until you got the report, but there was no way someone as astute as you wouldn't have been aware that this house needed a lot of work. You'll never admit it to me, but I'll bet there was nothing noted in the report that shocked you. You knew what you were bidding on when you made the offer."

"Yeah, Andrew. I knew the house needed work. I didn't know that some areas weren't even structurally sound. I never accounted for that." Craig's face flushed.

"Don't waste your breath or my time. I've seen you in action. You try to come off as a low-key, sweet guy, but I know the truth. You're a shrewd shark!"

Craig opened his mouth to speak and immediately closed it.

"I saw what you did to my agreement. You kept my team on

their toes changing all sorts of terms. I thought my attorneys were sharp, but they were like guppies in the water next to you. You ripped them to shreds."

"I did what I had to. My priority is to protect my client's best interest."

"You sure did. And you also opened my eyes. I realized something during the negotiations. I'd rather have you on my side than against it. I have a proposition for you."

Craig arched his eyebrows. "I'm listening."

"There is no way I'm going down twenty thousand dollars as you requested. However, I will drop fifteen grand. In return I want you to do some work for me when all of this is over. I think you and I will make a great team. Do we have a deal?"

Craig was silent for a moment. "Under one condition. Since the house needs way more work than my wife and I ever anticipated, I want to be able to visit the house with contractors before we close so we can get a head start on the planning."

"As long as your real estate agent accompanies you, I'm okay. You can have four visits. Does that work?"

"Make it five, and you have a deal."

CHAPTER TWENTY-FOUR

NO MATTER HOW HARD I TRIED, WITHOUT FAIL, I always managed to be late. Sure, I could have blamed it on a multitude of reasons: an unexpected issue at work, a massive traffic jam on the expressway, or Amanda needed some extra help with her homework tonight, but none of them would be the truth. The reality was I dreaded having to go to yet another Forest River PTA meeting at Jackie's house.

Most women in my position, knowing they intended to leave town, would have probably bailed on the PTA by now. I'd spoken to my sister tonight while I drove home from work, and she said that was what she would do if she were me. However, she didn't share my obsessive need to complete every task I was assigned. But most importantly, the motivation that caused me to join the team in the first place kept me attending these meetings. There were still months left in this school year, and I was determined not to do anything to alter Amanda's experience.

Craig and I had decided to hold off on sharing that we were relocating to anyone except our immediate family, a few select friends from work, and my childhood best friend. Kelly was guiding me on making the transition easier for Amanda since she too had to move at a young age.

This decision to stay quiet wasn't easy for me. Considering how cliquish and controlling the moms were, I feared if word got out we weren't long for the town, Amanda would be the odd girl out, since she'd instantly lose her long-term friend potential.

Most importantly, though, I didn't want my daughter to worry about having to leave everything she knew behind and start over in a new place with new people. I wanted her to enjoy every day of her remaining time in Forest River, carefree, the same way she always had.

Although Craig understood my feelings about not wanting to upset Amanda, he thought I was out of my mind when I flat out refused to utter a word about this significant life-changing event to my local friends. But he still thought half the stories I told him about the shenanigans that went on with the women were exaggerations. He'd die if he knew I always toned down my tales before confiding them to him.

I took a deep breath and smoothed down my wool jacket before I knocked on Jackie's front door.

She greeted me without a word or smile. She merely opened the door and stepped aside, gesturing for me to enter. Typically, she'd offer a warm greeting, complete with her customary air kiss. Tonight, though, she was icy cold, and I was confused and hurt.

Maybe I was reading too much into her reaction? "I'm sorry I'm late." I gave her a hug and an air kiss.

Instead of returning my embrace she remained rigid, her back ramrod straight. She broke free quickly and turned toward her den.

"Come on, Sydney. The others are waiting," she called out over her shoulder.

I followed her and tried to process what could have caused her to change her attitude toward me so quickly. I had no idea what I could have done.

"Hi, everyone." I plastered on a huge smile and waved to the group before I sat down on the sofa next to Trisha. The ladies all warmly returned my welcome, unlike our hostess. My stomach clenched.

"Can we please cut out all the chitter chatter, girls?" Jackie said, after an exasperated sigh. Then, for further emphasis, she started to clink her wine glass with a chopstick. "We do have a lot to accomplish this evening. I understand you all have so much to say to Sydney. Unfortunately, she was once again tardy. It isn't right our work should have to wait until everyone can have a chance to catch up with her. After the meeting, you can chat all you like. But for now, we have business to take care of."

"Wow. What did you do?" Trisha whispered to me. "I thought you were the teacher's pet?" She smirked and put a piece of eel sashimi on her plate.

"You got me," I replied, puzzled. Sure, I was five minutes late, but I was always five minutes late. Jackie's attitude was extreme, even for her.

Jackie shook her head. "Even though the event is scheduled for only a few days away, we have to make major changes to our Snack with Santa."

"What kind of changes?" Aimee's eyes bulged.

"For starters, the name." Jackie ran her fingers through her ash blond hair. Her blue eyes blazed when she stared directly at me. "Donna once again has caused us unnecessary drama. She decided that even though the school has been hosting Snack with Santa for the last thirty-five years, the name of the event is offensive to non-Christians."

"What?" we all asked pretty much in unison.

"Yes, you heard me."

"That's the craziest thing I've ever heard," Claire said. "Everyone loves Santa Claus."

"We know you sure do," Trisha said with a giggle, as Claire turned crimson.

In the few weeks since our last meeting, her husband had moved out of their house. Less than a week after his bags were packed, her boyfriend, Jake, who was scheduled to play Santa, moved his stuff in. I couldn't help but wonder if she even had time to change her sheets.

"I don't understand. Craig and I are both Jewish, and Santa has," I made air quotes, "come to our house ever since Amanda was a baby. He's more of a symbol of happiness and hope to all children than a religious icon."

"And you think I disagree?" Jackie sneered at me. "My husband is Jewish too, and like you, Santa has strutted his stuff down our chimney for years. None of this matters now."

"Isn't Donna a devout Catholic?" Stacey asked. "I see her and her family heading to church every Sunday morning like clockwork."

"Yes." Jackie paced the room. "She is. So, Santa probably doesn't offend her, or her precious daughter. She made a point of making sure everyone knew that her opinions weren't personal. She stated that others were offended, although she refused to name names. She stressed how diverse the town has become and pointed out that not only are there numerous Jewish kids, but also Muslims, Hindus, and Buddhist children at the school. She carried on how it was completely unfair to do anything remotely religious in a classroom setting."

"Maybe she has a point," I replied, before taking a sip of my wine. Was it worth running the risk of alienating anyone?

"I'm not surprised you agree with Donna." Jackie glared at me with pure hate in her eyes. "The principal is on your side, too. He was afraid to upset the other parents, so here we are. Your friend has made it her main priority to make my life miserable this year, and now all of us have to suffer."

"What are you talking about, Jackie?" I asked, but my question went unanswered.

Trisha whispered into my ear, "What is the 'your friend' comment about?"

I shrugged. "You've got me."

"So instead of having Snack with Santa, we have to have snacks with snowflakes." Jackie rolled her eyes. "Have you ever heard of anything more ridiculous?"

"So, are you saying Santa can't come?" Claire asked, wide-eyed.

Jackie continued, "Fortunately, Claire, even Donna can't stop Santa from coming. He is going to have to come quickly. There will be no time for him to mess around. He's going to enter and deposit his load."

Trisha poked me, and I struggled to keep a straight face. Aimee and Stacey caught our eyes, and we all lost it. Even Claire couldn't help giggling.

"Grow up, girls," Jackie scolded and looked right at me. "What is this? The third grade? I'm shocked at you all. Claire," Jackie bent down in front of the woman and looked her square in the eyes, "I'm so sorry for their inappropriate outburst. I wish you and Jake nothing but the best. You deserve to be happy and no one," again she caught my eye, "should make you feel uncomfortable."

"Thank you." Claire smiled demurely.

"Wow," Trisha said quietly to me. "Someone sure is on her majesty's shit list tonight. Come on, tell me, what did you do wrong?"

"I genuinely don't have a clue." My mind raced. I tried to replay the last few weeks. No matter how hard I wracked my brain, I couldn't figure out what I possibly could have done to offend Jackie so profoundly. Sure, I'd been distracted, but I still managed to make sure every parent committed to bringing in a special treat for the event. I'd also personally gift-wrapped half of the presents Santa was supposed to distribute to the children. Jackie had wanted to wrap them together, at her house, but I'd persuaded her to let me do my share alone over a one-week period. I'd explained I needed the time to juggle the task with my job and our holiday preparations. She seemed to understand, then.

Jackie cleared her throat. "So, as I was saying before I was so rudely interrupted, the name of the event has changed. And as a result, our theme has to change, too. Claire, I know you're always on top of your game and probably have already picked up the paper supplies, but you'll have to swap it out. We can no longer serve on Santa-themed plates. Instead, we have to use ones featuring snowflakes. The napkins and forks should no longer be red. They must be silver and pearl." She picked up a glossy picture and handed it to Claire. "Here is a picture of a table-scape I found on Pinterest. I'll need you to re-create it."

Claire nodded obediently.

"I already took care of getting our shirts re-made." Jackie handed each of us a shopping bag.

Aimee pulled hers out. It was a long sleeved, fitted tee-shirt, hot pink of course. On the sleeves and around the collar were various sized shiny snowflakes. Across the front left breast in silver letters it read: Forest River PTA. And on the back, also in silver, was a giant snowflake, and underneath it said: Snacks with Snowflakes December 18.

"They came out great," gushed Stacey.

"I know." Jackie nodded. "And finally, we'll have to re-wrap all the presents."

"Why?" My blood pressure spiked, and I bolted upright in my seat. Thanks to the specific instructions on how each package had to have a full Santa visible, it took me hours and hours to wrap the thirty-five presents I'd been assigned. I couldn't afford to waste more time on such an insignificant task, especially so late in the season.

"You can't seriously be questioning why, Sydney. How can you possibly think based on everything I explained we could hand out presents featuring Kris Kringle? Your buddy Donna would go berserk! And there's no way I'm about to allow any more unnecessary drama to occur over this event. I've already made the decision. All the gifts will feature snowflakes. I found the perfect paper. I have yours right here. I'd invite you to do it together, but I know how busy you've been lately. I don't want to interfere with your other commitments."

Was this a jab about my job? "I—"

Without giving me a chance to finish my thought, Jackie handed me a huge bag filled to the brim with rolls of wrapping paper, ribbons, and pre-made bows. Then she quickly moved on to other pressing PTA matters.

I remained quiet for the rest of the meeting, which was no easy feat. Trisha kept trying to egg me on. She made sure to keep pointing out all of Jackie's snide remarks as if I were incapable of picking up on our host's hostility on my own.

Finally, the meeting ended. They all rushed to the front door and bid Jackie a hasty goodbye. I, however, didn't move a muscle.

Jackie returned to the den and immediately started to clean up the assorted snacks from the coffee table. "Oh, you're still here?"

I grabbed two empty wine bottles and the tray of sushi and followed her into her kitchen. "I'm not going anywhere until you tell me what's bothering you."

"Bothering me? Nothing is bothering me, Sydney," she said into her humongous Subzero refrigerator. She didn't even bother to turn her head slightly toward me.

"Jackie, come on." I stood next to her, my arms folded across my chest. "Cut the crap. You and I and all the other ladies saw something's eating at you. So why don't you just spit out what it is so we can hash it out and move on?"

"What's the point?" She walked over to her large, white farm sink and began to rinse out the wine glasses.

I shut off the water. "Sit!" I scolded. I pointed to her gray granite island in the center of the room. I walked over and pulled out a high back, wood barstool and sat down. Reluctantly Jackie joined me.

"You're not going to let this go, are you?" She dried her hands on an ornate dishtowel. "Why do you have to be such a pain in the ass, Sydney?"

"Well, that's one way of putting it." I offered her a small smile. "I'm not trying to upset you…"

"Well, clearly it's too late for that now, isn't it?" She rolled her eyes.

"Apparently, it is. But, I have no idea why you're upset with me."

"Syd? You expect me to believe that? You know very well what you did." She looked away. "Honestly, I'm not upset with you. I'm taking my frustrations out on you. I'm furious with myself. I was such a fool to think our friendship was real."

"What are you talking about, Jackie? Of course our friendship is real." Well, at least I thought it was. How could a true friend turn on me so quickly without warning?

"No. It's not." She shook her head. "I started to let you in, Syd. I even spoke to you about Kansas and my grandmother. I felt like I could trust you. I felt as if you could understand me, the real me, not the persona I constantly try to portray. Wow, was I wrong."

"Why are you saying these things? Why do you doubt me all of a sudden?" No matter how hard I tried, I couldn't figure out what I could have done to cause this severe reaction. I never spoke about Jackie to another mother behind her back, nor did I repeat any of the stories she'd confided in me, like the bullying incident, with anyone.

She twisted the dishtowel. "You know why." Her eyes filled with tears. "I made this mistake once before. I allowed Donna to see my vulnerable side. And what did she do? She used everything she knew against me and stabbed me right in the back so her daughter could move up the popularity ladder at my Hayley's expense."

I touched her arm. "I still don't understand what happened to make you so upset."

She snorted. "Whatever you say." She got up off the stool and grabbed her iPad from the counter. She sat back down while scrolling on the device. "Maybe this will help jog your memory."

I took the tablet from her and looked at a picture that had been posted on Facebook about a week ago. I started to laugh.

"What's so funny?" she demanded.

"You. Seriously, this is what has gotten you so upset? A picture of me sitting in a restaurant with four other ladies having a glass of wine?"

"It's not just four other ladies. Look who you're sitting next to!"

"Yeah, I know who sat next to me. Donna was the one who invited me."

She got up, threw the towel down, and walked over to the sink where she began to wash wine glasses once more. "Perfect. You've proven my point. Now, please go."

I grabbed the dishtowel off the island, joined her by the sink, and began to dry the glasses. "What is your point exactly?"

She shut off the water, again, and walked back to the table. I followed her. "You've been blowing me off ever since you returned from your business trip, Syd. I invited you over here, so we could wrap the Santa, damn it, I mean the snowflake presents together, but you didn't come. You said you wanted to take care of them at your house instead, so you could squeeze the task in when you have a free moment. We haven't had lunch once since you returned to the States. Nor have we hung out in any manner, shape, or form.

"Our phone conversations have been pretty much non-existent. It's like you stay on the line only long enough for us to cover the bare necessities. Forget about discussing anything remotely personal; we hardly manage to make any small talk. I've tried to make dinner plans for all of us and—"

"And we have a date scheduled for next Saturday."

"Unless you cancel." She smirked.

"Why would I cancel?"

"I don't know. Maybe you and your new bestie will want to go out instead. You found time to go out to dinner with Donna and her posse when you didn't have time for me."

I clenched my teeth. "Are you freaking kidding me?" I pointed at the picture. "You're treating me like crap because of something you saw on social media? What are you, seven?"

She looked away.

"Look at me, Jackie." I spun her to face me. "Maybe you should get your facts straight before you start throwing out accusations."

"Are you going to sit here and tell me you weren't with Donna?"

"No. I was there long enough to chug a glass of chardonnay." I crossed my hands over my chest. "If you want to be mad at me for being distant, I can't blame you. I know I've been a bit out of touch. I'm sorry. I'm completely exhausted and extremely overwhelmed. Craig and I have a lot going on."

I was so close to telling her the truth about our pending move, but I couldn't bring myself to. "Things have gone berserk at both our offices. I wanted to take some time off either before or during the holidays, but now I can't. The holidays are racing toward me like a freight train, and if that wasn't bad enough, Craig's parents are heading to our house for a week right around the holidays because they have a wedding to attend. Craig's dad is a doll, but his mother is a pill."

"I get it. You're busy. Despite all your commitments, you still managed to find time to get together with Donna." Jackie pouted.

I chose my words carefully. I was furious with her, but I also realized why she was so upset. My sympathy outweighed my anger. Despite how hard she tried to fight it, deep in her core, she was a very insecure woman.

"It's really none of your business what I do, or who I do it with. I'm a big girl."

Hurt flashed again in her eyes, and I reached for her hand. Feeling like I was talking to my child instead of an adult, I said, "And my going out with Donna and her friends doesn't mean I like you any less. Donna had a little situation at the nail salon, and I managed to get her out of there before the scene she'd started escalated out of control. As a thank you, she invited me to join her and her friends. She wouldn't take no for an answer. She made it clear it was better, not only for me but all of us, if I went for a quick drink and made an appearance, rather than insult her by not showing up. Let's just say, I sacrificed my evening for the team. If I live to a hundred, I will never understand how you were friends with her. You two couldn't be more different."

CHAPTER TWENTY-FIVE

TELLING JACKIE I'D TAKEN ONE FOR THE TEAM had been the right move. Her anger and hostility had instantly faded, which was perfect. I couldn't handle any more drama. During the past few weeks, Andrew and Craig had exchanged numerous phone calls and text messages regarding the contract. For every change Craig made, Andrew added two. I would have lost my patience fast, but my husband was in his element, relishing every debate.

He tried to deny it, but I knew he enjoyed the challenge and his constant interaction with Andrew. On more than one occasion, I'd overheard part of their conversation. They were laughing and joking, chatting about everything except my future home. I saw the start of a budding bromance brewing.

Honestly, I never thought I would live long enough to see the guys come to terms and finalize the agreements. But Andrew's desire to spend the holidays with his daughter in Saint Barts, negotiation-free, trumped his desire to keep delaying the inevitable deal. So, on Christmas Eve morning, the contract was signed, sealed, and delivered.

To say Kara and Jon had been patient during this time would be a complete lie. Jon and Rosemary must have called Craig a hundred thousand times to check on the status of their contract. And every time Craig spoke to them, he gave the same canned answer: he'd sign the contract, soon. I didn't know how they kept their faith that soon would come. I admired their patience, especially since if I were in their shoes, I wouldn't have been as understanding. That was why, as soon as the contract on the Shells Point house was in perfect order, complete with both signatures, we signed and sold our home.

I didn't want Kara and Jon to suffer another second with uncertainty, although it was a very bittersweet moment for me. We hadn't set a closing date, but we planned on a quick one. If I got misty signing the contracts, I'd be a mess when the title changed hands and my house officially became theirs.

"Merry Christmas!" Kara sang as I opened my front door. She'd called me moments after the contracts hit her inbox and asked if she could stop by this afternoon on her way to her sister's house.

She placed her packages on the floor. I hugged her hello, as did Amanda.

"Give me your coat. Is Jon with you?"

"No. I dropped him off at Mia's already. He had some calls to make." She handed me her long, red wool jacket.

"Hey, there's a baby in there!" Amanda exclaimed and pointed to Kara's swollen stomach.

"Amanda!" I gave my daughter the stink eye.

"It's okay. You're right, Amanda, I'm going to have a little girl like you in a few months."

Amanda bounced in place. "Cool. I want a sister… Or a cat… But Mommy isn't giving me either one."

"Never say never." I smiled at my daughter. "Can you do me a favor and bring in the cookies we baked this morning?"

Amanda raced to the kitchen.

"Wow, Sydney!" Kara beamed and hugged me once again. "You're expecting too?"

I raised my hand to my mouth. "Oh, no." I grinned. "Amanda doesn't know, but we adopted a kitten. He was rescued from a kill shelter and is in foster care right now. We're bringing him home tomorrow." It was foolish of us to welcome a pet into our home now, with everything going on. I sure didn't need one more responsibility. But I was so worried about Amanda adapting to our new house, I wanted her to move in with a cherished pal.

"Here are the cookies!" Amanda announced as she placed them on the coffee table. I had already put out a pot of coffee and several bottles of water.

Kara and I sat down. "Amanda, see all the bags by the front door? Go get them. There're presents in there for you!"

"Kara," I touched her arm, "you shouldn't have."

"I wanted to. After all, finally getting your signatures on the contracts was truly a Christmas miracle."

Amanda's eyes lit up as she unwrapped the presents. First, she discovered an American Girl doll. Then she opened a package containing an enormous assortment of arts and crafts supplies. "Thank you, Kara!" Amanda wiggled on the floor.

"You're so welcome. But I have one more present for you."

I squinted at her as she rummaged through her Louis Vuitton Hobo bag. As far as I was concerned, she had already gone over the top.

Amanda unwrapped the small square box slowly. I wondered if she sensed it was an extra special gift. "Look, Mommy!" She held up a pink Hermes H bracelet for me to see. "Everyone gets one when they leave elementary school, but no one in first grade has one!"

My mouth hung open, and I placed my hand across my chest. "Kara, no. We can't accept the bracelet. It's way too much." I found our town's tradition totally absurd. What sixth-grader needed a bracelet that cost over six hundred dollars?

"Nonsense, Sydney." She tilted her head in Amanda's direction. "Look how much she's already enjoying it."

Amanda was performing a silent play showing off her wrist to her imaginary fans. "Besides, I think you'd have to tear it off her wrist to return it to me."

Kara didn't give me the chance to reply. She sat down next to Amanda and started opening the arts and crafts supplies. "Come on. Before your mom can cause any trouble, let's color. Can you draw Santa?"

I knew Kara well enough at this point to realize there would be no persuading her to take back the present, so I decided to enjoy the moment with her and my daughter. As they colored, we chatted.

"Where is Craig anyway?" Kara asked.

I twirled one of Amanda's pigtails. "On his way to the airport to pick up his parents."

"Oh, how nice you'll get to spend the holidays with them." She beamed.

"Well, that's sure one way to look at it."

***

"Sydney, I thought you said this coffee was fresh?" My mother-in-law pushed the mug I had handed her off to the side with a scowl. Coffee splashed from the cup onto the kitchen table. She didn't even bother to blot it with her napkin. She'd probably look less put out if I'd handed her a glass of poison.

I grabbed a sponge and cleaned up the spill. "I brewed the pot fifteen minutes ago, Brenda. Do you want me to make you something else?"

Craig's parents had been with us for over a week already, and I was actively counting down the remaining forty-eight hours until they, well she, returned to the Sunshine State. This had been the longest Christmas break of my life.

My father-in-law reached across the table, picked up his wife's discarded cup, and took a big sip. "I think it tastes delicious, Syd." He winked at me.

For the life of me, I couldn't understand how they'd stayed married for over forty years. He must have had the patience of a saint.

Brenda folded her arms across her chest, and glared at him. "Of course you like it, Maxwell." She scowled at him. "You accept everything handed to you. I still can't believe you weren't incredibly insulted that Sandra and Fred deposited us at that table with those random people."

My father-in-law shrugged. "They were nice. Besides, what difference did it make? You barely sat still the whole night. You were so busy yapping with all your girlfriends."

My in-laws were in town to attend Sandra and Fred's daughter's wedding, which had taken place three very long days before. Brenda and Sandra had been friends for years; my mother-in-law was incredibly insulted they hadn't been seated with her gaggle of girls. She refused to accept that her late response to the wedding could have contributed to the seating arrangements. She had rehashed this story countless times. I was going out of my mind.

"Oh, Amanda," I called out as my daughter entered the kitchen with the kitten in her arms. "Be careful how you carry Oreo. You shouldn't hold him like a baby. He may scratch you."

"Nope. He loves it." She leaned down and kissed his black and white head. She'd fallen in love with the feline the instant we'd surprised her. My mother-in-law didn't feel quite the same way about the creature.

I poured some cereal into a bowl for my daughter. "Put him down and have breakfast."

"Keep him away from me," Brenda said before taking a bite of her bagel.

I looked at my watch. "Eat up," I said to Amanda. "Once Daddy's out of the shower we're going to hit the road. Grandma can't wait to see you."

"Can I bring Oreo to Grandma's? She's going to love him!"

"No, sweetie, he has to stay here. Cats don't like to travel."

She looked devastated she'd have to leave the cat behind. She'd barely let him out of her sight since he'd joined our family. It would be difficult for her to return to school after the holiday break ended.

Craig and I were heading over to Shells Point to meet with Parker and a bunch of contractors. As per the agreement, we were able to get a head start on the design and renovation before we closed. I was so eager to dive into the project. Since Craig and I'd be preoccupied with the plans, we wouldn't be able to focus on Amanda, so we decided to drop her off with my mom on our way.

It was ironic: her other grandparents were in town, yet I had to schlep her all the way to my parents'. It made me so sad. Over the years, Craig had tried to hide his feelings, but I was always able to see through his act. It troubled him tremendously that his mother had a strained relationship with our daughter. Honestly, she didn't have a close relationship with any of her grandchildren.

I'd never doubted for a second that Brenda loved our daughter. But to me, she never acted grandmotherly. My mom had all the time in the world for her grandchildren, regardless of their ages. She spent hours playing with them and continuously begged my sister and me to let our kids stay at her house for sleepovers. Craig's mom, on the other hand, always seemed so uncomfortable around any of her grandchildren.

She went through the motions and would absently play a game or two with them. When she talked to Amanda or the others, she never appeared to listen. The kids, fortunately, didn't seem to notice she was never truly present, but as a parent, it was impossible not to see.

"I know you told us you were going to take her to your mother, but Maxwell and I were thinking maybe you should change your plan."

"Morning, Mom." Craig bent down and kissed her cheek before grabbing a cup of coffee.

"Change them how?" I asked.

"Maxwell and I are only going to be here for another two days. I think Amanda should stay with us. I thought we could take her to the mall, have lunch, and catch a movie. How does that sound, Amanda?" And while the question was directed to my daughter, my mother-in-law didn't take her eyes off mine, almost as if she were daring me to deny her the visit.

"Fun!" Amanda yelled out.

"Oh, that's so sweet of you, Brenda. But a day like that could be very exhausting. Are you sure you're up to it? You've never spent so much time with Amanda alone before. She can be a bit overwhelming."

"I've had children, Sydney. I can handle your daughter. Don't you want me to spend time with her?"

Was she trying to blame her blasé relationship with my kid on me? I silently counted to ten and chose my words carefully. "I'd love nothing more than to see you and Amanda get closer."

"Good. It's decided," Brenda said with a curt nod.

I picked up my cell phone to call my mother about the change of plans. I couldn't decide if Brenda really wanted to improve her relationship with my daughter or was in search of an opportunity to share pictures of her and her granddaughter on Facebook and make her canasta friends jealous. Either way, I'd lie if I didn't say I felt more than a bit unsettled.

CHAPTER TWENTY-SIX

"THIS IS GOING TO BE ONE EXTREMELY long day." Craig turned onto the road which led to our future home in Shells Point.

"I'm ready for anything." I took the final sip of my caramel latte and forced a smile.

"Come on." Craig gently patted my thigh. "Be honest. You're worried about leaving Amanda with my parents."

"Gee, Craig. When you put it like that, you make me sound horrible. I know she's going to be fine with them. It's just so out of character for your mom to want to spend alone time with her." I couldn't figure out what Brenda's motive was. Maybe she was jealous that Amanda was eager to spend time with her other grandparents?

Craig neared the end of the cul-de-sac and drove up the driveway. He parked behind a plumbing truck. Before exiting the vehicle, he reached into the backseat for his manila folder and notebook. "Parker's late as always, just like you." He smiled.

"I guess you have a thing for late women," I fired back.

"Funny." He leaned over and gave me a quick peck on the cheek before he gestured to the truck in front of us. "Our first appointment is already here."

I wrapped my wool scarf tightly around my neck and cursed myself for not dressing more warmly. It was frigid outside. The winds were ferocious, and the weather forecasters had predicted that we'd be hit with a blizzard tomorrow.

"Craig?" A short, stocky man greeted us enthusiastically. First, he shook my hand then he took my husband's. "I'm Dennis Healy. Great to meet both of you."

"Thanks so much for coming out so early today." Craig patted him on the back.

The first item on my husband's punch list for the house was to convert it from oil heat to natural gas.

"No problem. I only live a few blocks away. I got here a while ago and took a little walk around. I'm sorry, buddy, but you've got yourself a problem." He pursed his lips.

I had finally started to let my guard down and not worry constantly.

Dennis crossed his hands over his broad chest. "I checked the oil tank in the front yard, and it is bone dry."

Craig ran his fingers through his hair. He turned his attention back to the plumber and said, "I have a bigger problem than that."

Dennis raised an eyebrow.

"I don't own this house yet."

We'd only signed contracts; we hadn't yet closed. And until we closed, the house still belonged to Andrew, who was lounging on a beach right now.

"Oh, crap."

The men looked at each other with knowing eyes. I, however, was clueless about what they were trying to communicate, silently, with each other. "What does all this mean?"

Dennis turned to face me. With pity in his eyes, he merely said, "I'm sorry."

"Our broker is on her way," Craig said. "We won't be able to get inside until she shows up. Did you happen to look around yet?"

"Nope. I only checked the oil tank then went back to the truck to wait for you. I don't think the rest will be a mystery now."

"Unfortunately not."

Apparently, I was the only one not in the know. Sometimes ignorance was bliss. Between the cold and the uncertainty, I shivered.

"Do you want to come with us or would you rather wait in the car, Sydney?" Craig reached into his back pocket for the key.

I pulled my scarf tighter around my neck. "No, I'm coming." I followed the men down the broken, bluestone path, which led to the front door of the house. Both of their eyes were focused on the ground as they made small talk.

When the path ended, we stepped onto the damp ground and headed toward the rear of the house. The heels of my boots began to sink into the soft mud and grassy patches. Not only did I regret not putting on an extra sweatshirt this morning, I also wished I had worn old sneakers or better yet, waterproof boots. With every step we took, the wetness increased. "Did it just rain or something?" I asked.

"I wish," Dennis replied, with a small, sad smile.

Before I could ask a follow-up question, we approached the back of the house. Water was gushing out by the sliding glass doors that led into the ground floor area of the basement. The puddles were so large they resembled a small pond.

"And here it is." Dennis placed both hands firmly on his hips.

"Crap!" Craig reached into his back pocket and grabbed his cell phone. "Damn it! Where are you, Parker?" he barked into the phone. If his attitude toward her now was any indication of how he'd behaved while they were dating, it was no wonder she'd dumped him.

I reached for his arm and squeezed it, and he lowered his voice slightly. "Good. We're in the backyard now. We'll come around and meet you at the front door. We have a huge problem on our hands." He turned around to Dennis. "Our broker is pulling up the driveway. She's got the keys to the house, so we can see how bad it is."

Realization hit me like a ton of bricks. With no oil in the tank, there was no heat in the house. With no heat, the pipes were bound to freeze, and by the looks of the backyard, we were way too late to stop any damage. The house had already flooded.

"Parker, hurry up. Open the door already." Craig's left leg jittered so frantically it was like it had a mind of its own.

Parker fumbled with the front door keys. Craig's nervousness was clearly contagious.

"Calm down, Craig. You're making me crazy. Hey, Syd." She gave me a tiny smile when she successfully turned the key in the lock. Then she introduced herself to the plumber.

"I knew this was going to happen!" Craig shouted as spittle flew out of his mouth. "I emailed Andrew two weeks ago. I specifically asked him to check the oil tank and winterize the house. He assured me he'd take care of everything. He promised he'd arrange for fuel delivery. Well, he didn't! He had plenty of time to bust my chops over every single sentence of the contract. He had me jumping through more hoops than I can count, yet he couldn't deal with making one simple phone call? If I didn't have enough on my plate before, now I have to deal with this."

"Let's try to stay calm, okay, Craig." Parker gently placed her hand on his shoulder. "Let's first see how bad it is before we overreact."

Craig raked his fingers through his wild hair. I feared if we ever managed to make this move a reality, I'd have a bald husband on my hands. "We know it's horrible. The entire backyard looks like the Mississippi River is running through it."

"Parker is right. Let's get our heads on straight and start dealing with the problem," Dennis said as he faced Parker. "Where's the basement?"

She walked through the foyer, toward the den, then opened a door. Single file we followed her down the steep, creaky stairs. "Oh crap!" she exclaimed when she reached the bottom.

I felt my stomach drop to my knees. "What is that?" I pointed at the ceiling right above the bottom of the stairs.

"A water bubble that is about to burst." Dennis pushed his way ahead of us with Craig at his heels.

"Where is the main shut off?" the plumber asked.

Craig shrugged. He and Dennis took off in opposite directions.

"You should take some pictures, Syd. I'm going to call the seller's agent," Parker said and walked upstairs.

Dennis found the shut-off and the water miraculously stopped gushing, preventing further destruction. They went upstairs to determine what pipe had burst. Instead of joining them I stayed in the basement and sat down on a relatively dry step. I allowed the tears that had been threatening to fall for the past half hour or so to run free. I was so frustrated. It felt like every time we managed to take one step forward on this move, something went wrong. Were we making one big mistake by moving?

When my tears finally subsided, I surveyed the damage with fresh eyes. An odd calm washed over me. This wasn't the first flood Craig and I had dealt with over the years. When Amanda was an infant, a major storm had hit our town. For a full week straight, it had rained torrentially day and night. Our basement filled with about two feet of water. Like so many of our neighbors, everything we'd stored down there was destroyed. We'd also lost our water heater and other mechanics. Like now, it had been the dead of winter. It was such a grueling and daunting task to clean up the basement, but we did it.

When I compared the damage here to what we had to deal with then, I realized this wasn't actually all that terrible. In fact, strangely, the flooding bonded me a bit to the house. It was almost as if I felt like the structure needed us. I ended my pity party.

Dennis greeted me when I reached the top of the stairs. "Are you okay, dear?"

I nodded.

"Can you give my wife some lessons?" He let out a belly laugh at his joke. "You're much calmer than I expected. We found the burst pipe."

"Which one?" My heart pounded quickly in my chest.

Craig answered as his eyes danced. "In the master bathroom. We'll have to chop up the whole shower to fix it."

I narrowed my eyes and stared at my husband as if he'd lost his mind. He was barely able to control his glee.

"What's wrong with you? How can you be happy at a time like this? That was the only working bathroom in this place."

CHAPTER TWENTY-SEVEN

CRAIG DIDN'T HAVE TO SPELL ANYTHING out for me. I quickly realized why he was thrilled the burst pipe was in the master bathroom. It was the only room in the entire house that was in decent condition. And while it wasn't our taste, we couldn't justify changing it. We'd planned on keeping it as it was. Now we didn't have a choice but to redo it.

As soon as the plumber walked out the front door, Craig bombarded Parker with questions. His voice rose with each inquiry, while he walked in circles. "What happens now? It was sheer dumb luck we came by today. I don't even want to think about what this house would have looked like if we weren't here to shut off the main water valve. We can't leave it like this! What are we going to do? There's a blizzard heading our way tomorrow. The house needs heat!" He pulled out his cell phone and scrolled through a long series of text messages. "Look! Three weeks ago, I asked Andrew to make sure the house was ready for the winter. Apparently, he completely ignored me."

Parker raised her hands in the air. "I know. Please, try to calm down, Craig."

Parker had the patience of a saint. She never seemed to get frazzled, which I was incredibly thankful for, especially since my husband looked like he could stroke out at any second.

"Calm? How can I be calm?" Craig's eyes bulged. "I know what we should be doing, but I'm powerless. We didn't close! This isn't our house yet."

"I know. I already spoke to the other broker. She's trying to reach Andrew. As you know, he's out of the country. She told me she'd call me back as soon as she speaks with him."

Craig rolled his eyes. "Like she's going to have success contacting him. I'm not waiting for her. I'm going to try and call him myself."

"Good. Between both of you reaching out, I'm sure we'll hear something soon." She turned to me. "Oh, Sydney. You're freezing and soaked. I don't live far from here. Why don't you come over to my house and dry off? I'll give you a fresh set of clothes?"

"Thanks." I blew on my hands. "I think I should stay here. We have a lot of people scheduled to come, and I want to participate. Also, I don't think with the state Craig's in he should be trusted to be alone. I don't want him taking his frustrations out on some poor contractor."

"I can respect that." She gave me a closed mouth smile. "But there's no way I'm letting you stay here all day, dressed like you are. You'll catch your death." She met Craig's frantic eyes. "You don't need me for the meetings, do you?"

"Not at all." He snorted. "Andrew wanted you to be present because he didn't trust us alone at the house before we owned it. How ironic. He was afraid of us damaging the place?"

Parker rolled her eyes. "Well, I don't think a mess of this magnitude was part of his master plan, Craig." She massaged her temples. "It's a problem for all of us." She put her phone in her bag. "I'll be back in a little bit. I'm going to run over to my house and pick up a change of clothes for Sydney. Do you want me to bring you anything? I probably have a sweatshirt that would fit you."

"No, I'm good."

"Okay, suit yourself. I'll be back soon." She gave me a quick hug before she dashed out the door.

We waited for our next appointment in the car, with the heater at full blast, as Craig compulsively checked his texts. At one time or another, Andrew had hired a landscaper. By the look of the non-existent grass, he had last been here many, many years ago.

When the red landscaping truck made its way up the driveway, Craig and I reluctantly exited our toasty car. "Great to meet you. I'm Brian." The tall, thin man enthusiastically shook both of our hands. "I'm excited you're buying the house and planning to fix it up. I hate to see such a great piece of land be neglected. It's a crying shame. All this place needs is a little tender loving care, and it will be magnificent. So, tell me, what do you have in mind?"

Craig took off with Brian while I opted to remain in the car. Yes, I wanted to be part of the plans, but I also didn't want to traipse around in the mud any more than I already had.

My phone beeped with a text from my mother-in-law.

Have you checked the weather? They're predicting at least a foot of snow!?!?!

I fired off a quick reply.

I'm sure it won't be that bad. The weather people are never right. And they exaggerate!

I turned on the radio and found an all-news station. Sure enough, my mother-in-law was correct. The forecasters were urging everyone to brace for the blizzard.

"Your mom is starting to freak out about the snow," I said to Craig when he entered the car. He shivered and rubbed his fingers together for warmth. I raised the temperature then waved goodbye to Brian.

"She's not the only one. I'm worried too." He tightened his jaw. "I'm afraid we won't even reach Andrew today. And if by some miracle I speak with him, I don't see how he'd be able to arrange an oil delivery on such short notice right before a blizzard. If there is even a fraction of the accumulation they expect, and this driveway doesn't get plowed, it will be impossible for an oil truck to get here and fill the tank with fuel."

I scrunched my face. "Oh, I didn't think of that."

"I know." He pursed his lips. "I wouldn't expect you to. The good news is Brian used to do snow removal for Andrew, back in the day. So, I arranged for him to come by tomorrow to plow."

Another truck pulled into the driveway and Craig glanced at his watch. "Great. The electrician is right on time. Come on, Syd."

As soon as we finished scoping out the details of installing a generator and upgrading the electric panel, Parker reappeared. She carried a big shopping bag as well as two extra- large cups of piping hot coffee.

"You are a goddess." I took the bag and a cup. The coffee tasted amazing. "My husband's a fool. He should have his head examined for ever letting you get away."

"Yeah, but he did all right after all." She beamed. "I didn't hear anything from the other broker yet. Did Andrew call you?"

Craig sighed heavily and scratched the dark scruff on his chin. "No."

When I emerged from what would soon be my bedroom wearing warm, dry clothes, I found Parker, alone, leaning against a wall in the hallway. When we'd first seen the house, it had been entirely furnished, complete with pictures hanging on the walls. Now every room was empty, not even a folding chair remained. Andrew had rented every item to stage the house for sale.

"What'd I miss?"

Parker gestured to Craig who paced in the den. "Your husband is giving Andrew hell." She grinned. "I'll bet Andrew regrets calling him back right about now."

My phone beeped with a new text, once again from my mother-in-law.

Sydney, I tried to call you AND Craig. Neither of you answered!?!?!? We need to speak about the snow NOW!!!!!!

I bit down on my lip. Why was Brenda fixated on the snow right now? Shouldn't she be preoccupied with all the fun stuff she had planned for today with Amanda?

"What's wrong?" Parker asked as I started to reply. I wanted to make sure Amanda was okay.

"Craig's mother is having a meltdown about tomorrow's weather. I understand she's been living in Florida for years and a blizzard isn't at the top of her favorites' list, but she wants to have a chat about the forecast right away. I don't have the patience to deal with her. Besides, she's supposed to be on an outing with Amanda."

"Oh yeah, I forgot. The dragon lady was staying with you. I never understood what Craig's father ever saw in her. Thank goodness Craig takes after his dad."

As Craig's voice raised several decibels, I added, "Well, most times."

"Speak of the devil," Parker said with a chuckle when he entered the room.

He put his phone in his back pocket and grinned. "Wow, it felt great to ream Andrew out. Hopefully, it worked. He told me he'd call the oil company right away and beg them to make an emergency delivery. He's also going to call his insurance company and have them send over an adjuster. Then he'll contact a restoration company to cart away the wet sheetrock and sanitize the basement. Since he won't be back in the States for another week and a half, he asked if I could come by to let the people in and help deal with the situation."

"That's pretty nervy." I felt my temperature rise. How dare he expect my husband to clean up his mess! And how in the world was Craig going to manage to find the time to take care of this with everything else going on?

"I'm glad he's got balls of steel. This way we'll know for sure that everything is being taken care of properly. I feel much better this way."

"How many more people do you have coming today, anyway?" Parker asked.

"Let's see. We still have the architect, the kitchen designer, the HVAC guy, someone from the pool company, and a general contractor on their way. We'll probably be here at least another three hours."

"Is there any reason you need me to stick around the whole time? I never expected this to be a whole day affair. I have some other appointments scheduled, which I could always cancel if need be." Parker leaned against the front door.

"Feel free to go anytime. We can handle everything here. We'll even lock up when we're finished."

My phone beeped while I hugged Parker goodbye, once more. Before I could even scan the message, my phone rang. I didn't have to look at the display to know who was calling me.

I tried to keep my voice steady and calm. "Hi, Brenda, I was about to call you back."

"Yeah, right." She snarled. "Do me a favor and don't lie to me. I waited a full nine minutes since I sent my last text. I thought I made myself crystal clear exactly how important it was for me to speak with either you or my son immediately. Neither one of you could be bothered to see what was wrong. It would have been nice if you had enough consideration to call me back."

"I'm sorry. We've been tied up. We haven't had an easy time of it here."

"Yeah, well my day hasn't been a walk in the park, either. Right now, I need you both to untie yourselves and get home, pronto."

My mind raced as I imagined all the worst-case scenarios that could have occurred. "Home now? What's going on? Is Amanda okay? Did something happen to her?"

"Oh, your daughter is fine, but Maxwell and I have a plane to catch."

"A plane?" I repeated for my husband's benefit. "What do you mean a plane to catch? You guys aren't scheduled to fly out for another two days."

"Yes, but the blizzard is expected to start tonight, Sydney. There is no way I'm going to stay here for a snowstorm of this magnitude when I can be back in sunny Florida, sitting poolside instead. I called the airline. I was on hold for about forty-five minutes, and finally, I spoke with a delightful girl. She understood the severity of my situation. She worked some magic and got us on the five o'clock flight out. She didn't even charge us a change fee. Now that's wonderful customer service, don't you think?"

I looked at my watch as panic set in. "Brenda, it's already after one o'clock."

"Yes, I know, dear. That is why you, and my son, need to get home ASAP. A car is picking Maxwell and me up in an hour and a half to take us to the airport."

I couldn't decide who I was more upset with: my selfish mother-in-law or myself for being dumb enough to think I could trust her to look after Amanda. I struggled, unsuccessfully, to calm my racing heart. "Brenda, we're at least an hour away, and we have meetings scheduled for the next few hours. There is no way we can get home in time."

"Well, that's not my problem now, is it?" she retorted without one hint of remorse in her voice. "I have issues of my own to deal with today. You and Craig will have to sort this one out. Maxwell and I haven't even begun to pack yet."

I broke into a cold sweat. "How can you do this to us? How can you do this to Amanda?"

"I'm not doing anything to you or Amanda. Last time I checked, I didn't control the weather, dear. Your daughter is happily playing in her bedroom with Maxwell. Sure, she was a bit upset when I canceled our outings for today, but she understood Grandma had an emergency to sort out." She heaves a sigh as though I'm the one putting her out.

"You and my son either need to get back here in an hour and a half or figure out what you need to do about your daughter. Goodbye."

"She hung up on me!" I whirled on my husband and clenched my fists. "What is wrong with your mother?"

"Let me try to call her." Craig reached for my phone.

"Don't bother. She won't listen to reason. She's already made her decision. You know as well as I do it's impossible to get her to change her mind. Besides, she already changed her plane tickets. She is a piece of work."

I paced through the empty house. My shoes squeaked almost as loudly as my heart pounded. I was freezing and furious. "If she had any thought about flying home today, why didn't she say something? Hell, why did she convince us to change our plans? We were all set to drop Amanda off at my mom's today. We never asked your mother to spend the day with Amanda. She practically begged us. What do we do now?" I tucked my hair behind my ears as inspiration struck. "I'll call an Uber and head home."

"That's crazy, Syd. Don't you want to be here for the rest of the meetings?"

Had he lost his mind? How could he be thinking about anything but his daughter right now? "What difference does it make what I want to do? We can't leave our six-year-old home alone!"

"I agree, but aren't there other options? I know she doesn't usually work weekends, but maybe Sally can come over and stay with Amanda?"

"No, she's visiting her sister in Texas, remember? Her flight isn't due to land until late tonight." I clutched my temples. My head throbbed thanks to all the tension.

"What about any of Amanda's friends?"

"I guess I can call Jackie. Maybe Amanda can hang out with Cassidy until we get home. I hate to ask for a favor like this, especially at the last minute. And…" I paused. "I hate lying to her."

"So, tell her the truth." He ran his fingers down my cheek.

"I'm not ready yet. Jackie won't understand why we're leaving Forest River."

"You know her better than I do, but I think you're overreacting."

I knew he was probably right. But I felt like I was betraying her and the PTA ladies by having one foot out of Forest River. I knew I had to tell her the truth soon, but not today.

I dialed her number and waited. Just when I was about to hang up, she answered. "Hi, Sydney! Sorry, my phone was at the bottom of my bag. What's up?"

"Any shot you're at home?"

"No. We're at the mall. The girls and I needed some retail therapy to prepare for the storm. Most people hit the supermarket before the snow comes but not us! We hit the shoe department! We all hate the winter."

I picked at a cuticle. "Yeah, you're not the only one."

In a hushed tone, she said, "Hayley, see if the sales lady has these in a size seven and a half for me." Then louder, "Is something wrong, Syd? You sound upset."

"I am. Craig and I," I gave myself a second to figure out how to stretch the truth a bit, "made plans to spend the afternoon with an old friend in Shells Point. We arrived here a little while ago. Craig's parents were watching Amanda, but—"

"Are they still with you? Are they ever going home? You poor thing. Now I know why you sound so troubled." Jackie had the pleasure of meeting my mother-in-law a couple of days before when she'd picked up Cassidy. The entire time Jackie had been over, Brenda moaned and groaned. She didn't stop complaining once. "When are they getting out of your hair? I'll bet it can't be soon enough."

"I never thought I'd say this, but it's too soon." I filled her in on my in-laws' plans.

"You got lucky, my friend, if you ask me. I can't imagine you trapped inside your house with that woman during a blizzard.

There's not enough wine in the world! Let her hightail it out of here. Good riddance, I say! I'll head over to your place and grab Amanda. Cassidy will be delighted! Take your time and enjoy the afternoon with your friend."

"But you and the girls are shopping."

"And you think any one of us needs another pair of shoes?"

CHAPTER TWENTY-EIGHT

FOR THE FIRST MONTH AFTER THE FLOOD Craig and Andrew had been in constant contact, working together to get the water out and have the house sanitized. But once the house dried, they were at a standstill as they waited for Andrew's insurance company to settle the claim.

Usually, I wasn't a procrastinator. But my fear of jinxing anything outweighed my compulsive need to get things done quickly. As a result, I didn't pack one single belonging of ours. The thought of how much work I had ahead made me reach for the Reese's Peanut Butter Cups every evening. Fortunately, I had my PTA duties to keep my mind off my housing situation.

Jackie and I had spent days running all over town on a quest to find the perfect decorations for the Cupcakes with Cupid party. Historically the event was called Snack with Saint Valentine, but like she had with poor Saint Nick, Donna put the kibosh on the name.

Finally, as February came to an end, the men sorted everything out on the same day Amanda celebrated her seventh birthday. In an attempt to help ease the transition when we decided to tell her the news, we'd asked our contractor to build a replica of her future home. The unexpected gift was a huge hit. I just worried her eye for design would rival mine and Craig's.

All the birthday parties Amanda had attended this year seemed as if they were planned for the mothers' benefits, not the children. The mommies were in a silent competition to one-up each other, although none of them came anywhere close to topping Cassidy's bash, which had raised the bar incredibly high. So, rather than follow suit, Amanda celebrated her special day the opposite way.

Instead of clowns, magicians, or a portable petting farm, the entertainment committee was composed of only my mom, Craig, and me. The girls all came dressed in their favorite princess costumes. We played simple, old school games like pin the tail on the donkey, had a piñata in the basement filled with Amanda's favorite candy, made beaded necklaces and bracelets, and served plain pizza with a princess ice cream cake for dessert.

The days flew by, and I struggled to keep up.

"Oh my God!" Jackie squealed as we stood behind the stage in the elementary school auditorium. "Today is finally here!"

She gripped my arm so tightly that I feared I'd have to wear long sleeves to work for the rest of the week unless I wanted my co-workers to spread rumors. It was March nineteenth: the day of the penny auction.

"I can tell." I smirked. Jackie was barely able to stand still for a second. "Wow, you're even more excited than Amanda was when I told her she had a snow day last Wednesday."

"I know! Isn't it terrific?" Jackie turned so she could face the other PTA moms and opened her arms wide. "Ladies, all our work has finally paid off. It's our big day and the house is packed."

Aimee pulled back the thick, red velvet curtain and poked her head out to take a peek. "There isn't an empty seat in the house. There's even a crowd standing in the rear of the room."

Claire gave Jackie a big hug. "You did it once again. Tonight, as always, will be a huge success. We all know we couldn't have accomplished this without our queen!"

Trisha bent down into a curtsy. "Come on, ladies. Let's all hail our queen."

Jackie placed her hand over her heart and tried to act all humble, but anyone who'd ever spent more than fifteen seconds with her knew she was eating up all the attention. "Oh, guys. Stop it. We know this was a team effort and we should all be proud of ourselves." She slipped her arm around my waist. "I think we also owe a special thank you to Sydney. I still can't believe all the donations she managed to snag from the department store where her sister works. In all my years of running this event, we've never had so many high-quality items up for auction. The money we'll raise will mean an extra special second grade for our children."

A lump formed in my throat. "Thank you." I was afraid if I spoke more than two little words, my voice would crack, knowing Amanda wouldn't be returning to Forest River Elementary in the fall with her friends.

"Jackie, you were brilliant to have gotten the liquor permit and hire the bartender from Bistro Baron tonight," Stacy stated before taking a sip of the event's signature cocktail – the Forest River vanilla fig Old-Fashioned. By combining bourbon infused with three different fig varieties, homemade vanilla bitters, and a splash of club soda, he'd created magic in a glass. "Not only are the parents more than eager to plunk down fifteen bucks for a cocktail, but they also have no desire to leave the gym. I swear, they must have spent at least double the time this year checking out the items."

I glanced over at Trisha, who was feverishly counting on her fingers, as her mouth silently moved. She nodded. "If my calculations are correct, between what we have left over from the other fundraisers we've held this year, plus what we'll raise tonight, we'll be able to take the kids on the weekend trip to Disney."

"No way," Claire said. "No second-grade class has ever done the trip."

The current tradition was two weeks before graduation the Forest River Valley's fifth graders made a pilgrimage to Orlando to see Mickey. On a few rare occasions, the fourth graders also journeyed to Florida. I felt horrible Amanda would miss out.

Then I realized Amanda could still go. I could take her the same week.

Stacey studied her shoes as Jackie turned her attention back to the rest of us. "As I was saying, this will be the first second-grade class in the history of this school to make it down south. I, for one, am super excited." She sighed. "Cassidy is my last child to walk these halls, and I want nothing more than to have these next four years be magical for her." She held out her arms for a group embrace. "And thanks to my dream team, I have no worries. My goal will become a reality."

A tear silently ran down my check. I wanted the same for my daughter. I worried she'd struggle to make friends at her new school. It was going to be hard to be the new kid in town. Sure, she was a very social and outgoing child, but I couldn't help but remember my childhood. I never wanted Amanda to experience what I did. But most of all, I feared that she'd hate Craig and me for making her leave all her Forest River pals.

"Are you okay?" Trisha asked as soon as we separated.

"Yeah, I'm fine." I wiped my eyes. "Stupid contacts. I think I might have a rip in one," I lied.

"Well, buck up, my pup," Jackie chided. "It's show time."

The curtain slowly parted and Jackie took center stage. The ladies and I surrounded her. I spotted Donna seated in the front row. She had her arms folded across her chest, and she glared at Jackie with pure hatred in her eyes. Now that I knew the full story about what had happened between the ladies, my entire opinion of Donna had changed. It shocked me how Donna had opted to make Jackie's life difficult rather than just apologize for her actions. I worked very hard not to act any differently around Donna. After all, it wasn't my battle to fight, even though Jackie was my friend. And I didn't want to do anything to set Donna off any further.

Jackie dramatically cleared her throat. "Good evening everyone and thank you so much for coming to celebrate the first-graders of Forest River Elementary School. I want to give a special shout-out to Principal Williams." She blew a kiss in the older man's direction, and he blushed. "Your leadership makes this school a premier academic institute." She clapped her hands, and the audience erupted in thunderous applause. "Your never-ending attention to detail and your desire to always go the extra mile with your teachers is apparent in your every action." I gasped when she turned and winked at Ms. Collins. The beautiful twenty-three-year-old teacher turned a ghostly shade of pale.

"Oh my God! She has no shame," Trisha whispered in my ear.

The latest rumor around town was that our principal, a father of five, had left his wife of twenty-nine years and moved into the apartment of Ms. Cynthia Collins only two months after she'd started teaching at the school.

"I know." I smiled. "Which is why we love her. Jackie says what we all think."

Jackie screamed and raised her fist in the air. "Give it up for our teachers! They do it ALL!"

Ms. Collins looked like she wanted to die. Principal Williams must have sensed her distress. As if he didn't have a care in the world, he gently slipped his arm around her waist.

"Oh my," Jackie added and her mouth hung open. Subtlety wasn't her strong suit and every parent followed her gaze.

When the crowd settled down, she continued, "Really, what would the first-grade class be without the parents? You should all be very proud of the jobs you have done raising your children." She clapped her hands once more, and the audience followed suit. "We are so fortunate to have such lovely children in this grade. In all my years of being PTA president, I have never seen such a resilient and cooperative group. These kids have been asked to make many sacrifices this year, from lunch choices to holiday celebrations, and they have rolled with the punches and made the best of every obstacle thrown their way."

Trisha elbowed me when Donna mouthed, "Bitch."

Jackie was unfazed. "And now our children are about to be rewarded, thanks to your generous donations!" The crowd erupted in cheers. "Now who's ready to get this party started?"

Aimee cranked up the stereo, and we all broke into the dance we had practiced for the last few weeks. I didn't think I'd have the nerve to perform on stage. My jitters disappeared. Being surrounded by these other women whom I now considered dear friends eased all my fears. So far, in some fashion, we'd proven no matter what that we had each other's backs.

When the music stopped, each of us took our respective places behind the various podiums and turned on the microphones we wore on our shirts. The baskets were brought in and placed behind us.

Claire took center stage and cleared her throat. "Hello, Forest River! The first item we have up for grabs tonight is a black Bottega Venta Hobo bag with a matching wallet! Oh, and rumor has it there's a little something special in the wallet for our lucky winner, who is," she dug her hand deep into the glass bowl and pulled out a ticket, "number four-seventy-five."

"It's me! It's me!" a petite blonde in the third row yelled out. She started to jump for joy. Her husband gave her a huge victory kiss before she rushed the stage to claim her loot.

The excitement in the auditorium was contagious. The prizes blew the crowd away. I finally understood why Jackie and the others looked forward to this event every year. Knowing I was a significant part of planning it was such a satisfying feeling.

"We're winding down," I spoke slowly into my microphone with a very unsteady voice. For as long as I could remember, public speaking had always freaked me out a bit. I'd confided this to Jackie. I'd expected her to criticize me, but instead, she'd allowed me to go last. "That means only one thing. The best stuff is coming up! Who wants to spend a weekend with three of their besties at the Silver Door Spa in Connecticut?"

The crowd went wild.

"One lucky winner and her three guests will have a weekend full of wine, yoga, massages, facials, and of course manicures and pedicures." I reached into my bowl and pulled out a number. "The winner is lucky number twelve-forty-two." The crowd was silent. I cleared my throat. "I said the winner is twelve-forty-two." Again, crickets. "Twelve-forty-two, are you out there?" The crowd giggled, but no one stood up to claim his or her prize.

I glanced over at Jackie for guidance. She raised one finger at me. "Okay, let's give the winner another minute. Everyone, please double check your tickets." All the eyes in the audience were on me. I silently counted to thirty. "Okay then, twelve-forty-two is going once, going twice, and gone." The audience clapped and cheered, and I reached into the bowl and pulled out another ticket." I smiled. "Let's try this again. Number thirty-seven you're headed for the spa!"

"Yes!" Donna screamed at the top of her lungs. She immediately jumped up from her seat and ran onto the stage. She grinned at Jackie when she passed her. "Thank you very much, Sydney." She gave me a quick hug before she took the basket from my hands.

At the same time, Jennifer Davidson stood up and started to tug at her mini skirt in an unsuccessful attempt to pull it slightly down. Jennifer broke into a sprint and raced up the aisle. She frantically waved a ticket high up in the air

"Wait! Wait!" Jennifer shrieked and stumbled up the steps. "I have number twelve-forty-two."

"Yeah, but you didn't claim it." Donna clutched the basket close to her chest.

"Give it to me." Jennifer grabbed hold of the basket. She struggled to stay upright and wobbled on four-inch red stilettos.

"No! It's mine!" Donna fired back, her eyes full of rage.

"My number was called first," Jennifer slurred. "I won, fair and square." Jennifer was rumored to drink in excess and flirt with all the dads while under the influence. I assumed the other moms exaggerated, as usual, until I'd witnessed her antics first hand. She literally threw herself at Jackie's husband in a drunken stupor at the Forest River Country Club. Scott had handled the situation like a champ, but I was mortified for Jackie and Jennifer's husband, Bill.

Donna jerked the basket away from her with so much force Jennifer almost fell backward. "You snooze you lose, sweetheart. You had every chance to claim it, but you didn't, so take your hands off my prize."

My eyes ping-ponged back and forth between the battling ladies and the shocked audience. People pointed and shouted toward the stage, but I couldn't make out their words. Principal Williams, Craig, Scott, and a few of the other fathers who sat in the front row stood up. I held up my hand and locked eyes with my husband. I wanted to avoid having the dad brigade rush the stage.

I turned to Claire and covered my microphone. "What should we do?" It was up to the rest of the group to stop this madness. Jackie wouldn't be any help this time. I'd bet our queen relished watching her archenemy in an embarrassing tussle in front of the entire school.

Claire shrugged and tilted her head to the guys, then whispered in my ear, "Too bad we opted not to have a security team tonight."

As long as we obtained the permit from the village to serve alcohol, there were no requirements to have security present. I agreed with Claire. A burly bodyguard would have been useful right now.

No matter what I felt about either of these women, I couldn't stand idly by one more second while they both made fools of themselves. "Ladies, cut it out. Look at how you're behaving. You should both be ashamed."

"Give me my prize," Jennifer whined and reached again for the basket, unsuccessfully. She almost toppled over. Trisha rushed to her side and braced the fall.

"I think it's time you get off the stage, Jennifer, before you embarrass yourself any more than you already have," Trisha said firmly.

"Where the hell is her husband?" Aimee asked without first covering the microphone she wore.

"If he had half a brain, he'd be hiding in the boys' washroom," Claire replied. She too forgot about her mic.

The crowd burst into laughter, which Jennifer didn't even seem to notice. Donna, on the other hand, broke into an ear-to-ear smile.

"I'm not going anywhere until I get a prize." Jennifer began to stomp her feet.

"I'm sorry, Jen. I called your number at least ten times. You didn't claim your prize, so another winner had to be chosen." I turned to Donna. "Go."

She didn't need any urging; she quickly exited with the basket and a satisfied grin.

"I want a prize!" Jennifer started to cry. "I won a prize. I want a prize."

Jackie crossed her arms over her chest and rolled her eyes. The guys started to inch toward the stage. And while I loved the heroics, I didn't want them to have to carry Jennifer out. Thinking quickly, I turned around and grabbed the bowl filled with tickets for the spa package. I dumped the losing tickets on the floor. I selected a few flowers from the centerpieces around the stage and put them in the large bowl. "Jennifer, today is your lucky day."

CHAPTER TWENTY-NINE

I SIPPED MY WINE AND LOOKED AROUND THE Forest River Country Club. Even though we'd been guests of the Martins numerous times this year, I remained in awe. The main building, located in the center of town, was originally the home of a legendary businessman and avid art collector, as well as the first resident of Forest River.

The mansion covered over two hundred acres and had magnificent views of the river. Throughout the building were white marble floors and every floor-to-ceiling window was ornately framed with intricately carved mahogany wood. Crystal chandeliers dangled throughout the building, and exquisite artwork adorned the walls.

Craig and I had considered joining for about fifteen seconds when we'd first moved to town. But since Craig hated playing golf and I detested tennis, we couldn't justify spending the exorbitant membership fee. The club had a lot of cool weekend events, which fortunately we were able to enjoy, thanks to our friendship with the Martins.

Tonight, for instance, was their annual clambake. As our daughters enjoyed a night of magic and macaroni and cheese upstairs in the large game room, the grownups dined on steamed Maine lobsters, baked clams, and fried shrimp. There was also a phenomenal raw bar. I was thankful I had worn a dress tonight because after everything I'd eaten I wouldn't be able to button a pair of pants at this point. And, yes, I still hadn't begun my diet.

Two weeks had passed since the penny auction, and in five days we'd be closing on both houses. Tonight was also the night I'd decided to break the news to Jackie about our move.

When Craig and I had gotten engaged, I wanted to immediately call my parents and tell them our fantastic news. I knew they'd be delighted. They loved Craig practically as much as I did. However, he was adamant we had to share the big news with them in person. He wanted us to see their reaction.

For two whole days, I'd kept the secret. I'd almost caved and called my mother countless times, but since I didn't want to start my married life with a lie, I honored his wishes. He'd arranged for us to go to my parents' for dinner. As soon as we'd walked in the door, I'd wanted to blurt out everything, but he'd wanted no part of it. I could barely swallow my salad because I was too busy choking on our secret. But I waited until the proper time to tell them he'd popped the question.

Now I was waiting again, and it was killing me.

"Should we order another bottle of wine or just get some dessert?" Scott asked as he stretched his arms over his head.

"I don't want any more wine," I said, although, I probably should have taken him up on the offer. I could have used more liquid courage, but I didn't want to prolong the inevitable.

Jackie nodded. "I agree." Her eyes lit up. "Oh my, God, Sydney, did you hear what happened to Jennifer after the penny auction?"

I picked up my glass and drained the tiny bit of wine that was left over in my glass. Despite being friends with Jackie, I still missed out on most of the local gossip.

"No." The last time I'd seen the woman was when I'd escorted her off the stage.

"Her husband wasn't with her, or if he was, he walked home. She, on the other hand, was pulled over as soon as she exited the school parking lot."

Craig cringed. I knew him so well. I'd bet he was kicking himself for not making sure she didn't get behind the wheel. Instead, he'd immediately gone backstage with all the other PTA fathers and boyfriends to join us while we'd counted the money we raised, which was mind-blowing. There was no doubt the kids were going to see Mickey next year.

"She drove?" Craig widened his eyes.

Jackie nodded. "Yep, but thankfully not for long. The police received an anonymous tip about Jennifer's condition. So, the cops were waiting for her. No shock, she failed the Breathalyzer. The police brought her to the station, and they booked her. Her husband let her stay in the slammer overnight before he bailed her out."

"Wow." I blinked a few times and remembered how Jackie slipped away from the group right after the curtains had closed.

"Hopefully, it was the kick in the butt she needed to get her life on track. You won't be seeing her around the schoolyard for the rest of the term." Jackie added, "She's away, in rehab."

I gave my friend a knowing grin. She'd never admit it, but there was not a doubt in my mind she'd made the call to the police, and for all the right reasons.

"Well, if we aren't going to have more wine, let's get some dessert," Scott said and stood up.

The rest of us followed suit and headed to the large dessert table. Craig always ended up having ice cream topped with M&Ms and hot fudge. Scott and I typically filled our plates with various slices of cake and assorted cookies to sample. Calorie-conscious Jackie always ended up with fresh fruit.

"Are you okay?" I stared at Jackie's plate in shock. As predicted, she had a dish of strawberries and raspberries. But uncharacteristically, her fruit was covered in chocolate, and there was even a dollop of whipped cream on the side.

"I figured I needed something stronger tonight. Are you going to tell me what's bothering you, Syd?"

We all sat down, and Craig squeezed my leg under the table.

Before I could answer, she continued, "We're friends. Don't you think I can see through your act the same way you can see through mine? Please, don't insult me by lying. A blind man can see something is going on. You haven't been yourself all evening." She started to tick off on her fingers. "You've been quiet, and you turned down the offer of more wine. Usually, you and I always have another glass or two after we finish dinner. And you kept exchanging nervous glances with Craig. So, I'll ask you again, what's bothering you?"

I pinched the bridge of my nose. It was the time I had been

dreading. I had played this moment in my mind for months. And even though I'd rehearsed in my head what I would say a thousand times, I could never predict how Jackie would react. "Sorry, I should have known you'd be able to sense something. I wanted to wait until after dinner to tell you guys."

Jackie nodded. "Go on, girl."

I reached for Craig's hand under the table. "We have something to share with you both. Some big news."

"Are you pregnant?" Her eyes bulged, and her mouth hung open.

"Oh, no." I instinctively reached for my middle and feared I looked the part. Stupid diet!

"Please don't tell me one of you are sick. But if you are, don't worry. Scott's cousin is a renowned physician. We'll either get you in to see him immediately or have him recommend a specialist."

"Thank you, Jackie. You're very kind, but we're both healthy," Craig said.

"Thank God!" She placed her hand on her chest. "Then what is it?"

"Sorry." I took a deep breath and scratched my head. "So, here's the thing. Craig and I have had to make a very tough decision…"

"Oh no!" She held her head in her hands. "You're not getting a divorce, are you? Don't throw your marriage away. I'm sure you'll be able to work out whatever problems you have. Last year Stacey and her husband went to the most amazing marriage counselor. He saved their relationship." Jackie reached for her phone. "I'll text her this instant and get you his name and number. Please, don't do anything rash, Sydney. You two make the most adorable couple. Don't they, Scott?"

Scott leaned over and gave his wife a peck on the tip of her nose. "Yep, they're almost as cute as us." He took her phone from her hands. "Jackie, I think their marriage is solid. Why don't you let them speak instead of jumping to conclusions, okay?" Then he turned to Craig. "You'd better not be dumping Sydney, man, because then I'll look like the jerk."

Craig patted his pal on the back. "Don't worry, bud." He looked at me. "Do you want me to tell her?"

I wanted to scream "yes" at the top of my lungs. But it wouldn't be right for my husband to handle my dirty work. She was my friend; she had to hear the truth from me. "No, I've got it." I faced her and gave her a small smile, which I knew didn't reach my eyes. "I'm sorry, Jackie, it's difficult for me to discuss." I took a deep breath. "We always dreamt of building a house, and we found the perfect place. Well, the house is one step above being condemned, but it's located on a beautiful parcel of land."

She smiled widely. "How exciting. But I don't understand why you've been a bundle of nerves."

My muscles tightened, and I licked my lips. "The house is close to my job and near where my parents and sister live." I looked down at my napkin. "We're moving to Shells Point."

Jackie sat silent and stone-faced as she processed my news. My heart pounded so quickly in my chest I got lightheaded.

Her voice was emotionless. "Shells Point?"

I felt my face flush. "Yes."

Jackie slowly smiled and said the one thing I didn't expect. "I'm so happy for you!" Then she hugged me.

When I broke free from her embrace, a tear ran down my check. "You're happy for me?"

"Yes, of course I am. Why wouldn't I be?"

I should have listened to Craig months ago when he'd tried to convince me to open up to her. But I let my fears dictate my actions. I should have known better than to think she'd lash out at me just because I was abandoning the town and the PTA. Time after time she'd proven she did care about me, yet I still reverted to my old beliefs that she only had her own interests at heart.

"Sydney, you're moving to Shells Point, not Pluto. We'll still see each other, and the girls will always be friends."

I felt my body relax.

"I'm envious of you, accomplishing one of your dreams. But really, the important thing is that you're going to be living close to your family. Man, I'd do anything to have my grandmother back."

"So you're not upset with me?"

She dipped a strawberry in whipped cream and took a bite. "Why on earth would I be mad at you?"

"Um, because I'm going to have to leave the PTA."

"Oh Sydney, don't be so dramatic." She rolled her eyes. "Sure, the PTA is better because of you and your contributions, but it will go on without you."

"But..."

"I hate to break this to you, girlfriend, but you're replaceable. We all are, even me." She batted her blue eyes and grinned. "My grandfather used to say, 'You bust your butt every day working, and then three months after you left people struggled to remember your name.' His outlook was a bit harsh, I know, but it rang true." Her eyes filled with tears. "My grandmother also had a saying: 'No matter how much you rely on a person, there is always another person somewhere willing, wanting, and able to take on the same challenge.' She'd say the only people you can't replace were your parents because you only get two of them. And I know the hard way how correct she was."

I squeezed her arm. I couldn't even imagine how difficult her childhood must have been.

Jackie casually dipped another strawberry in whipped cream, and changed the subject. "So, who else knows about the move?"

"No one except our family. I wanted you to be my first friend to find out."

Jackie beamed. "Thank you. Wow, you have no idea how much it means to me I'm the first to know. Tell me more about everything! Did you just find this house? Are you going to put yours on the market?"

"Everything has been in the works for quite some time." I played with the cake on my plate. "We already have a buyer. We're closing on Thursday."

Her mouth dropped. It felt like an eternity had passed before she whispered, "Thursday?"

I couldn't look her in the eye. "Yes."

She looked dazed. "As in five days from tonight?"

I nodded.

"Wow." She pursed her lips. "Now I understand why you were so worried about my reaction to your big news." She pushed her plate to the side of the table. "You've got to be kidding me, Sydney."

Her eyes filled with tears. "Thanks for the notice."

"Jackie, wait..."

She pointed her finger at me, and her eyes protruded. "No, you wait. How could you do this to the team? How could you do this to me?" She shook her head. "We have two more months left of this term, and several PTA events scheduled, including field day. You think it's okay to announce after dinner that in five days you're fleeing town?" She clicked her tongue. "Nice."

"Wait, Jackie, you don't understand." I held up my hand. "We're closing on the house this week, but we aren't moving until after classes end. We'll be here until June."

She didn't say anything, so I continued. "We worked everything out with the buyers. They're purchasing our house this week, so we can turn around and buy our new one. Best-case scenario, we're looking at months of construction. We don't want to live through it. So rather than rent someplace else, the new owners are allowing us to stay in our home for three months after the sale. Amanda doesn't even know about the move yet. We're waiting until the last week of class to tell her. We want her to enjoy the rest of the school year without having to worry about the future. She'll start camp up in Shells Point right after we move. Hopefully, she'll make some new friends before starting second grade."

Jackie massaged her temples. "So you'll still be participating in the PTA until June?"

I nodded.

"You're not abandoning me?"

My eyes welled. I hated that I'd hurt her. "Never! I'm sorry. I should have told you about the move months ago."

"Yeah, you should have."

I smiled.

"So, who are these people who bought your house anyway? Do they have kids? I'll need a PTA replacement."

I chuckled. "Their names are Jon and Kara Cuttinham. They're a lovely couple. She just gave birth to their first child, an adorable little girl named, Emma, last week." I reached for my bag to get my phone, so I could show her the picture that Craig had taken of us at the hospital. "It's funny. I feel like I'm leaving my house in good hands."

She enlarged the picture, and her eyes clouded over. She angled the phone, so her husband could see the picture. "I know her. She's Mia Montgomery's sister."

As Jackie said the name out loud, a chill ran down my spine. I finally realized why the name had always sounded familiar. Mia Montgomery was the mother who'd lied to the school psychologist last summer about Hayley, and the catalyst for Jackie and Donna's falling out.

I covered my mouth with my hand. The woman I had spent most of the term thinking of as a devil would be spending holidays at *my* home with *her* family. Oddly, I felt at peace. After all, if not for Mia, Donna and Jackie wouldn't have had a feud and I'd still be friendless.

CHAPTER THIRTY

I OPENED THE KITCHEN CABINET AND PULLED out two wine glasses. "So how weird do you feel right about now?" I asked my husband.

It was Thursday night, and we had come home from the closings about fifteen minutes before. Craig and I no longer owned this house. Jon and Kara did.

Craig remained silent. He studied the contents of our wine refrigerator. He pulled out a very old bottle of Bordeaux, one that we had saved for more years than I could remember. "I think I'm a bit numb, honestly." He poured us each a glass and handed me one.

I sniffed the wine before I raised my glass toward his as memories of all the years we'd spent in this room flashed in my mind's eye. "Well, to what should we drink? The end of an era?"

"Nah, I think we should drink to new beginnings instead."

I smiled and took a sip of wine, which was as delicious as I had hoped it would be. "We've sat in this kitchen a thousand times over the years. But right now, the room feels completely different to me, foreign almost." The tears I'd tried so hard not to shed all day finally fell freely down my face. "Craig, this is no longer our home."

"Oh, Sydney." He put his arms around me, and I sobbed. He whispered into my hair, "This will always be our home, no matter what. We made this place what it is. It was our vision, and our hard work allowed Jon and Kara to fall in love with this house. And because we did such a phenomenal job, they paid us a boatload of money."

"Daddy, why is Mommy crying?" Amanda asked as she walked into the kitchen, clutching Oreo, the cat.

"Because she's happy," Craig replied.

I smiled at my daughter for good measure and wiped the tears from my cheeks.

"That's dumb." She puckered her lips.

I kissed the top of her head. "Well, sometimes grownups act silly just like little girls. How does pizza sound for dinner?"

"Yes!" Amanda pumped her fist into the air. "With pepperoni?"

"Of course." After the emotional day I'd had, the last thing in the world I wanted to do was cook.

I went over to the refrigerator and pulled out some baby carrots for Amanda. "Go finish your homework in the den and snack on these for now. I'll order dinner in a little bit."

As soon as Amanda was out of earshot, Craig said, "Remember, Syd, we aren't going anywhere for quite a while. We'll be here for another three months or so. You'll still make lots of new memories here. But it's also time for us to start making new memories in Shells Point."

Craig and I had both taken off work so we could spend time at our new house. We were going to do some minor demolition before our contractor arrived Monday morning.

I smiled before I remembered the first item on my agenda. I had to clean up one bathroom to use. I couldn't continue to run over to Burger King every time I had to pee.

Craig's phone chirped.

"Who texted you?"

Craig chuckled. "Andrew. He asked if I missed him yet."

"What are you two going to do with yourselves now the deal is complete?"

Craig and Andrew had had a lovers' quarrel after the flood, but once the water was out of the house, the two of them rekindled their bro-mance.

"Don't worry. Andrew and I are still going to be in touch. Since the house transaction is behind us now, I'm planning on heading over to his office toward the end of next week to meet with him. It looks like I'm going to start doing some work for his company."

I beamed at my handsome husband. "I don't know how you do it, but you are the only person I know who can manage to score a client while buying a house. This has been a very bizarre experience, don't you think?" During the past few months, I think I'd felt every possible emotion from sadness to euphoria. And now, since almost everything was behind us, I felt an odd sense of relief. There was no turning back, and no more second-guessing our decision. We were officially Shells Point bound.

Craig grinned at me. "I know. After all the documents were signed, Walter pulled me into his office."

Walter was my husband's mentor and the senior partner at the law firm where Craig worked. Walter was also the attorney who'd handled both of our closings today. "Wally said that he's been practicing law for close to fifty years and has never witnessed two transactions like ours. Usually, there's some tension or hostility in the air during the closing. The sellers felt they should have gotten more money for their homes while the buyers felt like they overpaid for the property. Walter said he's never seen a closing where everyone involved seemed like they were best friends."

"Walter's a sweetheart, but I did start to worry Kara had managed to get on his last nerve." Walter was such a down-to-earth, kindhearted guy. I'd hit it off with him right away, and like my husband, I was sad to know he planned to retire soon.

"I won't lie. Walter was starting to lose his patience with you both. He tried to hide his frustration, but I could see the expression on his face. Not that I blame the guy for getting annoyed. Seriously, the two of you couldn't stop babbling and giggling. You and Kara were way worse than Amanda and Cassidy any day."

I jabbed him in the ribs. "Oh, and you and your BFF were better behaved? When Andrew busted out the cigars and the bottle of champagne, I thought Walter was going to have a coronary."

Craig tried to keep a straight face. "Well, Andrew did get bubbly all over the conference room table."

"Fortunately, Parker was quick on her feet and grabbed some tissues. She saved Andrew's hide." I took a sip of wine as a small smile spread across my face. "Speaking of which, did you happen to catch a glimpse of how Parker and Andrew were gazing at each other?"

He nodded. I had made subtle hints to Parker about Andrew for weeks. She paid attention. She came to the closing all decked out in a low cut, black wrap dress. I thought she looked beautiful. Based on how Andrew could barely take his eyes off her, he shared my opinion.

I poked my husband in the ribs. "And you thought I was crazy when I suggested we should set them up."

His phone beeped again with another text message.

I cocked my head to the side. "Andrew, again?"

"Yep. And you were on to something. He's having dinner with Parker on Sunday night." He paused briefly. "I guess everything is finally falling into place."

I nodded.

"Sydney, it's time." His eyes pleaded. "We need to tell Amanda the truth. She's smart. She'll sense something is going on."

My heart pounded in my chest. I remembered the pain when my parents sat me down and told me Kelly was moving away. I felt it was too soon to spring this on Amanda. I wasn't ready to subject her to that type of stress, not yet. She had several more months left in the term, and I wanted her to enjoy every second. There was no way I was going to ruin the rest of the school year for her.

CHAPTER THIRTY-ONE

"OH, SYDNEY." Jackie breathed a sigh of relief as soon as she laid eyes on me. Hastily, she grabbed hold of my arm and practically dragged me up the school's central staircase.

It was the crack of dawn on a Saturday morning in the beginning of May. I'd reluctantly left my family who were fast asleep. "Good morning to you, too," I managed to utter before I yawned, deeply. I was bone tired.

Craig and I had spent pretty much every free moment we had in Shells Point. Jackie had been fantastic and invited Amanda over most weekends so we could do work around the house. I was sore in places I didn't think I even had muscles.

"I was so worried you'd be late, as usual. But look at you! You've done me proud this time, Sydney. Here's your prize, my friend." She handed me an extra-large cup of coffee from the local deli. "I thought you'd need this."

I took the cup and held it with both hands. It was unseasonably cold for a spring morning. "Forget about all the mean words I had running through my head. I thought you were insane for dragging me out of bed at this ungodly hour of the morning. I've completely forgiven you." I took a sip. "Thanks. I so needed this." I'd had no time to put on a dab of lip gloss this morning yet alone brew a cup of coffee.

I glanced at my watch. Despite Jackie's panic, it wasn't even six o'clock in the morning. "Remind me again why we're here at the crack of dawn. You do realize it's a Saturday, don't you? Shouldn't we still be in bed catching up on our beauty rest, or at least binge watching Netflix before we have to tackle countless loads of laundry, make breakfast, and head to yet another birthday party?"

"Oh please." She shook her head from side to side and made a clucking sound. "We have no time for sleep. As it is, I already cut you slack because you work full-time and you've also been running yourself ragged at that new house of yours. I should have forced you to meet me here at five-fifteen to guarantee we'd be the first two mommies in line."

She looked around the empty parking lot. "But usually the vultures don't start appearing until after six, so I figured we'd still be safe. I've been keeping a close eye on cars that have arrived, and I think we'll be okay. Hopefully, we won't be in for any unpleasant surprises."

"You do take the spring concert seriously, Jackie." Not that I was surprised. Jackie took everything Forest River Elementary seriously.

"Ah, it must be nice to be so innocent, Sydney." She linked her arm through mine. "Listen up. We don't have any choice but to be vigilant about obtaining tickets. You know the deal, right?"

I shrugged. Since Amanda had inherited my atrocious singing voice and Craig's non-existent musical ability, neither one of us had any fear of not being front and center for her premier performance. Of course, we didn't want to miss seeing our little girl up on stage with her classmates singing her heart out. But both my husband and I would have been perfectly content to be seated anywhere in the auditorium, even way in the back, especially if it meant having a few more seconds of shut-eye this morning. But I didn't have the heart to turn Jackie down when she'd invited me to wait in line with her for tickets. As progressive as our school was, I was shocked they didn't sell tickets online. Then Jackie shared how several years ago when they'd tried that approach, a mother was busted for trying to recreate the tickets on her printer so her entire extended family could experience her son's trombone solo.

We walked up the stairs toward the fifth-grade classrooms, which were located all the way in the rear of the school. "Why are we going upstairs? I thought we'd get the tickets near the auditorium."

"You should count your lucky stars every day that you have me to show you the way. What would you ever have done without me?"

What would I do without her next term? I'd lived in this town for ten years, yet I honestly hadn't known what to expect when Amanda had begun first grade. I loved being able to experience the ups and downs of the parental drama with a friend. It would be so odd to be alone, again, but this time in a new place. Should I join the PTA again?

I followed Jackie down the long corridor.

"The school only allows parents to get four tickets to any show. It doesn't matter how many kids you have performing or if the parents are separated and remarried. Four tickets are the limit, no exceptions! The rule is nuts if you ask me. I've been trying to petition to change the policy for the past six years, to no avail. The school board simply will not budge. Since the tickets are given out on a first-come-first-serve basis, if you aren't in the front of the line, you risk ending up in the nosebleed section behind a bunch of iPads and screaming toddlers."

My eyes narrowed, re-reading the school's parent manual in my mind. "I thought siblings weren't able to attend the show. Isn't that why there's a special performance scheduled for the morning before the concert, so other children can see it without taking up seats?"

Jackie took a deep breath before gazing up at the ceiling. She looked like she was saying a silent prayer before she opened the door to the classroom, which had a large sign announcing in red letters: "Get your spring concert tickets here!"

"Oh, thank God!" she exclaimed when she surveyed the room and only found three other moms ahead of us. She greeted the ladies with dramatic air kisses before turning her attention back to me. "Where was I?"

"iPads and kids coming to the show."

"Oh, yes. Bless your heart. You can be so naïve sometimes." Jackie smiled sweetly at me.

I arched an eyebrow dramatically, although I wasn't insulted. By now I knew Jackie well enough to know she meant no harm. She was only being playful.

" I don't mean anything bad, obviously. But the school year is coming to an end, and you're still giving the parents in this town the benefit of the doubt? Haven't I taught you anything this term?"

"Um..." She'd taught me a lesson all right, but not the one she thought. I learned first impressions weren't always accurate, and often it took a lot of time and effort to understand a person.

She placed her hand on her chest. "Not everyone is as understanding as I am, you know."

I coughed, in an unsuccessful attempt to cover up my chuckle. "Yeah, understanding is the first word that comes to mind when I think of you."

She smiled. "More than three-quarters of the parents ignore every rule. The spring concert is practically an invitation for horrific behavior. What I have seen go on in that auditorium over the years would make your hair stand on end!" Her eyes bulged. "More children than I can count have been snuck into the shows. When Hayley was in second grade, she had a singing solo. I couldn't even hear one word of her performance because some toddler in the back pitched such a fit. Then when Hayley was in third grade, our entire house came down with the stomach flu. It wasn't pretty." She grimaced. "I could barely make it out my front door, let alone get to the school in time to get tickets. So, we had horrible seats. We were stuck all the way back in the fourth row!"

"That doesn't sound so bad to me."

"Oh, if you were stuck back there, you'd realize how awful it was. I couldn't see a thing."

"Hey, ladies," Trisha practically sang and joined us in line.

I hugged her, and Jackie gave her an air kiss.

"Wow, it's sure getting crowded in here." She waved to a few women around us before opening a large paper bag. "I brought bagels. Jackie probably won't be caught dead holding a carb, but I thought you might like one, Sydney."

I eagerly took the bag. "Thanks, I'm starved." Jackie, as predicted, declined graciously.

"So, was the queen filling you in on the drama of spring concerts past?" Trisha elbowed Jackie's shoulder.

I nodded.

Trisha bounced on the balls of her feet. "Did she tell you about the time she almost got into a fistfight?"

I nearly choked on my bread. "What?"

"Trisha, you are such an exaggerator." Jackie gently slapped Trisha's arm. "It wasn't that bad."

"Okay, whatever helps you sleep at night, darling." Then Trisha turned to me. "You missed the good old glory days, Sydney. You probably can't imagine, but once upon a time, Mrs. Martin here wasn't as in the know about all things Forest River Elementary. When Hayley started kindergarten with my Emma, we were two regular mommies. But then she joined the PTA with a vengeance. Hayley has an amazing singing voice."

Jackie blushed. "She takes after me, you know."

"Yeah, well, unlike her mom, she was painfully shy. She took the stage—"

Before Trisha could complete her thought, Claire and Stacey appeared. Claire called out, "Hey, guys!"

"I can't believe how crowded it is here already," Stacey said. She glanced at her watch. "We had to park our car two blocks away! What are we talking about, ladies?"

"The time Jackie almost got into a fistfight?" I replied, although it came out more like a question. I no longer wished to be tucked under my covers. I was enjoying every second with my friends. Part of me wanted to freeze this moment. I wanted to halt time a lot lately, so I could make certain moments linger.

I'd spent so much of the past seven years living my life in a blur, trying to cram as much as humanly possible into a day. I'd missed out on so much in the process, like having dear girlfriends. It wasn't until you knew something was about to end that you realized how fortunate you were to have had it in the first place.

"Oh, yes!" Claire grinned and put her arm around Jackie's waist. "Good times!"

Trisha cleared her throat. "So, I was saying, Hayley was super shy. As soon as she walked onto the stage and saw the number of people in the audience, she must have gone into shock. The spotlight shone on her little face, and she struggled to make a sound. She kept opening and closing her mouth silently."

"There were tears in her eyes." Jackie sniffled. "I did what I had to do to help her."

Trisha struggled to keep a straight face. "Oh yeah, little miss thing over here stood up, raised her hands high in the air, and started screaming, 'You can do it, Hayley,' at the top of her lungs. And when that didn't work, she started singing the song. Eventually, Hayley joined in, but Jackie kept on standing and singing." Trisha started wiggling in place. "She even did a cute little dance."

Jackie giggled.

"It was charming, actually," Stacey added.

"Yeah, it was adorable for a couple of seconds." Trisha put her hands on her hips. "Until the other parents started to get upset. They yelled at Jackie to sit down. Of course, Jackie refused. The lady who was sitting behind her was the mother of a fifth-grade bully, and pushed her. Jackie turned around and stood up on her chair, her fists raised. She was like eleven months pregnant with Cassidy at the time. Her stomach needed its own zip code, but she wasn't going to let that stop her. Thank goodness Scott was there. He yanked her off the chair before she drew any blood."

"Oh, my God!" My mouth hung open. "This happened?" I wished I'd known Jackie back then. I loved how these women had so many shared moments, of themselves and their families. It made me sad to think my time with them was so limited, and all I'd have to look back on was this one short year.

Jackie pursed her lips. "Yeah, it was a fun night. Hayley ended up crushing the performance and had a solo every year since. I can't believe this will be her last year to get up on this stage." She wiped a tear from her face.

"Getting emotional?" Aimee tucked an arm around Jackie's waist. "I know how you feel. I cried on my way here this morning too. I can't believe this will be Kyle's last drum solo. How are our little ones heading into junior high, especially since we haven't aged one bit?"

I cried on my way over to the school today, too. I experienced the same mix of emotions as the mothers of the older kids. This would be Amanda's first and last spring concert at Forest River Elementary School. It was my one and only chance to huddle up with the ladies and gossip as we waited to get our tickets. Guilt nagged at me: I hadn't yet confided in the group that we were moving.

"Okay, this is ridiculous already!" Donna exclaimed and marched over to our party.

"What is your problem this time?" Jackie asked her former bestie.

"If you want to know, you." Donna pointed her index finger at Jackie's chest.

Jackie giggled. "Oh, how original. Okay then, have a nice day." She chuckled before looking away.

"Seriously, Jackie. Who do you think you are?" Donna shoved her slightly. "Do you have any respect for anyone besides yourself and your friends? Look around! The line for tickets extends all around the building. But do you care? No, you let your pals stroll in and cut in front of everyone else."

"Mind your own business, will you?" Jackie crossed her arms over her chest. "You never had an issue when you were able to sleep late and still get front row seats thanks to me, did you?"

Donna opened her mouth to speak, but Jackie didn't give her a chance. "No, you didn't. You used to show up so late there were times I thought we'd finish getting our tickets before you even arrived. But you were always so thankful because we had your back. Well, you're not part of the group anymore, Donna, and the only person to blame for that is yourself."

"You are such a bitch."

Jackie batted her eyes. "You know damn well I didn't start this. You did. You can call me all the names you like. I don't care. Nor do I care about you, or the fact that you'll be sitting in the last row for the concert. Now, please leave us alone and return to your spot in line on the curb."

Donna let out a huff and walked away.

"She is sure a piece of work," Aimee said.

"Yep." Claire nodded. "But she does keep things interesting. I'm sure Donna's stewing right now. It should be interesting to see if she pulls a stunt next year. Perhaps she'll draft another petition?"

"Whatever she has in store for us, we'll handle it! She can't beat this team!" Stacey shouted.

"To the team!" Trisha cheered, and everyone raised their fists high up in the air. I joined in half-heartedly and prayed I was able to keep a poker face.

"Come here." Jackie pulled me off to the side. "Are you ever going to tell the others you guys are moving?"

I nodded. "Yes, soon." Jackie had been pressuring me to tell everyone about our pending relocation for a few weeks, but I wasn't ready.

"I sure hope so. The ladies have a right to know you're leaving. You owe it to them."

"Yes, I know. I just want to wait a little longer, until we're closer to the end of the term. I don't want to tell Amanda yet."

I'd voiced my concerns to Jackie several times already. She knew I was concerned about my daughter being so worried about moving she wouldn't be able to focus on school or enjoy the time she had left with her friends. I felt if I waited until right before classes ended, she would cope better, especially when we told her about the fantastic summer camp she was going to attend in Shells Point. I was afraid the more people who knew we were leaving the more of a risk someone would slip and say something to Amanda.

"It's your call, but for the record, I disagree with your approach. Forget the fact you're now part of this team." Jackie pointed at the others. "The ladies are also your friends. I can't even imagine what they'll think when they find out you've been keeping this big secret for months. You're not being fair to them."

I sighed deeply and returned my half-eaten bagel to the bag. I had lost my appetite. "I know." Was I making a mistake keeping this secret? Was I destroying all the friendships I had made this year? Would my plan backfire? I wanted to protect my daughter, but would I hurt her instead?

"We have our last meeting of the year two weeks before field day, to finalize all the plans." Jackie folded her arms across her chest and glared at me. "You'd better be ready to fess up by then. If not, I'll take matters into my own hands."

Jackie let her words linger as she rejoined the group. I remained in my spot, frozen. Had I misjudged Jackie? Should I have trusted her with my secret?

CHAPTER THIRTY-TWO

I STARED AT MY LAPTOP AND RAN my fingers through my hair. My mother was right. As far back as I could remember, she'd warned my sister and me to be careful about doing repeated favors for others. Before we were born, she'd worked full-time as a legal secretary. One day, a girl who'd been assigned to work for another partner at her firm had called out sick. My mom covered for the woman and when she came back three days later, the attorney asked my mom to handle the girl's tasks for him. When she'd questioned him, he'd declared she was better and faster than his secretary.

Which was pretty much the exact situation I was currently dealing with. When I was first assigned the task of composing the letter bashing the best friend ban earlier this term, I should have muddled my way through it instead of drafting a masterpiece. Because if I'd failed, Claire, the former scribe of the PTA, would have been sitting at her computer right now, completely stressed out, instead of me.

It was the first Friday of June, and I wished I had a pause button to slow down the passing days. We'd decided to tell Amanda about the move this weekend. Then I'd fill the ladies in on Monday at our final PTA meeting of the year, as Jackie had requested. She was right: I owed it to them to be upfront.

Craig and I had both taken off from work today to try to get some much-needed packing done. He had made remarkable headway in the garage and basement, while I'd spent most of the day fretting about composing a stupid email. I glanced at the clock on the wall. It was almost four pm. Amanda and Sally would be home from ballet soon. I needed to get this email out before they returned.

Satisfied I had followed instructions and thoroughly shamed the parents who didn't follow through with their required contribution to the group gifts, I crumpled up my notes and hit the delete button. I felt so free when I erased the entire email. My year as a PTA member was coming to an end, and it was high time I was finally my own person. I'd written a second email my own way, not how Jackie had instructed. I re-read the message one final time.

To: Parents
From: Sydney_Clayton
Date: 5/15
Subject: There's not only one way to show gratitude
Dear Forest River Parents,

Time sure flies! It feels like yesterday I stood in front of my house, frantically snapping photos of my daughter as I tried to capture the mix of emotions associated with the first day of school. In what feels like the blink of an eye, she outgrew that perfect outfit, and the school year is rapidly coming to close.

My daughter had a fantastic year at Forest River Elementary, just as I hope your children did. We are so fortunate to live in a town where our educators value our children as if they were their own. Our sons and daughters receive not only a fantastic education, but they are also privileged to participate in extraordinary extracurricular activities, as well as go on once-in-a-lifetime field trips.

At the beginning of the term, the class mothers addressed how much money was needed for the end of year group gifts. Unfortunately, the majority of the parents have not sent in their checks. We will extend the deadline for donations until Wednesday at 3:00 PM. Any child whose parents contribute by that time WILL have their name listed on the class card.

If you opt out of participating, either for financial or other reasons, we do hope you consider showing your children's teachers your appreciation in another way. After all, there shouldn't be only one way to say THANK YOU.

Warm Best,
Your PTA Board,

Jackie Martin – President
Claire Conroy, Trisha Dickens, Stacey Williams, Aimee Roberts, &
Sydney Clayton

"Please don't tell me you've been sitting here in front of your laptop for the last two hours?" Craig slumped on the sofa. He looked exhausted.

"Um, guilty as charged." I gave him a small smile. "But check it out." I pointed to a small box in the corner. "I packed up all my files and office supplies."

"And I should be proud of the milestone?" He yawned.

I scratched my head. "Well, I did take care of all our winter clothes, too. I didn't only pack them up, I also sorted through everything and prepared a big bag of stuff to donate."

"Well, I guess that's something. But seriously, you need to stay focused. We're in the home stretch now. In less than a month we're moving. We're running out of time, so we have to make every second count. Which is why we took today off from work so we could pack, remember?"

I opened my mouth to speak, but he didn't give me a chance.

"And yes." He pointed toward the box in the corner. "I know you did something today. But you've been locked up in this room for," he squinted at his watch, "close to two hours writing an email."

"I was also messaging with Parker," I announced proudly. "Things are going great with her and Andrew. She seems so happy ever since they started dating. They went to a charity event last weekend! Do you want to see a wonderful picture of them?" I navigated to Facebook, but my husband didn't budge.

"No. I'm happy for them, but who are you trying to fool? I'm sure you chatted with Parker, but I know how you roll. The bulk of the time you were locked up in this room you were typing up some cockamamie PTA email."

"Well, I—"

"Why do you care so much what these people think? We're leaving in less than a month. You'll probably never even meet most of the parents you had to contact. And for the ones you do know, except maybe a select few, how likely is it that you'll ever have anything to do with them again?"

A tear rolled down my cheek. "Yeah, I know." I sniffled. "You make excellent points, and I think you perfectly summed up why writing this email was so difficult for me." I looked around the room. "No one knows we're moving. I want the other parents to know how much I appreciate the faculty at Forest River Elementary and the quality of education our daughter has received. And when people find out we're moving, I don't want anyone to think I didn't take my PTA duties seriously, because I did, Craig. I did."

At first, my work with the team was an obligation I'd resented. I looked at it as a waste of hours I didn't have. However, as the months passed, I realized I couldn't have spent my time in any better way. I dedicated so much of my life to my career, and while my accomplishments were rewarding, guilt always gnawed at me because my job caused me to miss out on so many moments of Amanda's life. All the satisfaction I felt professionally paled in comparison to my pride in helping make sure her school experience was extra special. Also, it didn't hurt that I genuinely ended up liking the ladies a lot.

"I know, sweetie." My husband stood up and walked behind me. He gently began massaging my tense shoulders. "I've been wondering about something."

"Mmm?" I murmured and rolled my neck.

"Are you planning on joining the PTA up in Shells Point?"

I tucked a strand of hair behind my ear, and nodded. "I think so. How funny is that? To think, only a few months ago I was complaining about being bullied into participating. And now," I reached over to the edge of my desk and clutched a picture Craig had taken of the group right after the penny auction, "I can't imagine not being part of the team. I never felt like I had any true friends in this town before. And now, right before we high-tail it out of here, I finally do." I sniffed.

I realized that having a group of gals to let off steam with and run ideas by, not only made me a happier person, but it helped me be a better mother. When we moved, I would try to reach out to people more.

"Sydney!" Sally yelled from downstairs.

I hadn't even heard the front door open. I looked at my watch. It was four-fifteen. If they left ballet right after class had ended, they probably got home about fifteen minutes ago.

"Craig! Sydney! Craig! Do you hear me? Where are you? We're home." Sally yelled out again, her voice louder and higher pitched. She never called out to us when she entered the house. My heart pounded double time in my chest. Something must be wrong with Amanda.

CHAPTER THIRTY-THREE

WHEN I SAW SALLY PACE BACK AND FORTH at the bottom of the staircase, I knew my suspicion had been correct. I quickened my walk, as did Craig. A glass of milk and a plate of cookies was sitting on the coffee table, but Amanda was nowhere in sight.

"Sally, is something wrong?" Craig asked.

Her gray curls bounced as she nodded. "Yes, I think so. Something upset Amanda, badly."

"What happened?" My heart pounded furiously in my chest.

"I don't know." She picked at an imaginary piece of lint on her baby blue cardigan. "When Amanda got out of ballet class, her eyes were all puffy and red, and she was crying. She refused to look at me, let alone tell me what happened. She stared out the car window silently the whole ride home." Sally pointed at the table. "I made her a snack, but when I brought it down to the basement, she told me she didn't want to eat. She never refuses Oreos. They're her favorite. I tried to play with her, but she begged me to leave her alone, so I came back up here, and called for you." She glanced at the gold watch on her wrist. "I'm going to cancel my doctor's appointment."

Don't be silly." I touched her arm. "You should go."

Sally, unfortunately, wouldn't be staying with us once we moved to Shells Point. We had hoped she'd consider it; she had been part of our family since Amanda was six months old and I'd returned to work full-time. But we weren't shocked that she felt the commute would be too much for her. What did surprise us was how our departure ended up being the motivation she needed to retire.

"Okay." She put her pocketbook on her shoulder. "Please text me later and let me know how Amanda's doing."

Amanda sat on the floor in the playroom section of the basement, with Oreo the cat on her lap, surrounded by her Barbie dolls. But she wasn't playing with any of them. Her favorite stuffed rabbit, that she'd had since she was a baby, sat abandoned by her side. Her chin rested on her knees as tears ran down her cheeks. She stared at the dollhouse we'd bought her for her birthday, which was a replica of our future home in Shells Point. It was like she wanted her favorite toys to give her comfort, but they weren't cooperating.

"What's wrong, baby?" I squatted down.

She shook her head.

Craig joined us on the floor. "Amanda, come on. Talk to us. We know something's bothering you."

"No." She sobbed into her knees.

I gently tugged at one of her dark brown pigtails. "Sweetheart, we can't help you feel better if we don't know what's making you so upset. What happened in ballet class today? I know you were late. Sally told me you forgot your book bag at school, and she had to circle back to pick it up before bringing you to dance class. Did Miss Stephanie make you feel bad because you were tardy?"

Amanda's teacher was a prima ballerina, who began to teach after an ankle injury had forced her offstage. She was incredibly talented and expected a lot from the girls. I felt she took class a bit too seriously, but my daughter loved going.

Amanda whispered, "No."

"Did you miss the barre exercises? I know you love them the most."

"Yes, Mommy, I did. But that's not what's bothering me," Amanda whined.

"Progress," I mouthed over her head. "Okay, then tell us what's making you so sad."

Slowly, Amanda lifted her head. Her green eyes were red and swollen. "The girls were sitting in a circle doing stretches, and when I walked in, they all started to whisper and point at me. Then Miss Stephanie made us all practice our positions, but they kept acting mean. I thought Ms. Stephanie would get mad, but she didn't." She swiped at her tears. "She didn't care. She just kept telling us to redo our pirouette. After class ended the girls ganged up on me and told me a bunch of lies."

I gulped and locked eyes with my husband. He pulled Amanda onto his lap and kissed the top of her head. "What kind of lies?"

"They said I wasn't gonna be with them in second-grade. They said we were leaving Forest River. Forever! I said they were wrong. They called me stupid!"

"That bitch!" I put my hand over my mouth, but it was too late.

Amanda giggled half-heartedly. "Daddy, Mommy said bad words." Amanda loved to rat us both out when we misbehaved.

"I know, sweetie. Mommy does that sometimes."

Amanda turned to face her father. "I'm not stupid, am I?"

Craig kissed her cheek. "Of course not, baby. You're a very smart girl. You get your big brains from me and your good looks from your mommy." I punched him playfully for suggesting I wasn't smart, but my action was only for Amanda's benefit. I felt like the most idiotic mother in the world. Why had I waited so long to tell Amanda the truth? And why had I trusted Jackie with my secret?

"Then why did the girls say I was dumb? They're the ones who don't know anything. We're not going anywhere!" Her bottom lip jutted out defiantly.

Craig glanced at me over her head and whispered, "It's time. I'll start."

I closed my eyes and exhaled. I had dreaded this conversation for months, and I was relieved he was going to be the one to start it. On any given day he was far more clear-headed and rational than I ever hoped to be. And right now, I was too livid to form coherent sentences, let alone comfort my daughter properly. I had tried so hard to keep our move a secret, so we'd be able to protect Amanda. And now, thanks to that gossiping queen, our daughter found out the truth in the worst possible way.

"Amanda, we have something to tell you."

Her eyes widened like saucers, and she started to bite her nails.

"Stop that, sweetie." I took hold of her hands. "It's going to be okay."

Craig continued, "Mommy and Daddy should have been the ones to tell you the exciting news. We're very upset the girls beat us to it." He glared at me over her head. "It never should have happened that way, because they don't know the real story, only tiny parts of it. Are you ready for the full truth?"

She shrugged her tiny shoulders. "I guess so."

Craig pointed toward the dollhouse. "If you could live anywhere besides here, where would you want to live?"

"Nowhere," she said with a frown. Besides inheriting my looks, she'd also managed to get a stubborn streak.

"I know you don't think so. But come on, play along with Daddy, okay?"

He tickled her gently and angled his head toward her dollhouse. "If you had to live in another house, what would you want the house to look like?"

Yeah, Craig was great at leading the witness. Amanda picked up his clue, and pointing toward the toy, she said, "Like that."

"Well, guess what?" Craig's green eyes sparkled. "When we move, your new house is going to look exactly like it!"

Her mouth opened and closed. She studied her father. "How? It's only a toy."

"Well, Mommy and I..." The doorbell chimed, interrupting Craig briefly, but we both ignored it. "There is a house very close to where Grandma Phyllis and Grandpa Carl live. And it looks just like this one. Can you believe it?"

She wrinkled her forehead as the doorbell rang again.

Craig continued, "And when I say close, I mean you'll be able to see them every single week. In fact, they'll even pick you up after school some days."

Amanda let out a small yelp and her eyes danced. "Cool."

"I know. And you are going to..." Craig stopped in his tracks as the doorbell continued to chime. He turned to me. "Go answer the door. Whoever's there isn't getting the hint we don't want to be bothered. They're driving me crazy. I've got this."

"You sure?" I stood up, reluctantly. I wanted to be part of the conversation.

"Go," he replied sternly.

I kissed Amanda's cheek and walked toward the staircase. I turned back and saw Craig whispering into Amanda's ear. Her cheeks brightened. My pulse slowed. I felt a small bit of relief by the time I reached the top of the stairs, even though the bell kept ringing. I opened the door without bothering to look at who was standing on the other side.

She barged right in. "Sydney, Cassidy told me what happened at ballet today. How—"

My ears pounded with blood, and I felt like all my extremities were on fire. "How could you have done this?" I screamed. I didn't think. I reacted. I raised my right hand high in the air.

CHAPTER THIRTY-FOUR

"SLOW DOWN. IT'S THE SECOND TO LAST HOUSE on the left," Jackie said. She pulled down the sun visor and wiped away a remaining trace of smeared mascara.

I still trembled slightly. I couldn't believe I'd almost resorted to violence. When Jackie had appeared at my front door, I was completely blinded by rage over a perceived betrayal. Thank God, seconds before I did anything I would later regret, I opened my eyes wide enough to see she was as upset and traumatized as I was.

I was furious with myself. How horrible was I that I'd immediately assumed Jackie had blabbed about our move? Every event which had taken place over the past nine months flashed before my eyes like a lousy made-for-television movie. Time and again, I'd seen first-hand that she wasn't a villain. Instead, she'd proven to me she was someone who had my back, always.

Fortunately, I didn't do anything I'd later regret. Instead of slapping her, I had wrapped my arms around her tightly, and we'd both cried. When we broke the embrace, I realized what had occurred. Jackie had come to the same conclusion earlier, and she confirmed my suspicion.

We had waited until Amanda regained her composure and Jackie cleaned up her running makeup before we got in my car and drove across town.

"Do you want me to do the talking?" she asked as I parked in front of a massive brick McMansion.

Although I would have loved to sit back and enjoy the show, this was my battle to fight. "Thanks, but I have to do it." I flashed her a small smile. "You can introduce us, though."

"You got it, girl." She squeezed my shoulder.

I stood off to the side as Jackie rang the doorbell. After a moment, a tall, incredibly fit, blonde opened the door. Dramatically she looked Jackie up and down. She crossed her arms over her chest. "Well, this is an unwelcome surprise. What are you doing here, Jackie?"

"Great to see you too, Mia. Don't worry. I have nothing to say to you." She gestured toward me. "My friend, Sydney Clayton, however, has a lot to say." While their daughters had made amends, Mia and Jackie were still at war.

"Sydney Clayton?" She gave me the once-over. "*The* Sydney Clayton?" She flung open the screen door. "Come inside. I'm so happy to meet you."

Jackie and I exchanged sideways glances as we entered her home.

As soon as we settled in her living room, Mia said, "I have no idea what you're both doing here. Nor do I know why you're together. Regardless, you have no idea how happy I am that my sister is moving to town, especially now that Emma was born. I wanted her to return to Forest River so badly. Kara was so picky about where she wanted to live. I never thought I'd see the day." She rolled her eyes. "And then with all the dramatics with the sale, I didn't want to get too excited, but finally, it's a done deal!"

"So you know all about what transpired when Kara was looking to buy my house?" I asked.

"Of course." She smirked. "We're sisters. She tells me everything."

"So you knew she agreed to keep the transaction confidential, even after the closing."

"Yes, of course." She crossed her legs and sat up straight in her chair. "You didn't honestly expect her not to tell her sister where she was moving, did you?" Mia sneered.

I tucked a strand of hair behind my ear. "Of course I knew she told you. The same way I told her I was coming to see you today. What I'm not okay with is the fact that you broadcast the news."

"I did no such thing," she said adamantly.

"Oh really?" I began to bounce my leg.

"You didn't tell anyone, Mia?" Jackie chimed in. "Are you seriously going to sit here and lie to our faces?"

Mia remained silent.

I thought carefully before I spoke. "Moments ago you told me you were so excited to meet me. Aren't you even a tiny bit confused why we showed up now? Especially since I know your sister is home in her apartment with her baby girl and not visiting you?"

Mia said nothing.

"I hoped you'd have owned up to what you did and would have taken responsibility for your actions. I guess I was wrong to have given you the benefit of the doubt. Your sister spoke so highly of you, so I wanted to think you were as wonderful as she said you were. But let's face it. When someone shows you who they are, you should believe them. My bad." I looked her square in the eye, "And while we'd never met, you showed me who you were when you pulled your little stunt last year. Fortunately, Hayley moved on. She's fine. Your actions didn't damage her one bit. I pray my kid ends up being as lucky."

Mia blinked rapidly. "What happened to your child? Kara loves your daughter."

I gritted my teeth. "My daughter went to ballet class today and came home with her world turned upside down. My husband and I were planning on telling her this weekend that we were moving away from Forest River. I was dreading breaking the news to her, but now I don't have to." I glowered at her. "Now she knows. She found out from the girls in her class."

Mia pinched the bridge of her nose and closed her eyes.

I leaned in. "I'm going to ask you the same question one more time, Mia. This time, I'd appreciate the truth. Who did you tell?'

Mia fidgeted. "I told a bunch of people that my sister was moving to town. How could I not? I was beyond excited." She wiped a tear away. "No one questioned me, except for one person. She grilled me. All she wanted to know was which house my sister bought. She wouldn't take no for an answer, so I told her. I regretted it instantly, especially when she said her daughter was friends with your kid. I swore her to secrecy. I should have known better than to trust her."

Jackie rolled her eyes. "Yeah, I'd think you'd have better betrayal radar by now."

Even though I already knew whom she confided in, I needed confirmation. "Give me a name, Mia. Who did you tell?"

She looked at her shoes. "Donna."

CHAPTER THIRTY-FIVE

THE SATISFACTION I FOUND WAS FLEETING. More often than not, the best revenge was to remain silent and put on a happy face. Nothing irked a miserable person more than seeing others experience joy. And at this point in time, all I wanted to do was enjoy my life.

I had no idea which one of us Donna wanted to hurt more: Jackie or me. But the truth of the matter was, I didn't care. For about fifteen seconds I thought about confronting her. But with everything else going on, I didn't have a second to spare, let alone waste, on her.

While Jackie and I pieced together what had transpired at ballet class, Craig calmed Amanda down. I didn't know what he'd said exactly, but he'd managed to transform her fears into excitement. Amanda couldn't wait to start a new chapter of her life in Shells Point, and eagerly counted the days until she would begin camp.

She was even looking forward to beginning second-grade at a new school. We told her she could have a party in the fall so her new Shells Point friends could meet her old Forest River pals. She and her squad had been planning it ever since.

The other PTA members had been equally supportive. During the last few weeks over countless bottles of wine, the ladies and I had gone through practically every single article of clothing we owned. My friends and I had laughed and cried while we played keep or toss. When it came time to bubble wrap all our wine glasses and good china, we'd formed an assembly line. All the tasks I had dreaded having to tackle alone quickly became fun. I stopped feeling sad we were leaving our home. Instead, I was delighted to have the opportunity to make new memories with my dear friends.

I squinted in the bright sun as Trisha deposited a box of trophies onto the large table, which we'd set up off to the side of the soccer field. Today was the last Forest River Elementary School event I would participate in.

"It has to be a thousand degrees today," Trisha said. She pulled her blond hair into a ponytail.

"Field day always is." Aimee grabbed scissors and sliced open the box. "It's like the weather gods try to punish us or something every single year. Wasn't it fifteen degrees cooler yesterday?"

Stacey nodded in agreement and helped Aimee set up the trophies on the table. "It sure was."

Jackie and I had just finished unloading bottles of water. She walked around to get a better look. "Great job, Trisha!" She beamed. "The trophies look amazing." She held one up for me to see.

"Nice," I said softly. I was trying very hard not to get emotional, but it wasn't easy. There was only one more week left of school.

Jackie studied the second-place trophy for a second. "I can't believe we have the same battle every year."

"I guess some things will never change," Claire stated with a satisfied grin. "But we always manage to win, don't we?"

"Yeah, we win!" Jackie announced. "Winning is a huge part of sportsmanship. What's the point of competing if there's nothing to gain by winning?" Jackie gestured to a few frowning women who stood huddled together, off to the side of the field watching a group of kids compete in a three-legged race. "All those whiny moms who carry on how every child should get equal ribbons. They're so worried about making someone feel bad. They make my blood boil."

"I know," Trisha added. "I get they don't want their children upset if they don't perform well, but kids need to learn they have to work hard to make something of themselves."

Stacey chimed in, "Also they need to know not everyone is great at everything. When I was little, my parents made sure I knew my limits. They saved me a ton of embarrassment." She giggled. "And thank goodness Sydney's parents did the same. Could you imagine if they let her grow up thinking she was able to sing?"

The ladies began to laugh. Several months ago, these guys had forced me to break my rule about singing in public. It was Stacey's thirty-eighth birthday, and to celebrate she'd dragged us all to a local bar, on karaoke night. No matter how hard I'd tried to convince the girls I could carry a five-hundred-pound man easier than I could carry a tune, they hadn't believed me. The more I protested, the more insistent they became. Finally, thanks to a shot or two of tequila, I succumbed to peer pressure and gave them what they wanted. I didn't even last a full verse before Jackie had to rush up to the microphone and rescue me. She belted out the song, and I silently swayed to the music. I was too mortified to lip-synch.

"Sydney? Are you okay?" Jackie asked.

I hoped she wouldn't notice that a tear had escaped.

"Oh, Syd." Stacey stroked my arm. "I'm sorry. You know you can't sing. I didn't mean any harm."

I laughed and cried at the same time. "It's not that. It's everything else." I took a deep breath. "Standing here with you guys, knowing that in less than a week we're leaving this town, everything hit me hard. I'm going to miss you all so much."

Jackie put her arms around me and hugged me tightly. "It's okay, Sydney."

I clung to her. Then, one by one the other ladies joined in. After a moment or so we broke apart.

Jackie put her hands on her hips. "Now get yourself together, girl."

Aimee handed me a napkin from the drink table, and I took it gratefully.

"You may be moving, but you're not getting rid of us so easily. In fact, I already have some notes jotted down for you." Jackie reached into her back pocket and pulled out a sheet of hot pink paper. "It's regarding an email that we need written by the first week of school. It's going to take Claire a bit of time to get back into the swing of being our scribe. I assured her you wouldn't mind helping out a bit until then."

Claire rolled her eyes. "Yeah, Syd, it may take me the full term to get my writing mojo back. Feel free to carry on and continue handling all the email demands from our queen for me."

"Okay, guys. Enough of this sentimental bull." Trisha pointed toward the field where most of the mothers stood. "Do you see what

I see?"

Donna stood on the field watching a group of first-graders compete in the crazy clothes relay race.

Stacey raised her hand to her forehead to block the sun. "Is she holding a dog?" she asked.

"She was." I pointed while she placed her pooch down.

We all stared in silence as the Bichon Frise lifted his leg to urinate on the grass.

"You've got to be kidding me!" Jackie screeched. "What is wrong with that woman?"

"A lot," I replied. She was one person I wouldn't miss when I left town.

Donna picked up her pup and walked toward us.

"Oh, this should be good." Claire took a step backward.

Without making eye contact, or saying hello to any of us, Donna reached for a bottle of water.

"Um, excuse me. What are you doing?" Jackie asked.

"Taking a bottle of water. Isn't it obvious?"

Jackie folded her arms across her chest. "Yeah, Donna. I can see that. The question is why."

"I don't understand," she replied and stroked the dog's head. "How many reasons could there possibly be for someone to take a bottle of water? I'm not planning on using it to shower."

"Unless Jackie dumps it over her head," Trisha whispered in my ear.

"Oh, don't play dumb with me, Donna." Jackie shook her head. "You know perfectly well the water is for the children, so they don't dehydrate."

"I'm fully aware, Jackie. I may not have been part of the PTA this year, but I've spent enough years behind that table to know the purpose of the water."

"Good. So now please step away from the table."

"I will do no such thing," Donna replied, defiantly.

"I've asked you nicely. You don't want to upset me, Donna, do you?"

"I don't care one iota about you or your feelings. With all your so-called powers, you still can't do anything to hurt me."

GO ON, GIRL 227

Jackie's face turned beet red. She struggled to keep her composure while Stacey reached into her back pocket and pulled out a five-dollar bill. "Donna, go buy yourself a drink from the vending machine by the cafeteria."

"I don't need your money." Donna kissed her dog's head. "And I'm not missing any more of the races. I have no time to waste on you or your petty nonsense."

"Let it go," Claire whispered to Jackie.

"You're right." Jackie smiled, sweetly. "Take the water, Donna, and get out of our sight. It's not worth a fight. We have more important things to do this afternoon, like make sure you get your mangy mutt off the field." Jackie scrolled through her phone and showed Donna the picture she'd captured of the dog peeing. "Do I need to remind you pets are prohibited on school grounds?"

"Oh, Clarence isn't a pet." She batted her eyes. "He's a service dog."

"He's a what?" I couldn't remain silent one second longer.

Donna put her dog on the ground and pulled a red plastic bowl from her bag, which she filled with the water she'd fought so hard to obtain. The dog drank with greed. "You heard me. Clarence is here for emotional support for both Julia and me. You have no idea how difficult this year has been for both of us. Oh, wait. Maybe you all do know because you're responsible for our pain." She slowly made eye contact with all of us.

My pulse raced, and my heart pounded in my chest. I wanted to pummel her. "You know, Donna, I felt sorry for you earlier in the term. I came to your rescue in the nail salon when you were acting like a raving lunatic. And even though she was late, I should have let Jennifer walk off the stage with the prize at the penny auction. Instead, I placated her, so you could enjoy the spa weekend. I figured you could use an escape from here." I shook my head. "Time and time again, I've tried to be nice to you and your daughter. And how did you thank me? After you found out from Mia we were moving, you told your seven-year-old kid and encouraged her to tell the other girls the big news. Did you think that would help her take Amanda's place in the group once we left town?"

Donna opened her mouth to speak, but I didn't give her a

chance. "Don't even try to defend yourself. I'm sure you didn't realize it at the time, but Kara and I are friends."

Donna's eyes widened.

"I spoke to Mia. She told us everything," I spat.

Donna's face turned purple.

"How do you know she's not lying?" Donna picked up her dog and caressed his neck. "See, this is what's wrong with you people. You never give me any credit. You speak to some stranger for like five minutes and take their word for gospel. You've known me for years, Sydney Clayton. Yet you toss my credibility out the window as if it was garbage."

"You need a good hard look in the mirror." I took my sunglasses off. "Yes, I only spoke to Mia for a few minutes. And in that time, I saw how deeply she cared about Kara. She'd never intentionally hurt her sister. The fact that Amanda and I were affected was an unfortunate coincidence to her. You, on the other hand, are always right in the middle of the drama, playing the poor wounded person. You thrive on the attention, and so does your daughter. I may have fallen for your act earlier this year, but I see you crystal clear now. And while you may blame us for your misery, you've brought everything on yourself." I put my arm around Jackie's waist. "I'm sorry our friendship upsets you. One day maybe you'll realize what it means to be a friend."

CHAPTER THIRTY-SIX

I FILLED MY PAPER CUP WITH MUCH-NEEDED caffeine before I disconnected the coffee maker. The machine was one of our few remaining personal items that we hadn't already packed. During the past few weeks, we'd gradually moved most of our stuff to Shells Point. We wanted to put away as many of our belongings as possible before moving day. So today, all that was left were a couple of boxes and the bulk of our furniture.

Craig supervised the moving company and had everything under control. Amanda trailed behind her father with her iPad, determined to capture the final few moments at home on video to share with her friends.

I opened our back door and walked toward the center of our yard. All our outside furniture was already in the moving truck, so I sat down cross-legged on the grass. I took a sip of coffee and looked around. I dialed the phone and my eyes prickled with tears.

"How are you holding up?" Jackie asked by way of a greeting.

I plucked a blade of grass and held it tightly in my hand. "Not so great."

"Oh, Syd," she cooed.

"I can't stop crying, Jackie. I don't know what's wrong with me."

Her voice was steady and strong. "There is nothing wrong with you."

"I kept wandering from room to room. It's empty, and it's breaking my heart. This place was more than a house to me; it was home. There's not one room that wasn't full of memories. How can I walk away? How can I leave everything behind?"

"Sydney, your memories will come with you. You'll always have them, no matter where you live. And you will make new ones in your new house."

I knew she was right. Still, tears streamed down my cheeks.

"Come on, Sydney, don't cry. You know as well as I do that moving is the right thing for you and your family. You and Craig didn't make this decision lightly. Think of Amanda. It will be amazing for her to be so close to your parents. And since your office is much closer to your new home, you'll be able to spend more time with her too. She'll be so much happier."

I sniffled and clutched the phone tightly. "I know."

"Listen to me. You're sad now, and you have every right to be. Moving is one of the most traumatic and emotional events in life. But it's also an exhilarating time, one that you should try to enjoy. You guys are about to begin a new chapter of your life, in a new place that you and Craig spent so much time and energy designing. Each day you'll make new memories there. And, while it will take some time, soon that house will become your home."

As I spoke to Jackie, I felt myself relax slightly. She validated my feelings and eased my nerves. Life was crazy. Nine months ago, I couldn't stand her. I'd tolerated Jackie and let her push me around because I felt like I had no choice if I wanted my daughter to be happy. But now, the thought of living so far away from her was very upsetting to me. I was comforted, though, because I had complete faith that distance wouldn't break our bond. "You're right, but I'm going to miss so much more than just this house."

"And I'm going to miss you too." Her voice cracked. "But we'll still see each other. You invited us over next weekend for dinner, remember?"

"Oh, yeah." I giggled and prayed I'd have a working kitchen by then. Although the bulk of the construction had been completed, there was still a lot of work left to be done.

She sighed deeply. "Sydney, remember, life is short. We make decisions every day. You and Craig decided to move, and you know it was the right choice."

"You're right, Jackie. And I have one more decision to make. I can sit here on the phone with you and waste the last few minutes I have at home being miserable, or I can choose to be happy and remember all the good times we shared here. I'm choosing to be happy."

"Good for you. Go on, girl."

"Jackie, one more thing. I love you."

I hung up the phone before she could respond. I walked back inside my house and took one final look around. The rooms were all empty, but our memories would always remain. I wiped a tear away and picked up my daughter. I kissed her on top of her head while Craig put Oreo, the cat, in his carrying case. I reached for my husband's hand. And I smiled. "Come on guys. Let's go home."

THE END

KEEP READING FOR A PREVIEW OF
PLAN BEA

PLAN BEA

"OH MY GOD!" I jumped up from a deep sleep and turned on the light over the bed. My heart beat a mile a minute as my stomach took a nosedive. No good ever came from a call in the middle of the night. Trust me, I knew. I learned that lesson the hard way, twelve years ago.

Thankfully, the phone was on Cole's side of the bed. I knew it was probably silly of me, but when we moved into this house, we placed the phone on his side of the bed for this very reason. I wanted my husband to be the first line of defense if the police or a hospital called with an emergency in the middle of the night. I didn't think I was emotionally strong enough to experience that again.

Two rings.

Three rings.

Why was Cole letting the phone ring so long? I didn't want the kids to wake up. It would be impossible to get Harley back to sleep.

As the fourth ring began to sound, Cole thrust the phone at me. "It's for you. It's Beatrice."

"Mom. What's wrong?"

"Wrong? Wrong?" she repeated in a singsong voice as if I was deaf. "Why do you always assume something is wrong, Annabel?"

"Um, maybe because you're calling me in the middle of the night?"

My mother let out her slow, sarcastic chuckle. You know, the kind that made you feel insignificant and so inferior. I should have been used to it by now, but sadly, I was not.

"Annabel, really? Middle of the night, aren't you being a bit melodramatic? It's what time? It's only —"

I glanced at the cable box across the room. "Ten-thirty, Mother. To you, it may not be late, but Cole and I were both asleep. With work and two kids, we're exhausted by the end of the day. Call us crazy, but we like to go to bed at a reasonable hour."

Cole was watching me. As I covered my face with my hands and shook my head in frustration, he must have realized my mother was being her usual self. He flicked off the light and rolled over. He'd be snoring in moments. I'd be lying if I said I wasn't jealous.

My mother exhaled. "I guess I can understand, although I really do think it's too early for you and Cole to be sleeping. You know Annabel; you really do need to keep that husband of yours happy. I would think you'd have other things to be doing at this time of night if you know what I mean."

"Mother, I'd love to debate our sleep patterns with you, but I guess that's not why you called, especially at this hour."

My mother and I never called each other just to talk. In fact, I didn't actually remember the last time either one of us spontaneously picked up the phone to have a little mother-daughter chat. Our calls were all business, prompted by life events, breaking family news, or just plain old forced. In fact, we have a standard fifteen minute "touching base" phone call each Thursday, precisely at eleven forty-five in the morning when my mom drove to the nail salon for her weekly manicure.

"You're right, Darling. I did have a reason for my call. I have big news for you. Very exciting news, I must add."

"Okay. I'm all ears." I said as I flopped back against the bed and pulled the covers up to my chin.

"Remember the lovely gentleman I told you about? Walter?"

"The one you met a couple of months ago when you went on that cruise with the ladies you play bridge with?"

"Yes!" She exclaimed. "That's him. Well guess what?"

I couldn't help it and I certainly didn't mean it, but a huge, loud yawn escaped my mouth. "Sorry, Mom. I don't know, and I'm too tired to play guessing games." I glanced over at a snoring Cole. Lucky bastard.

"Okay, I had such a great time on the cruise with him. If you remember, we met by the pool bar. I know everyone says the cruise line has impeccable service, but I didn't experience it. The staff wouldn't last fifteen minutes at the club that's for sure. Good help is so hard to find these days. Anyway, we both must've been waiting for the bartender for a full five minutes. Five minutes! Can you believe it? When he finally came over, we both blurted out our order at the same time. Turns out, we both ordered the same drink! We began laughing the moment the words left our mouths."

"Yes, you told me this." While my mother had no patience listening to me discuss my children, my husband, or really anything going on in my life. But when it came to one of her stories, you'd better pay attention... Well, unless Marcella, her manicurist, was waiting. In that case you got a free pass. One thing to know about my mother, Beatrice Buchanan, she has two conversational speeds. One was slow and drawn out, and the other was slower and more drawn out. There was no point in trying to rush her. So I laid my head down on my pillow and prayed I wouldn't doze off before she got to her point.

"Oh yes. I did mention it, didn't I? But it bears repeating. So after we got our drinks, we sat down together. The cruise ship had these amazing chaise lounges. They were so comfortable, way more comfortable than the ones they have at the club. Walter sat in the sun, but I was under the umbrella. You know, Annabel, I've haven't sat in the sun in twenty-five years. You should take a lesson from me if you don't want to be all wrinkled up when you are my age."

I grunted.

"So, as I was saying, once we started talking, we just couldn't stop! He was so interesting and funny. I was kind of shocked—you know most people aren't worth paying attention to. Anyway, one drink led to another and by the second gin martini, I was feeling a little tipsy, but I was having a blast!"

"I know, Mother. You told me this story already, right after you got home from the trip. Can we please cut to the chase?" I felt bad that I rushed her but I was fading fast. I feared this could go on for hours.

"Annabel, please. Let me tell my story, maybe if you stopped interrupting me I could finish."

Why did I even bother? I couldn't decide if I should stay in bed or go downstairs and brew a cup of tea. Maybe snack on some of those double-chocolate chip cookies I made this past weekend. I decided to forgo the snack, once I'm out of bed there's no chance of getting back to sleep.

My mother continued. "Where was I anyway? Oh, yes. I remember. We decided to meet up after dinner. As I ate, I wished I had arranged to have dinner with him instead of the ladies. You know I love the girls, but can they gab. I swear if I heard one more word about Miriam's granddaughter's college acceptances, I would've had to abandon ship. Stella was no better. She just couldn't stop talking about her son's promotion. And don't get me started on how Wilma kept droning on about her daughter's new house. She carried on so much you'd think she discovered a new continent, I mean really it's just a house. Some people are so self-centered."

I couldn't even reply for fear of what I would say.

"As soon as dinner ended, I ran back to the room to fix my face. The sea air really wreaks havoc on your makeup, you know. I met Walter in the lounge. We ordered an after dinner drink; it sat there untouched. There was a five-piece band, and they were playing the oldies. He asked me to dance, and let's just say that man can really trip the light fantastic. Before I knew it, it was the wee hours of the morning. I don't remember the last time I had so much fun. We were docking in Cozumel the next day. I was supposed to spend the day with the girls. But I couldn't handle being with them one more minute. Did I mention how annoying they were?"

"Yes, you did."

"Oh, well instead I stayed on the ship with Walter. Best. Decision. Ever! Let's just say for the rest of the cruise I didn't have to hear anymore about the great Harvard/Yale debate. I spent all my waking and," Beatrice paused to clear her throat, "my non-waking hours with him."

"Mother, please. Can we not go down that road, again."

"Okay, okay." She chuckled before continuing. "As I was saying before you interrupted me again, I started to worry as the trip came to an end. I didn't want to lose Walter. But, as usual, my worry was for nothing! Walter lives in Manhattan. We've been seeing each other ever since we got home. And... get ready for it..."

I stifled another yawn. "I'm at the edge of my bed."

"Walter asked me to marry him!" Beatrice screamed so loudly into the phone I was surprised she didn't wake up Cole. I glanced over at him; he was still fast asleep.

I sat straight up. "He what?"

"You heard me, dear. He asked me to marry him. And I said yes! But it gets even better; I need your help. I don't want to discuss it over the phone. Prepare dinner tomorrow night. Walter and I are coming over. I want you to meet him, and I want to go over what I need you to do for me."

"But—"

"No buts. Dinner. Tomorrow. We'll be there at seven o'clock. Oh and one more thing: no carbs. I have to watch my weight. I'm going to be a bride, you know."

ACKNOWLEDGMENTS

Thank you so much for reading *Go On, Girl*. I hope you enjoyed reading about this crazy cast of characters as much as I enjoyed writing their story. Moms always say they don't have a favorite child, but I like to buck tradition – By far, I love *Go On, Girl* the best.

I can't take credit for the story, though. Truth is always funnier than fiction, and while I took a lot of creative liberties, most of what occurred in Forest River was experienced by my friends who generously shared their tales of motherhood with me. Tania Schwarzwald, thank you for messaging me the day your phone exploded with carpool drama. You were joking that I could write a book about the experience, but I took you up on your suggestion. Thank you, Heather B, Melissa P, Tonya R, June C, Fran V, Lissette H, Melanie G, and Helene W for all your inspiration.

Carl, Hannah, Paul, and Brianna – thank you so much for being such cuties. Amanda wouldn't have had such a dynamic personality without you guys! Allison P and Diane L – thank you for helping me find my new dream home and welcoming me into the world of real estate. #FollowTheOrange

To the two people I love most in the world: Marc and my mom, Loretta – thank you for all your love and support. You've both had your hands full with me this year. Sorry. It has been a challenging time, on many levels, but knowing you were both always in my corner kept me going. You both always know what do to lift my spirits and motivate me to continue to run full speed ahead, and man, I'm running!

Meredith Schorr, thank you for your friendship, wisdom,

inspiration, for always being there for me. Not only during our last visit when you put up with my painting a wall in my kitchen, but you also recommended Sam…. You are a wonderful friend…

Samantha Stroh Bailey, thank you for being the best editor ever! You've worked tirelessly on helping me mold and shape this story, and your insights and recommendations were terrific. You've pushed me so hard, and I've learned so much from you.

Greg Simanson, once again thank you for creating the cover of my dreams. You are so talented and have the patience of a saint.

A huge hug to the members of my street team, everyone who keeps me company on social media, and all the book bloggers out there! You guys are amazing. Keep writing.

If you enjoyed *Go On, Girl*, it would mean the world to me if you left a short review on any retail website and/or Goodreads. I love to chat and stay connected to readers. You can find me on Twitter @feelingbeachie, or on Facebook. My blog is Feeling Beachie or email me (hilarygrossmanauthor@gmail.com). To find out about new releases (including *Plan Dee*) join my mailing http://eepurl.com/brlroD

XOXO,
Hilary

50495686R00135

Made in the USA
Middletown, DE
25 June 2019